Crime & Modernity

Continuities in Left Realist Criminology

John Lea

SAGE Publications
London • Thousand Oaks • New Delhi

First published 2002

Apart from any fair dealing for the purposes of research or
private study, or criticism or review, as permitted under the
Copyright, Designs and Patents Act, 1988, this publication may
be reproduced, stored or transmitted in any form, or by any
means, only with the prior permission in writing of the
publishers, or in the case of reprographic reproduction, in
accordance with the terms of licences issued by the Copyright
Licensing Agency. Inquiries concerning reproduction outside
those terms should be sent to the publishers.

 SAGE Publications Ltd
6 Bonhill Street
London EC2A 4PU

SAGE Publications Inc
2455 Teller Road
Thousand Oaks, California 91320

SAGE Publications India Pvt Ltd
32, M-Block Market
Greater Kailash – I
New Delhi 110 048

British Library Cataloguing in Publication data

A catalogue record for this book is available
from the British Library

ISBN 0-8039-7556-2
ISBN 0-8039-7557-0 (pbk)

Library of Congress control number available

Typeset by SIVA Math Setters, Chennai, India
Printed and bound in Great Britain by Athenaeum Press, Gateshead

Crime & Modernity

Contents

Preface and Acknowledgements

This book has been with me for some time. Its inspiration is twofold. The first is a desire to consolidate the theoretical gains of the Left Realist criminology of the last two decades which, it has always seemed to me, centre around the perspective known as the *square of crime* (Lea 1987, 1992; Young 1987, 1992). The study of crime is grounded in a framework of interaction which includes, besides the familar dyad of offender and victim, the state and the criminal justice agencies themselves together with the publics and communities within which crime and crime control take place, as active participants in the construction and regulation of criminality. This framework can of course be deployed in an analytical way, to enable the contributions and interactions of these various participants to produce changes in crime rates. This was the main emphasis of an earlier contribution of mine (Lea 1992).

However, the present period has seen the problem of crime take on new dimensions besides the traditional issues of rises and falls in the amount of criminal activity. The increasing normalisation of crime, its relationship with economic activity, survival of poor communities, the changing methods of operation of the criminal justice agencies, all point to a sea change in the relationship between key forms of criminality and other aspects of the social and economic system in which crime is less an episodic and rude disruption of normality and increasingly one of its salient features. There is a need, therefore, for a framework within which such changes, and their relationship to wider developments in contemporary capitalist societies, can be located and understood.

This brings me to the second inspiration for my argument, namely, the necessity of history. To understand the changing relationships between criminality and other socio-economic processes, an historical approach is absolutely necessary. It is a core argument that many of the changes taking place at the present time re-present aspects of modern capitalist societies in their formative stages. This involves abandoning an analytic in favour of a chronological approach. The square of crime thus reappears as the social relations of crime control, a set of social relations through which societies deal with a large part of their interpersonal conflicts and harms as crime, and by means of criminal justice. These relations have their distinct historical preconditions in the processes of modernisation beginning, in Britain, in the seventeenth and eighteenth centuries and which are today becoming exhausted.

Aware that I have only scratched the surface of the task I set myself, I ask attentive readers to prepare themselves for loose ends, unfinished arguments and no doubt flagrant contradictions. But if I have conveyed an orientation, a way of thinking about the subject matter of criminality and its complex relations with the process of modernisation and the crisis facing contemporary capitalist societies, then I will have achieved something.

I would like to offer thanks to all those friends and colleagues with whom conversations have helped me on my way and who commented on all or particular parts of the manuscript. Trevor Bark, Keir Sothcott and the 'social crime' seminar were a constant source of encouragement. Leo Zeilig and Patrick Slaughter read all or parts of the manuscript and saved me from many lapses into incoherence. Sue Lees read everything and tried her best to force clarity on my prose and arguments. All faults are mine alone.

John Lea
August 2001

1
Practical Criminality

In his essay entitled 'Who thinks abstractly?', Hegel provided us with the following description:

> A murderer is led to the place of execution. For the common populace he is nothing but a murderer. Ladies perhaps remark that he is a strong, handsome, interesting man. The populace finds this remark terrible: What? A murderer handsome? How can one think so wickedly and call a murderer handsome; no doubt, you yourselves are something not much better! This is the corruption of morals that is prevalent in the upper classes, a priest may add, knowing the bottom of things and human hearts. One who knows men traces the development of the criminal's mind: he finds in his history, in his education, a bad family relationship between his father and mother, some tremendous harshness after this human being had done some minor wrong, so he became embittered against the social order ... and henceforth did not make it possible for him to preserve himself except through crime. There may be people who will say when they hear such things: he wants to excuse this murderer! ... This is abstract thinking: to see nothing in the murderer except the abstract fact that he is a murderer, and to annul all other human essence in him with this simple quality. (Hegel 1817/1965: 116–17)

Hegel's aim here was to show that the common-sense view of abstract and concrete thought is the inverse of reality. The criminal appears as a very 'concrete' phenomenon: the murderer on the tumbril, the defendant in the dock. However, in order to focus on this one aspect of his identity, his criminality, others have to be suspended and annulled. His criminality has to be abstracted out from the complex of other characteristics which make him what he is and be regarded as dominant. In the criminal trial, of course, some of these other characteristics, such as his unhappy childhood, may re-enter the frame in a subordinate role as mitigation. While they do not influence the initial characterisation of our individual in terms of his crime, they represent a move towards a more concrete and many-sided view of his nature. For Hegel concrete reality is not something we start off from, readily given to observation, but which we arrive at as a conclusion.

But the important point for us here is that this process of abstraction is the foundation stone of modern law and criminal justice. All societies have some notion of 'crime' and individual redress of interpersonal conflicts and harms. But in pre-modern society this is usually integrated into other social relations such as status and kinship, etc. It might be one thing to rob or kill a member of your own family, another to rob or kill a stranger; one thing for a nobleman to harm a peasant and something quite different for a peasant to harm a nobleman or a priest. The focus on the criminal identity of the individual was less sharp and was still locked into other contexts and characteristics of the individual. It was of course much harder to think abstractly in a society where nearly all social relations were interpersonal ones of status and submission. By contrast, in modern society where a large proportion of relations are ones involving passing strangers, or individuals whose relationship centres around a single dimension of work or economic exchange, it is far easier to think of people abstractly because we know so little about them anyway. So when they kill, it is the killing that defines them. If a mediaeval king or the lord of the manor killed, then it was hard for all those under his personal rule to forget that even though he had killed, he was still the king or the lord of the manor.

The assumption that criminality is largely an individualistic response, which does not have to be individualised by the powers that be, is easily made. Most social mechanisms involve the actions of individuals in one way or another but it does not follow that it will be the individual who is constructed as the responsible agent as opposed to families, communities, ethnic groups or more impersonal market forces. Older, pre-modern forms of 'crime control' such as ethnic warfare, feuding, vendetta, etc., testify to the essential modernity of criminalisation and its link to the emergence of the notion of the free individual and the abstract legal person. In addition, and again this is easily taken for granted, crime is usually seen as an episodic disruption of an otherwise harmonious ongoing process. This is linked to its nature as individual act rather than ongoing institutional or social process.

It is also linked to the existence of the *other*, the stranger. In the closed mediaeval village community in which the status of all individuals was known and integral to their being, harms and wrongs had to be dealt with *in terms of* their status rather than through its negation. Conversely, those from outside the community tended to be feared and 'criminalised' quite irrespective of their actions. Modern society makes possible the re-production of individuals as 'criminal other' even before the judge, let alone the state, has decreed it. Modernity provides the resources and possibilities for this in the notion of the free individual as abstract person, half-way, as it were, to criminalisation. The issue for the modern court is whether the right individual has been taken: the one who actually committed the offence. If so, the status as criminal is assured automatically by their actions. The degradation ritual of the court confirms what has already taken place as a social interaction. Alternatively, because criminalisation has already occurred as a social fact, the modern court – at least in the more progressive jurisdictions – need not overly preoccupy itself with such ceremony and can become an altogether more 'humane' place.

Thus the process of abstraction – we might call it the *criminalising abstraction* – which establishes the identities of those who violate the criminal law as criminals irrespective of other characteristics they might have, that leaves, in the words of the great eighteenth-century jurist Cesare Beccaria, 'no further care to the judge than to examine the acts of citizens and to decide whether or not they conform to the law as written' ([1764]1996: 7), is not simply a logical process. The content of abstraction, what is included and what is excluded, who can in actual practice be criminalised, is a social, historical and political process. It is a question of power and imagery. On the one hand the emergence of the rule of law, the doctrine that all killers from the king to the merchant to the landless peasant, will be treated as murderers in the same way by the courts is rightly held to be one of the great achievements of modernity, of the Enlightenment. Its historical precondition is the emergence of the doctrines of individualism and universal human rights. These were based in turn on the ascendancy of capitalist market relations in which individuals related increasingly as abstract legal persons, citizens, buyers and sellers of commodities, bearers of rights and obligations irrespective of other differences and characteristics. Without this the rule of law would be impossible in anything other than a tautological sense. Law is the counterpart of political economy (see Fine 1984; Pashukanis 1978). On the other hand, however, the *content* of the criminalising abstraction is never free of the imagery and practice of power. Who can be criminalised; who is virtually 'pre-criminalised' irrespective of their actions; and who can only be criminalised with great difficulty, if at all, irrespective of what they do. These forces, at play within the relationship between formal criminalisation and the substantive character of *criminals*, reintroduce the older issues of social status and identity into the newer abstractions. Modernity is contradictory from the outset. It is not simply a break from the past but its reworking into new configurations.

The rule of law and legal equality is also the counterpart of the modern democratic state. Modern states are democratic in so far as the people, through their representatives and with the departure of God and the king, become the ground of the legitimacy of the state and its laws. The state as the most powerful agent in society, freed from *direct* appropriation by powerful individuals or social groups, is thus in a position to apply the criminalising abstraction consistently. The powerful state, supreme power within its national territory – and frequently beyond its borders – is an aspect of the dual nature of modernity. On the one hand modernity brings the emancipation of the individual from the hierarchical ordering of feudalism and, on the other, the need to secure social order by regulating this process through the various apparatuses of law, discipline and regulation. Hence modernity, as it developed in western Europe during the eighteenth century, is a dual process of liberation and disciplinisation (Wagner 1994). The modernity of criminalisation lies precisely in its subordination of the freedom of the individual to the interests of social stability. It is achieved by the criminalising abstraction which singles out individuals, annuls other aspects of their character and circumstances – be it social status, life history or control over resources – and holds them responsible for their actions in accordance with a general rule of law that recognises their right, as free individuals, to equal treatment. However, since *capitalist* modernisation is carried, initially, by a particular social class, the bourgeoisie, those freedoms, and also the potential criminalisation of their misuse, are not distributed evenly.

This gives modernity a decidedly dark side. As far as criminal justice is concerned, the criminalising abstraction is, firstly, never entirely consistently applied. It is subject to key exclusions. Some, such as women in the marital relationship, are effectively precluded from claiming victim status in the case of violence from their husbands, while the working class bears throughout the early stages of modernity the status of the already criminalised having, for the bourgeoisie and its magistrates, no other identity than the criminalising abstraction itself – in the form of the *dangerous classes*.[1] Simultaneously the upper echelons of the bourgeoisie by virtue of their social status are able to deflect the rigours of criminal justice to a considerable extent. The content of the criminalising abstraction varies. The poor working-class criminal takes on an exaggerated animal status as brute while the female offender is defeminised as 'mad'. But quite apart from exceptions and exclusions, the very working of a system of universal human rights and legal rules serves to reproduce as well as ameliorate the substantive social inequalities and injustices alongside which they function. The Napoleonic Code, which in its impartiality prevented rich and poor alike from sleeping under the bridges of Paris, is the best known illustration. The enlightened magistrate responds by taking into account the poverty or other disability of the offender as mitigating circumstances at the stage of sentencing. Of course what circumstances count as disability or weakness is itself an issue of power. The Victorian moral reformer could look with sympathy upon the poverty of the poor waif who stole a loaf of bread. By contrast only very recently have such problems as long-term violence by husbands to wives, when the latter turn to what would otherwise be simple premeditated murder, begun to be regarded in a similar light.

It is nevertheless a mistake to see the development of criminal justice and the criminalising abstraction as simply the perfection of a mechanism of repressive social control. The importance of seeing modernity as a process involving simultaneously mechanisms of liberation and disciplinisation (Wagner 1994) is that neither must be seen as entirely obliterating the other. Indeed each affects the working of the other. If the exclusions mentioned above give a hollow ring to wide areas of so-called liberation, the working of the mechanisms of discipline and regulation have to come to terms with the dynamics of liberation. One side of this is that the masses benefit from the rule of law and the criminalising abstraction. As far as the working class was concerned the rule of law, as the historian Edward Thompson put it, was 'an unqualified human good ... [which] ... while it did mediate existent class relations to the advantage of the rulers ... mediated these class relations through legal forms which imposed, again and again, inhibitions upon the actions of the rulers' (1977: 264-5).

At the same time the masses have to be progressively brought into and mobilised as part of the process of control and regulation itself. This is well understood in areas such as the progressive extension of the franchise and the legitimation of independent working-class organisations such as trade unions and labour parties. Also understood is the area of social policy (in the most general sense of the term) as the development, during the late eighteenth and nineteenth centuries of a concern with *governmentality* (Foucault 1979, 1991); with the mobilisation of a wide range of disciplinary mechanisms, including private institutions such as the family to secure participation and conduct, in a process of essentially self-regulation or 'self-carried power' (Foucault 1977: 201).

Traditional jurisprudence and political science have conspired to see criminalisation as the unproblematic application of clear categories of criminal law exhaustively analysable as discourses and practices of the state including, where changes in the boundaries of criminality are at issue, through the formal legislative process. Such a focus is one-sided. The state remains of course the central institutional locus of the criminalising abstraction precisely because it rises above the particularities and conflicts of society. But it is effective only to the extent that its actions are reproduced and reinforced by a whole complex of attitudes and behaviours in society as a whole. Criminalisation involves much more than the agencies of the state, including their informal and discretionary modes of operation. It is more accurate to say, with Nicola Lacey, that the 'very subject matter of criminal law and criminology appears to slip through our fingers as "criminalisation" is revealed as consisting of a number of interlocking social practices whose operations leave the boundaries of "criminality" anything but precise' (Lacey 1995: 17). These practices, like the informal and discretionary mode of operation of criminal justice agencies, should not be seen as imperfection or dilution of criminalisation but rather its essential dynamic. It cannot function in any other way. The working of criminal justice cannot be properly understood except as a set of social relations of which the state is only one component, albeit a very powerful one. This becomes clear if we consider two important arguments which at first sight appear to move off at a tangent. The first concerns the practical boundaries of criminalisation and the second the issue of alternatives to criminalisation as a response to individual conflicts and harms.

Reconstructing crime

The understanding that criminalisation is governed by the substantive inequalities of power in modern society can lead obviously to the attempt to find a new set of foundational principles from which to deduce what activities are crime. It takes the form of an attempted return to one side of the dualism of modernity; the discourse and practice of liberation and the inalienable human rights that are its foundation. The motive for such a strategy, among criminologists, is usually one of discontent with the idea of subordinating the subject matter of study to whatever the actually existing criminal law, with its biases and power effects, happens at a particular time to define as crime.

One of the classic formulations, within Anglo-Saxon criminology, of the strategy of reconstruction was provided by Herman and Julia Schwendinger who argued that radicals should reject existing criminal law in favour of a wider definition of crime as violation of basic human rights:

> Basic rights are differentiated because their fulfilment is absolutely essential to the realisation of a great number of values ... [hence] the right to racial, sexual and economic equality. The abrogation of these rights certainly limits the individual's choice to fulfil himself in many spheres of life. These rights therefore, are basic because there is so much at stake in their fulfilment. It can be stated ... that individuals who deny these rights to others are criminal. Likewise social relationships and social systems which regularly cause the abrogation of these rights are also criminal. If the terms imperialism, racism, sexism and poverty are abbreviated signs for theories of social relationships or social systems which cause the systematic abrogation of basic rights, then imperialism, racism, sexism and poverty can be called crimes according to the logic of our argument. (Schwendinger and Schwendinger 1975: 136–7)

In the period since the mid-1970s there has, on the face of it, been considerable progress in areas involving human rights. Many states have, for example, made renewed efforts to criminalise racist or sexist practices, and there has also appeared to be considerable progress in the criminalisation of human rights violations in the international sphere. The reappearance of war and ethnic conflict in eastern Europe, conflicts in Africa, the ending of military dictatorships in Latin America, have all provided contexts in which the notion of *crimes against humanity* has gained ground (see Robertson 1999). However, the practical problems facing the embryonic international institutions and those who claim to act on behalf of the 'international community' help to illustrate some of the problems with this position[2] and enable a deeper grasp of criminalisation as a social process involving, but extending well beyond, the state.

The main concern of the Schwendingers' argument was of course less a call to action on the part of states to extend the boundaries of criminalisation than a call to radical criminologists to extend the boundaries of their studies well beyond those of the official discourses of criminal law and criminal justice agencies. One of the obvious problems was that the discipline of criminology might wander so far from what was publicly seen as crime as to leave the discipline in an 'idealist limbo' (Clarke 1978: 44; see also O'Malley 1988). But more important, there are severe problems facing even powerful state institutions in attempting to extend the boundaries of criminalisation in the name of human rights. To take an example current at the time of writing, the International War Crimes Tribunal based in The Hague may issue warrants for the arrest of various Balkan gangsters and warlords, and even heads of state, on charges of crimes against humanity arising from recent conflicts involving ethnic cleansing and genocide in parts of former Yugoslavia. The problems of enforcement of such warrants are of course considerable and obvious. NATO troops in the region may be a rather ineffective police force, particularly as regards tracking down individuals – not a traditional military skill. Other key practical assumptions of criminalisation become obvious by their notable absence. Normally criminal justice agencies attempting to apprehend criminals can rely on at least some sections of the public to report sightings or other information and be prepared to give evidence, appear as witnesses, etc. If, by contrast, sizeable populations vehemently reject the legitimacy of the International War Crimes Tribunal as an agent of western imperialism, characterise the individuals concerned as national heroes rather than criminals, and see charges of 'war crimes' simply as thinly veiled imperialist aggression led by the United States, then criminalisation as a practical process faces considerable obstacles. These are compounded if the military commanders of NATO troops in the area, mindful of other political considerations transmitted down other chains of command, refrain from seriously searching for the indicted war criminals because the actual arrest of the latter might precipitate a political crisis of unpredictable outcome, then even the very label of 'war criminal' stands in danger of becoming de facto meaningless. Finally, others, in particular the victims of activities of the indicted war criminals, seeing the impotence of the 'international community' to enforce its warrants may take matters into their own hands and re-launch guerrilla warfare or engage in assassination attempts. In this worst case scenario any notion of criminal justice is rapidly displaced by considerations of low intensity warfare, vendetta and feud. This is more than the simple issue of whether the law will be enforced, but rather whether the criminalising abstraction itself can be effectively sustained. The socio-political preconditions for criminalisation are graphically illustrated in their very absence.[3] There is more to the extension of criminalisation than the activities of the state. The extension of human rights and the criminalisation of their violation remain at the level of rhetoric if they are not articulated *both* in the practical actions of the state *and* in the dynamics of social relations.

A further set of issues concerns the nature of criminal activities themselves. The criminalising abstraction is concerned with individuals, or entities that can be practically presented as individuals, for the purposes of allocating responsibility. Problematic situations and conflicts can only be dealt with as crime if they can be made to fit this conception. The attempt to criminalise the unintended consequences of the working of organisations is fraught with problems. 'Rights cannot be enforced if no one can be held responsible for their infringement' (Benton 1998: 167). The area of corporate criminality furnishes many examples. Even harder is to retain any recognisable notion of criminality in dealing with the outcome of market forces and the general unintended consequences of basic economic processes such as capital accumulation. Yet the table of human rights presented by the Schwendingers includes such entities as imperialism and poverty. In certain circumstances these can be presented as the results of actions by identifiable individuals or corporations. For example, multinational companies paying below poverty wages in poor countries could be prosecuted for violations of minimum wage legislation. However, if the corporation is considerably more powerful than not only its victims but also the local state and criminal justice system, this will be less likely even if such legislation is in existence. Such incidents as the Bhopal pollution disaster in India in 1984 in which the alleged criminal negligence of a large multinational corporation allowed escaping toxic gases to kill and maim thousands, provided a graphic illustration (Pearce and Tombs 1993). While powerful offenders bring problems in their wake, the attempt at criminalisation at least makes sense both on an intellectual and a policy level. However, to the extent that world poverty is a result less of the criminal negligence of particular large corporations than of the normal working of market forces and the process of global capital accumulation, the strategy of criminalisation encounters severe difficulties. If companies wilfully violate minimum wage legislation, that is one thing, but if those companies go bankrupt as a result of changes in market conditions, that is quite another, and there is little scope for criminalisation. To regard the growing immiseration of the world's population as 'criminal' in anything other than a diffuse moral or polemical sense of the term is therefore quite misleading. Neither is it obvious that the attempt to coerce such phenomena into some form of criminological perspective, as opposed to the political economy of global capitalism, serves any purpose other than confusion.

If the absence of the social preconditions of criminalisation has a negative side where it impedes the advance of criminalisation in defence of human rights, then it has a positive side in impeding the ability of authoritarian regimes to disguise their ruthless denial of human rights as some form of crime control. An authoritarian political regime may desire to criminalise the activities of those courageous individuals engaged, often with the tacit support and admiration of large sections of the population, in what in liberal democracies would be legitimate oppositional politics. The benefits to the regime and its public image both nationally and abroad are obvious if it can claim it is dealing with a problem of criminality. But when such a process of 'crime control' is subject to close inspection it begins to become clearer what is taking place in practice. Who, for example, will report such 'crimes' to the authorities and provide corroborating testimony in court? The regime finds that an army of spies and informers will be necessary, their information will be largely fabricated and distorted, uncorroborated by witnesses other than those already in the employ of the political police, and will usually be protected from any process of cross-examination or other scrutiny in court. The judicial proceedings will be a grim parody of due process while the only victims of the process will be seen by the mass of the population to be the very 'offenders' themselves. In such situations, as in South Africa under the apartheid regime or in Chile under Pinochet, the violation of human rights and the attempted portrayal of any form of oppositional activity as crime earned worldwide condemnation. The visibility of oppression in these cases lay not only in the periodic revelations of torture, disappearances and deaths in police custody and the tireless work of those who had the courage to expose such occurrences, but also in the inability of the regimes to present their activities in the last analysis as crime control whatever the law stipulated. This was notable in the South African case, where state oppression was heavily codified through criminal law and surrounded with the trappings of legality. What was missing were the social components of criminalisation which prevented political and legal closure.[4] As Habermas (1976) remarked, efforts by states to engage in 'ideology planning' may well deploy a battery of strategies which include the use of law. However, such processes come up against severe limitations in that *'there is no administrative creation of meaning … .* Cultural traditions have their own, vulnerable, conditions of reproduction. They remain "living" as long as they take shape in an unplanned, nature-like manner' (1976: 70). Criminalisation cannot be controlled solely by the state. When it flies in the face of popular sentiments, grounded in determinate social relations, then it becomes something else.[5]

Authoritarian attempts at criminalisation are of course an extreme case. In democratic societies the process whereby criminalisations that have fallen foul of changed culture and attitudes fall into disuse is not dissimilar. If an activity becomes socially accepted and decriminalised in popular opinion, few people will report the offence, police and judicial authorities will become reluctant to prosecute and when they do there will be widespread disapproval with such prosecutions being regarded as a waste of time and public resources. The social underpinnings of criminalisation begin to crumble. Eventually, the criminal law itself may be changed. Such may well be what is happening to victimless crimes such as cannabis smoking in many western democracies. There is thus an objectivity to what is or is not 'crime', but it is not an objectivity simply enshrined in actually existing criminal law nor simply in a higher set of a priori principles of human rights. The objectivity is rather located in social relations, in how a variety of social actors respond to situations which they may well regard as the violation of human rights.

Deconstructing Crime

The same issue of the basis of criminalisation in social relations rather than in either state edicts or abstract conceptions of human rights, is illustrated by the converse strategy of attempting to dispense with criminalisation altogether as an ineffective and oppressive method of dealing with harms and conflicts. Starting from an attempt to subvert the disciplinary side of the dual nature of modernity, the argument has been classically stated by the Dutch abolitionist lawyer, Louk Hulsman, who argued that the

> categories of 'crime' are given by the criminal justice system rather than by victims or society in general. This makes it necessary to abandon the notion of 'crime' as a tool in the conceptual framework of criminology. Crime has no ontological reality. Crime is not the object but the product of criminal policy. Criminalisation is one of the many ways of constructing social reality. (Hulsman 1986: 34–5)

Abolitionism is the practical policy and deconstruction the theoretical orientation. This view starts from the opposite end of the argument to the 'all human rights violations are crimes' approach. The criminal justice system, rather than arising to deal with the objectively pre-existing problem of crime, insists on stamping the label of crime on a diversity of otherwise quite incommensurable forms of activity. In fact we can deal with conflicts and harms, argues the abolitionist, without falling foul of the dark side of the criminalising abstraction; the forcing of similarity in the face of difference. Hulsman urged us to dispense altogether with criminalising terminology and deal directly with the underlying reality of a diversity of problematic situations, conflicts, harms and 'trouble' in relations between people, each with its own dynamics and appropriate forms of solution. The practical implication is that we should seek to abolish the criminal justice system as it now stands and transform its agencies into resources for the resolution of conflicts without attempting to impose any external definition on what those conflicts might be. It should be entirely left to individuals to decide they have a conflict, or are involved in a problematic situation with others. The role of the state would be purely that of facilitating the parties coming together. At its most radical, abolitionism might be seen to involve the abolition of the criminal justice system altogether in favour of decentralised dispute-resolution systems, while its minimal version would advocate rather a dissolution of criminal law into various forms of victim-initiated civil litigation.

On an obvious level Hulsman is absolutely right. It is not individuals who carry legal classifications around in their heads. The victim of 'crime' often indeed knows only that a rather unfortunate problematic situation has arisen. It is the criminal justice system that decides that it is burglary rather than criminal damage, actual rather than grievous bodily harm and so on. For abolitionism the injunction on the participants in a conflict situation to remain passive in the face of the criminal justice system and its legal categories is replaced by a more active mobilisation in which the state takes a back seat. It brings the parties together but then they have to work out the nature of their dispute and how to resolve it. This type of thinking has, like the human rights approach, not been without influence. Recent decades have seen the proliferation of various schemes, often with overt state support, for community mediation, restorative justice, reintegrative shaming, etc. (Matthews 1988; Braithwaite 1989; Ness 1990; Hahn 1998). In the latter case there has been explicit interest in forms of communal dispute resolution to be found in traditional communities among native peoples, a pre-modern theme to be found in some abolitionist writing (Christie 1977). If there is consensus about what is or is not a harm and the community has sufficient resources to sort out low-level conflicts and apply reasonable censure, then abolitionism makes sense. The systems of conflict resolution that predated the criminal justice system may exist and function alongside and in ambiguous relationship to it.

The weakness of abolitionism is generally considered to lie in its assumptions about power relationships in modern industrial capitalist societies (Lea 1987). The idea that disputants can come together and resolve their conflicts presupposes a particular social structure in which people both have the time and energy to pursue their cases through civil justice or whatever other reconciliation mechanisms predominate, and the power to define what is or is not problematic or harmful and what constitutes a satisfactory outcome to mediation processes. What is presupposed is some version of reflexivity akin to Habermas' *ideal speech situation* of open, power-free communication in an as-yet-to-be-realised final perfection of a modernity of rationally communicating free individuals (see Habermas 1987). However, such conditions are, currently, rarely achieved. Even within the relatively cohesive localised communities already mentioned, the dominant definitions of what is problematic frequently exclude whole areas of activity that certain groups see as harmful and wrong. The most obvious example is violence against women. It is hardly surprising that a powerful tendency in feminist politics has been for more, rather than less, criminal justice intervention and application of the criminalising abstraction in the private sphere of the family and of gender relations generally. In a similar vein, as regards much harm inflicted on the weak by powerful corporations, the popular demand is less that the parties to the dispute be left to sort out their problematic situation than that corporate executives be hauled before the courts and fined or imprisoned; in other words that the criminalising abstraction is forcefully applied in a consistent manner. The issue is not that the criminal justice system deals with such matters in a more just or effective way, but that the disputants themselves lack the power and resources to sort out their conflicts. Such resources could be returned to them but not without a fundamental reorganisation of society. Even where, as in both the area of sexual violence and corporate victimisation there has been considerable development of an organised social movement, the goal of the latter has usually involved the strengthening of criminalisation (see Pitch 1995).

Thus the critique of both reconstructionism and deconstructionism leads to the same conclusion: that of the dependence of criminalisation on a certain set of social relations of power and interaction which call it into being and which are necessary for its practical working. From a reconstructionist perspective the ability to change the parameters of criminalisation, either in the interests of human rights or in the interests of their suppression, is crucially dependent on the degree to which wider social relations will provide practical support for new extensions of criminalisation. From a deconstructionist perspective the issue is the inability of actually existing power relations to enable a decentralised system for dealing with harms and conflicts in relations among and between individuals and organisations without recourse to the criminalising abstraction administered by a criminal justice system – or something closely resembling it – centred in the state.

However, there is an obvious though important qualification to be made. This relationship of mutual interdependence between criminal justice and social relations of power and culture, which is but a particular example of the general relations of separation and interdependence between the state and civil society characteristic of modern society, is an historical phenomenon. It is not in the nature of things but the product of a particular historical development. Thus abolitionism is only wrong to the extent that it advocates the possibility of dispensing with criminal justice and criminalisation *in the existing form of society*. As a critique of the repressive nature of criminal justice and a prefiguration of a more egalitarian society, it is an important standpoint. Neither is the argument that there is presently no alternative to criminal justice and criminalisation a denial of the oppressive nature of much crime control by existing states. It is rather to point to the contradictory phenomenon of dependence upon oppressive institutions by virtue of the fact that the organisation of socio-economic and political life in modern capitalist society has deprived the mass of people of any alternative. People hand over their problems to the criminal justice system because they have been deprived of the power to do otherwise. As the Soviet legal theorist, Evgeny Pashukanis wrote:

At the Hamburg Congress of Criminologists in 1905, van Hamel, a reputable representative of the sociological school, declared that the main obstacles to modern criminology were the three concepts of guilt, crime and punishment. If we freed ourselves of these concepts, he added, everything would be better. One might respond to this that the forms of bourgeois consciousness cannot be eliminated by a critique in terms of ideas alone, for they form a united whole with the material relations of which they are the expression. The only way to dissipate these appearances which have become reality is by overcoming the corresponding relations in practice, that is by realising socialism through the revolutionary struggle of the proletariat.... The concepts of crime and punishment are ... necessary determinants of the legal form from which people will be able to liberate themselves only after the legal superstructure itself has begun to wither away. And when we begin to overcome and to do without these concepts in reality, rather than merely in declarations, that will be the surest sign that the narrow horizon of bourgeois law is finally opening up before us. (Pashukanis 1978: 184–8)

It is this historical dynamic which is the main orientation of our argument in this book. The social relations which necessitate criminal justice have a history, they are part of the development of modernity and their crisis is part of the crisis of modernity. It should not be thought that a crisis in the social conditions which sustained criminalisation and criminal justice is automatically a precursor of the type of harmonious interaction prefigured by abolitionists. Something altogether different may be on the horizon. But this is part of our later discussion. Our task now is to specify with some greater rigour just what are these social relations of criminalisation and crime control to which I have been referring.

The Social Relations of Crime Control

A purely juridical perspective, concerned with the administration of the law, generally deals with a concept of the criminal offender as already in court, and spends little time thinking about the processes, and particularly the informal ones, whereby he or she arrived there. Yet a glance around the criminal court will reveal the importance of the working of a whole series of social mechanisms and relations. Present are not just the judicial and legal professionals but the defendant, and perhaps the victim as chief witness for the prosecution. How did they get there? Who reported the crime and why, and in the face of what obstacles, or under the pressure of what inducements? A central part of the case of the prosecution or defence may hang on the testimony of witnesses. How did they get there? Why were they prepared to get involved? Why were they prepared to give statements to the police? What obstacles were placed in their way or what pressures forced them to comply? Investigating magistrates, lawyers and police officers may have an implicit understanding of these mechanisms since a good part of their working life is spent dealing with them – gathering information leading to an arrest, securing the appearance of a reluctant witness in court or dealing with victims whose fear of the police may be even greater than their fear of reprisals from their attackers.

This complex of social relations which makes criminalisation an objective possibility I shall call the *social relations of crime control*: an ensemble of actors, roles and interactions which sustains the application of the criminalising abstraction and the management and control of criminality. We can describe the basic dynamics at work in a schematic or ideal type form as a 'square of crime',[6] a system of interaction between four participants; the state and the criminal justice agencies, offenders, victims, and the various publics and communities involved in the control of various types of crime.

The state and the public

The social foundation of modern crime control is that various types of conflicts have been handed over to the state to sort out. To use Nils Christie's (1977) terminology, *our* conflicts have become *their* property. This handing over has various preconditions. Firstly, the categories of criminal law deployed by the state must bear sufficient correspondence to popular conceptions of guilt, justice and harm that citizens will identify broadly the same acts as crimes as the state, and broadly agree with the types of punishments and sentences meted out by the courts. This is often regarded as guaranteed in liberal democratic regimes by the legislative process together with the assumption of a natural consensus around *primary* criminalisations such as murder and theft (see Cohen 1988). Even where this agreement exists, the public must accept the legitimacy of the criminal justice system and the activities of its various officials. This can vary within wide limits, from a rather unlikely confidence in both the competence and the professional integrity of criminal justice personnel to the more realistic scenario of a feeling that there is simply no alternative in dealing with a particular situation to that of calling the police. The crime control activities of the criminal justice agencies cannot be separated in practice from other activities in which they may be engaged. If a community is systematically harassed by a racist police force who label its young men as already criminalised then that community will be reluctant to call upon or give evidence to the police even where serious victimisation has taken place. Such communities may prefer to deal as far as possible with their own conflicts and troubles.

There is, and this will be discussed more fully later on, a whole host of habits of conduct that citizens must adopt in order to function as an adjunct rather than as rival, or hindrance to the state. How people use and conceptualise public space, read signs of disturbance or irregularity and what consequent action they take, in particular as regards the transmission of information about crime to the criminal justice agencies, are all crucial components of the techniques of governance which extend beyond the agencies of criminal justice and other branches of the state apparatus and permeate the public, local communities and families.

The state and the offender

Which law violations and problematic situations can be effectively criminalised is an important question of power involving both the state and the public. As far as the state is concerned, notwithstanding formal injunctions (present in some criminal law jurisdictions) on the public prosecutor to pursue all reported crimes, the key issue is that of discretionary behaviour. What crimes and the criminality of which social strata will be the practical focus of police action is a key variable. It is generally assumed that whereas offenders are usually more powerful than their victims, they are weaker than the state. Those in danger of criminalisation have differing resources to mount a counter-attack. The young street criminal from a poor community certainly has no power and in any case usually has an already pre-criminalised social status. Others, such as organised crime syndicates, may not avoid criminalisation, but may be able to neutralise its effects through corruption and intimidation both of criminal justice agencies and community and private organisations. Others, such as prestigious business leaders and politicians or impeccably respectable husbands are able to deploy their social status as a mechanism with which to deflect in a number of ways the criminalising abstraction. For example, in criminal trials of highly respectable financiers for various business crimes there is often a lingering assumption that really they should not be in court at all and that the matter could sensibly have been dealt with in some other way. Similarly, the ways in which rape trials usually reproduce rather than equalise the power relations between men and women, leading to the criminalisation of the victim rather than the offender, are well known.

The weakness of the offender in relation to the state is therefore a crucial component of the social relations of crime control. It enables the criminal justice system to reconcile respect for the rule of law, and hence sufficient public support to enable a flow of information about crime to the authorities, with the requirement to control crime effectively. The public could collaborate with the police without fear of reprisal from the weak offender or fear that the police themselves were corrupted by the offender. Conversely, the police could rely on a flow of public information available without intrusive surveillance on their part, and in sufficient quantity and quality to persuade a jury to convict even if the offender chose to remain absolutely silent throughout the entire proceedings as was his right. Not only therefore do the rights of due process and respect for civil liberties not interfere with the effectiveness of crime control but the former are conducive to the latter. Respect for due process and civil liberties secures the public legitimacy of criminal justice agencies and enhances the public willingness to collaborate with them. The weakness of the offender complements the role of the community as an agent of informal non-coercive control in enabling the reconciliation of law with order. As noted above, in the case of more powerful offenders this is problematic.

The state and the victim

Victimisation is not simply an automatic effect of the criminal action. Victim is a legal category and a social role requiring a certain type of action in relation to the state authorities, namely, passivity. This involves the handing over not only of technical aspects of criminal investigation and establishment of guilt, but also of the moral righteousness at harm suffered, to the criminal justice system (Christie 1977; Elias 1993). It is the state that is injured by crime. In most western criminal jurisdictions the victim takes a passive role as chief witness for the state, though as I shall note later this is beginning to change. Victim is also a social category, a status. To claim the status of victim in the eyes of the state – and the community – requires a certain type of behaviour. A transition must be made from 'sufferer' to victim (see Grant-Stitt 1989). The 'victimising abstraction' parallels the criminalising abstraction and in a similar way involves social power relations and cultural attitudes. The individual or individuals concerned need to act in certain ways in order effectively to secure victim status. Nils Christie identified the *ideal victim* as 'a person or category of individuals who – when hit by crime – most readily are given the complete and legitimate status of being a victim' (Christie 1986: 18). To achieve such status the victim must be seen to be acting in certain ways: for example, doing something entirely respectable at the time of the crime and having no complicating personal relationship with the offender which might cloud the issues of criminal responsibility. The effect of cultural stereotypes and power relations in the criminal trial process itself is no more clearly illustrated than in cases of rape where the matter before the court frequently shifts from the actions of the alleged offender to those of the victim (see Lees 1996). Victims themselves may not wish to claim full victim status and may aim, at least initially, at an alternative status such as that of disputants. Victims of domestic violence, for example, may call on the police but not wish to assume the full implications of a status as victim of crime, rather wishing the police to simply 'calm down' the situation (Hoyle 1998). That choice may, of course, itself be the effect of power relations.

The public and the victim

The relationship between the public and the victim reinforces and reproduces that of the state. The public must identify with the victim. This is

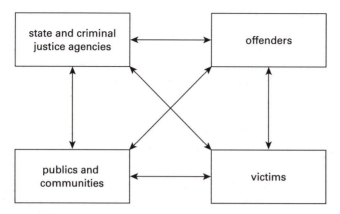

Figure 1.1 *The social relations of crime control*

particularly important in equating the power balance between situations where weak victims encounter powerful offenders. Where, for example, the victim's dependence on the offender will act as a barrier to the claiming of victim status, then the surrounding community must give sufficient support to provide testimony on behalf of, or put sufficient pressure on, the victim to compensate for this dependence. Conversely, the public may obstruct the claiming of victim status through techniques of blaming in which the victim rather than the offender comes to be regarded as the cause of the crime. Such an ideological construct needs to be carefully distinguished from the fact that many offences may arise out of prior interaction in which both victim and offender participate. In cases where the victim is absent, such as homicide or so-called 'victimless' crimes, the community has to substitute for the victim in various ways through reporting and providing evidence. Often the public will take the form of a geographical locality, of a local community of neighbours or perhaps work associates who witnessed the crime, saw something suspicious, etc. But many crimes take place elsewhere than in the victim's own locality or workplace. Members of a wider and more amorphous public must be prepared to respond to police requests for information. It is not so much the location as the activation of community that is important as far as the social relations of crime control are concerned. The forms of behaviour required of the victim – passivity, unambiguity of relations with the offender – may well be required by the community also. By this mechanism social relations of power are reproduced within criminal justice. The community may make or unmake victims. The positive side may be where victims are unaware of what is happening to them except as a result of public mobilisation, as in many cases of corporate crime concerned with pollution or the sale of dangerous goods. The negative side is seen in the denial of victim status through racism or the reinforcing of sexist assumptions concerning culpability in domestic violence or rape cases.

The public and the offender

Ideally, the relations between citizens must be such that anyone who commits a recognisable harm can be criminalised and their other identities and attributes placed in suspension or mobilised to give substantive content to the criminalising abstraction. The application of criminalising abstraction by the community is central to the whole process of crime control. The process of fitting a particular situation to the legal categories involves a complex play of power and conflict both in respect of the relation of the offender and the victim to other members of the community and of the latter to the state. Criminalisation involves the fitting of *trouble* or *problematic situations* into the straitjacket of criminal law categories and the effective recasting as criminals and victims of individuals about whose lives and affinities a great deal may be known in a cohesive community. This is the core of the criminalising abstraction. It is not that the public or the victim must first perform this abstraction and then call the police. Rather, the decision to call the police is the first step in a process one of the possible outcomes of which may be the criminalising abstraction. Cohesive communities may have a variety of complex relations with their own troublemakers. They may be simultaneously fearful of and yet benefit from certain forms of support rendered by local 'villains' which may range from sorting out petty violence and squabbles to providing a supply of cheap stolen goods. In business a certain distaste for illegal violations and corrupt practices of colleagues may be more than compensated for by the feeling that such matters should be handled in-house and are no concern of prying outside institutions such as the criminal justice system. But to the extent that the latter is able to function, the community at some stage must disconnect from the offender; it must tolerate the interventions of the state, the police and perhaps others, such as defence lawyers, knocking on doors, asking questions, taking statements, etc. It must learn to participate in the crime control process on terms set by the state. Nevertheless, even when the police are not called, the role of local communities and families, or business communities, as agents of informal social control of potential offenders is a crucial part of crime control. These structures of informal power enable the preservation of liberal legality by moderating any tendency on the part of the state to a coercive authority, and the abandonment of the rule of law and civil liberties, in the interests of all-embracing crime control.

> Liberal legality would prove too delicate for a society founded on coercive authority, were not this authority embedded indistinguishably through discipline in the domain of the normal, of the unremarkable. (Fitzpatrick 1988: 190)

The offender and the victim

Finally, the ideal victim might be thought to be paralleled by the ideal offender as outsider and stranger with no complicating relations with either the victim or the surrounding community. This situation may be approximated in street theft or household burglary by a stranger from another community, or in a clear case of financial fraud perpetrated by a group of professional criminals on a company. The offenders can be criminalised immediately by both victim and surrounding community because they have no other identity arising from a relationship with victims or other members of the latter's social network. However there is a paradox in that the more the offender fits the category of stranger, and is therefore most easily criminalisable, the less information there will be which will enable him or her to be tracked down. The highest rates of crime cleared up by police tend to be where, as in the majority of homicides, the victim was known personally to the offender and the friends, neighbours and relatives have much to say on the matter. But in homicide or brutal violence it is the abhorrent action which demonises and criminalises the perpetrator whatever else his relations with the local community. Even people who have difficulty in coming to terms with the fact that 'such a nice family man as Dr X' could possibly have turned out to be a killer, have no problem in applying the criminalising abstraction where the crime is so horrendous a disruption of civilised normality as to unambiguously dehumanise and demonise the perpetrator. However, in communities where violent death is a much more normal part of the brutality of everyday life, a murder may be less of a departure from normality.

The idea that crime exists as a distinct entity outside of this complex of relations, waiting, as it were, to be discovered by them, is revealed in the use of the term by both criminologists and criminal justice agencies of the phrase 'the dark figure of unrecorded crime' to refer to matters which are not reported to the criminal justice agencies and processed as crimes. In a strict sense this is a meaningless discourse. Not only is it not clear whether such problematic situations, if reported, would have stood the test of due process in the courts (Lacey 1995), but it is also often not clear how such events would have been conceptualised had they actually been reported and acted upon through the normal channels of criminal justice. For example, respondents to victim surveys, even though the forms of victimisation they are asked to report are usually focused on criminal law definitions, may report incidents to interviewers that they would not report to the criminal justice agencies or which would not have been regarded as crime had they done so. What interviewers are picking up may be in many cases not so much 'unreported crime' as some of the silences and power effects of the social relations of crime control.

We have described the social relations involved in criminalisation and crime control in rather ideal typical form. Actual reality departs from them in various ways even in situations where they are hegemonic. But that is precisely an illustration of their precariousness as condensations of social interaction. A number of aspects of their working can be underlined. Firstly, they sustain an organised system of moral censures which underpin criminalisation. As Colin Sumner has argued, '[t]he sociology of crime and deviance must ... become a sociology of social censures; their structural roots, institutional forms, discursive and practical meanings, systems and policies of enforcement, hegemonic functions, effects and significance for "offenders", and normative validity' (Sumner 1990a: 26–7; see also 1976, 1990b). Censure takes a practical form as the identification and labelling of offenders, their segregation and classification as individuals engaged in distinct types of activity – the application of the criminalising abstraction. Secondly, they function as a structure of communication. The flow of information about 'crime' or 'suspicious events' from the public to the criminal justice agencies, and the structuring and tutoring of public suspicions through requests for information or observations by police or collaborating media institutions, helps to sustain a common language of criminality, together with the renewal and updating of criminal stereotypes. Finally, the social relations of crime control are a mechanism of power involving the handing over of discourses and activities to the state, the abdication of the power and right to settle conflicts and the consignment of such activity to negative connotations of vigilantism and 'taking the law into your own hands' when it should be in the hands of the state, and the forcing of difference and diversity into the universalist discourse of criminal law. The positive effects of power include the rule of law and the overcoming of difference by that same discourse. But state power and the discourses of criminal law are part of 'a dense web that passes through apparatuses and institutions, without being exactly localised in them' (Foucault 1979: 96) but a web which is located in the dynamic of the social relations of crime control as a whole. The object of state activity, of public policy can therefore never be simply the articulation of criminal law and legal power but the wider task of 'government' of this structure of relations to ensure its reproduction and functioning.

Crime and Modernity

The study of interactions between the components of the social relations of crime control to reveal the various power effects internal to their operation is part of the task of a criminology dedicated to 'a fully social theory of crime' (Taylor et al. 1973). The study of the development of these relations in order to specify their conditions of existence is part of the wider task of an historically informed social theory of modernity. In the rest of this book the aim is to make a contribution to this latter task by linking some of the main developments in the social relations of crime control with the wider changes associated with the contradictory unfolding of modern capitalist societies. The main thrust of the argument will be as follows.

The social relations of crime control, despite being a key aspect of modernity, take a long time to develop and only ever develop partially, meeting with numerous resistances and obstacles. That is the result of the contradictions and tensions of a modernity whose principal engine of development is the accumulation of capital. Nevertheless, during the long period embracing, in England, the latter part of the eighteenth and most of the nineteenth century the overall tendency was towards their consolidation. Partly, this was a result of conscious social engineering, of a *modernising offensive* (Wagner 1994: 20) led by the enlightened sections of the bourgeoisie which involved reforms aimed at the education and socialisation of the working class and the reorganisation of the urban environment. This strategy was possible, indeed it only occurred because, the requirements of profitable capital accumulation and the reform of cities and social life were tied to one another. The first required the second. Capitalist expansion itself provided the resources and needed the results of the process. This was the period in which capitalism, still infused with the dynamism celebrated by Marx and Engels in the early pages of the *Communist Manifesto* of 1848, was revolutionising the forces and relations of production.

The consolidation of the social relations of crime control is inextricably bound up with these developments. Changes in the structure of cities, communities and in personal behaviour made possible a clearer marking out of the criminal, clearer definitions of crime, and boundaries of legitimate and criminal violence in private and public space. Meanwhile the agencies of criminal justice and social welfare spread into working-class communities and partially displaced traditional forms of autonomous conflict resolution, relegating the latter to the status of auxiliary or *informal* social control. At the same time within the bourgeoisie itself the development of restraint, the calming of the wild excesses of an earlier period of 'primitive accumulation' and a framework of legal regulation of economic practices made headway. All this is part of what might be considered one of the greatest projects of the first stage of modernity, that of the governance of civil society. These dynamics will be the theme of Chapter 2.

But the new forms of freedom and emancipation resulting from capitalist modernisation were accompanied by new forms of exploitation, impoverishment and conflict. Crime control was, and of course is, penetrated by these in a number of ways: by the contrast between the benefits of the rule of law and the criminal justice system as a mechanism for the protection of the powerful; by the continual weakening of the social relations of crime control in the face of powerful offenders or community sanctioned *social crime* as modes of resistance and survival among the poor. Criminalisation never loses its status as a contested process despite its overall tendency towards stabilisation. This will be the main theme of Chapter 3.

The middle of the twentieth century is the high point of what Peter Wagner (1994) terms *organised modernity*. Through the turmoil of the inter-war period the Keynesian welfare state emerges as a mechanism for social and economic stabilisation. Full employment, Fordism, and a process of breakdown in class and regional cultures through mass education and social and geographic mobility seemed, for a time, to have permanently subdued the conflicts and contradictions of the first phase of modernity. This enabled a further stabilisation of the social relations of crime control through the strengthening of consensus around definitions of criminality, the institutionalisation of urban structures and forms of behaviour conducive to crime control. At the same time social planning enabled the welfare state to join the criminal justice system as a conflict regulation mechanism. The period of the 1950s and 1960s in particular was one in which criminal justice issues were progressively depoliticised and unproblematic. The social relations of crime control could be virtually taken for granted except in a few backward areas of older cities, or regions on the periphery of modernisation which could be seen essentially as hangovers from the first stage of modernity or even pre-modernity. Nevertheless steadily rising rates of crime pointed to important fissures in the stabilisation process. Chapter 4 will attempt to draw together some of these themes.

But this period was short lived. In reality large areas were never touched by expansion, but in any case from the last quarter of the twentieth century modernity has moved into a new type of crisis. The dominant forces have been fragmentation and a weakening of the type of social structure that underpinned the social relations of crime control. This rupture in the dynamics of modernity has been sufficiently profound to have given rise to a plethora of new terminologies and discourses – for example: postmodernity, late modernity, late capitalism, postfordism, risk society – all of which attempt in one way or another to grasp the dynamics of a real crisis in the modernisation process. The ingredients of change are reasonably clear: globalisation, the dismantling of the welfare state, changes in the organisation of urban life and class structure, changes in gender relations, all associated with the changed dynamics of capitalism. These developments, it will be argued, are characterised by a disruptive tendency in which the relationship between the development of capitalism and the development of society has changed. Whereas during the nineteenth century the expansion of capital accumulation, despite its contradictions, did lay down the conditions for social cohesion, stable communities, continuities in social and economic life, the forms in which capital now develops on a global scale tend to undermine these older stabilities. Capitalism no longer develops the social productive forces, or at least not in the same way and not in a way compatible with recognisable forms of social stability.

The impact on criminality and its control is considerable. There are, it will be argued, two tendencies gathering pace. Firstly, a reintroduction of some of the obstacles that the nineteenth-century development of crime control had to overcome: blurred boundaries between criminality and normal activities and social relations; crime as an increasingly functional as well as a disruptive element in the survival of both poor communities and powerful corporations;

fragmentation of communities and urban space which disrupts stable forms of governance of crime while the latter itself increasingly functions as a form of governance. Crime, by becoming increasingly normalised, begins to lose its distinct identity *as crime*. Secondly, the same dynamic necessarily characterises the control of crime. The expansion of the latter to the management less of a distinct criminality and increasingly of the poor as a whole, who now reassume the old nineteenth-century mantle of the *dangerous classes*, blurs the boundaries between crime control and more general social regulation which is itself fragmenting and pluralising under the impact of changes in the nature of global capital accumulation.

The discussion in the remaining chapters will attempt to unravel some of these themes. None of this will of course appeal to those who see crime as an unproblematic legal category and crime control as simply a technical solution to an essentially unchanging problem. But for others it might serve as a set of pointers to a more developed understanding of the role played by criminality in the development and crisis of modernity.

Notes

1 This will be discussed further in Chapter 2.

2 The Schwendingers' argument was one of a number of contributions seeking to emancipate criminology from too close, or indeed any, dependence on existing criminal law categories. Their view that the concept of crime itself should be extended to embrace all human rights violations is paralleled by the more recent argument of Henry and Milovanovic (1996) who wish to define crime as 'the expression of some agency's energy to make a difference on others and it is the exclusion of those others who in the instant are rendered powerless to maintain or express their humanity' (1996: 116). See also Pepinsky (1974) who wished to substitute 'exploitation' for crime as the object of study.

3 That such a state of affairs, rather than being symptomatic of the gradual emergence of a system of global criminal justice to regulate the affairs of the international society of nation states, portends the future for crime control within nation states themselves, will be argued in Chapter 7.

4 A society in which social support for repressive criminalisation functioned effectively would not be unlike Daniel Goldhagen's controversial portrayal of public participation in, and support for, Nazi extermination of the Jews (Goldhagen 1996). For a critique of the argument see Finkelstein 1997.

5 The dynamics of authoritarian criminalisation will be further discussed in Chapter 3.

6 This account of the social relations of crime control is derived from earlier work in the tradition of Left Realist criminology The emphasis in the latter was on the use of the 'square of crime' as a framework within which to study the various interactions which constitute the crime control process (Lea 1992; Young 1987, 1992). The emphasis in the present work is that of the historical constitution, development and crisis of that system of interaction itself.

2

Modernisation and Crime Control

The previous chapter described how in modern society criminalisation involved a set of social relations and roles which secured the position of the state, the criminal justice agencies, as the source of legitimate remedy for interpersonal conflicts and harms. The dependence of criminalisation upon the working of the social relations of crime control, obvious as it may seem to any criminologist, lawyer or police officer with a minimal sociological imagination, has important implications. The first is that crime is not a form of action which exists prior to the institutions and social relations which deal with it. Abolitionists are right to insist that, on the contrary, we have 'crime' because we have criminal justice systems. It needs to be added that we have 'crime' also because a certain set of historically constituted social relations underpins such systems and enables them to function. Any attempt to change legal definitions of crime without reference to whether the social arrangements to practically criminalise the activities they refer to exist or can be easily established, is inevitably flawed.

Having established this, we can move on to consider the question of what broad social changes tend to consolidate the social relations of crime control, and which undermine them. This takes us to the heart of the study of the development of capitalism and modernity. In short, it is crucial to see the social relations of crime control as having a history rather than being just 'there' in one form or another in any society. Clarity concerning the relation between the development of criminalisation and the development of capitalist modernity will enable an understanding of the signficance of current social transitions and crises for criminal justice.

This, however, is easier said than done. It is hardly contentious that, for example, the processes of political representation and negotiation charac-teristic of modern democracies have specific historical preconditions; that they did not exist during the Middle Ages. Criminalisation is different in that something resembling 'crime' and mechanisms for its control can be uncovered in nearly all historical periods. People have inflicted violence on one another and appropriated one another's personal effects since the beginning of time. Historians can thus research the factors governing the rise or fall in rates of homicide or theft in the mediaeval or early modern period, giving the impression that what is being talked about is essentially the same phenomenon as crime in the nineteenth or twenty-first centuries.

Histories of criminal law and administration are easily constructed from the standpoint of gradual progress in devising incrementally improved solutions to a problem which remains essentially unchanged. The aim of this chapter, therefore, is simply to illustrate that the modern form of crime control is historically distinct and based upon particular social and economic developments. The account which follows, based largely on the English experience, is certainly not intended as a contribution to historical criminology – no new facts are unearthed and the work of established historians has been blatantly pillaged in order to construct the argument.

Pre-modern Crime Control

The structural features of pre-modern society in western Europe – taken for our purposes as referring rather loosely to the mediaeval and early modern periods – which most concern us in attempting to understand the dynamics of crime control are the predominance of social interaction through localised and personal relations. Thus mediaeval society was largely a system of private power; of the particular loyalties and bondage of specific communities to their seigneurs rather than a framework of universalised legal relations between abstract citizens. There were no citizens but, rather, separate communities with their specific obligations and loyalties. This had of course a profound impact on the nature of criminality and its control.

This localised nature of social relations meant that notions of the criminal were heavily overlaid with other categories of outsiders to be feared. Mediaeval Europe was plagued by anxiety about strangers (Bloch 1961). Outside the walled town or manorial estate bandits and robber bands existed as professional organised groups beyond the law. But the strangers and outsiders also included beggars, vagabonds and generally people without a community or seigneur who were often regarded as illegal and criminalisable (Jütte 1994). These, including the mad and the sick, all tended to be dealt with as one mass. The predominance of personal and communal relations resulted in a particularism that militated against the notion of criminal as a distinct identity. On the one hand all strangers might be regarded with suspicion and denied rights, while within the community censure tended to take a concrete form, as between relatives or family members, focusing on the act in question and involving all aspects of a person's status and relations with others as part of the characterisation of what had taken place and how it should be dealt with. This could be seen in the nature and operation of the criminal law which 'was often modified by local custom, local laws, and local opinion on what might be the best way of dealing with specific offenders and offences.' (Sharpe 1996: 103). The essential relationship was the particular conflict between victim and perpetrator. The modern unified and distinct concept of crime awaits the centralisation of the state, initially in the form of the centralisation of monarchical power and subsequently the modern nation state (see Spierenberg 1984; Ness 1990).

Well into the modern period many laws themselves lacked generality and only applied to specific places or situations, something which formed an encumbrance for later modernising reformers. As late as 1826 Robert Peel complained in a parliamentary debate on the reform of the felony laws that previous legislators 'did not think in terms of general codification.... If an offence were committed in some corner of the land, a law sprang up to prevent the repetition, not of the species of crime to which it belonged, but of the single and specific act of which there had been reason to complain.' (Emsley 1996: 204). In other words, criminal law by no means traditionally presented a set of universalistic definitions of and injunctions against 'crime'. To produce such a system was precisely the task of the reformers and codifiers. A general notion of crime and an accompanying clear social identity of criminal offender applicable to all norm-violators were subordinate to these localised relations well into the early modern period, such that

> [h]istorians anxious to study crime in the sixteenth, seventeenth and eighteenth centuries must first realise that their subject was not known then by that name. The word was current, but it lacked precise meaning.... In studying crime we therefore study something like an artificial construct, a compound comprising breaches of the law which at the time of being committed were regarded as diverse and separate (Elton 1977: 5).

Nevertheless, even if concepts of crime were different or more blurred, individuals were named, denounced to the authorities by victims and community members who would then appear before court to testify against them. The lack of a modern precision with regard to criminality did not negate the existence of some variant of the criminal sanction; rather it determined a marked lack of precision in its deployment regarding both frequency and the range of individuals and their interpersonal conflicts and harms. It is at the level of social relations – between communities and offenders, communities and centralised institutions of control – that an understanding of such dynamics must be found, rather than, for example, in notions that the pre-modern system was simply 'inefficient'.

Community and Offender

In the modern world in various places, such as traditional working-class communities, we still find a good deal of ambivalence about, for example, crime committed against outsiders, or in some other part of town (see, for example, Evans et al. 1996; Walklate 1998). Nevertheless, in most areas the social relations of crime control are sufficiently grounded that people are prepared – they have few other options – to hand over the problem to the state and to accept its definitions and processes. In pre-modern society it was the ambivalence that was uppermost. Not only was the general apparatus of the state usually distant and weak, but a society based on localised personal obligations sustained blurred boundaries and ambiguities about many forms of illegality, particularly if directed at those outside the network of localised relations. These constituted a far more diffuse set of obligations than that of the modern legal code and which allowed a considerable space, both geographical and moral, in which observance and non-observance could co-exist. As Foucault observes, pre-modern society was characterised by a sanctioning of 'popular illegalities' in which

> each of the different social strata had its margin of tolerated illegality: the non-application of the rule, the non-observance of the innumerable edicts or ordinances were a condition of the political functioning of society … illegality was so deeply rooted and so necessary to the life of each social stratum, that it had in a sense its own coherence and economy.

The result was that

> criminality merged into a wider illegality, to which the lower strata were attached as to conditions of existence…. Hence an ambiguity in popular attitudes: on the one hand, the criminal – especially when he happened to be a smuggler or a peasant who had fled from the exactions of a master – benefited from a spontaneous wave of sympathy…. On the other hand, a man who, under the cover of an illegality accepted by the population, committed crimes at the expense of this population, the vagrant beggar, for example, who robbed and murdered, easily became the object of a special hate. (Foucault 1977: 82–4)

This generalised pragmatic attitude towards illegality was not restricted to the poor and marginal groups but included 'village worthies … who moved in and out of crime as need and opportunity dictated' (Hanawalt 1979: 114). Likewise, 'in the Middle Ages, the upper reaches of English landed society had felt no qualms about breaking the law … violence was common, usually in pursuit of local prestige or power, local office holding, parliamentary elections, the short circuiting of law suits, disputes over boundaries or real estate' (Sharpe 1984: 202; see also Elias 1982; Gurr 1989). Where violence – and this goes for other criminalisable acts – are regularly resorted to and by large sections of the population, there are considerable impediments in the path of regarding them as a distinct form of criminal behaviour. The focus remains at the level of particular actions which for one reason or another are proceeded against. Crime, in short, was normalised.

Community and Sovereign

The second respect in which the social relations of crime control appear in pre-modern society in a blurred or partial form concerns the mechanisms of control over illegal or other deviant acts. The most important aspect is that the community itself, rather than the state, is the principal agent of regulation. This should be distinguished from the modern sense in which local communities or families may exercise an informal social control which is to be contrasted with the formal social control exercised by the state. Communal regulation was inherent in the localised and particularistic nature of norms and sanctions. Furthermore, the 'state', particularly under feudalism, is hardly the same type of entity as in modern society. Even where fairly strong centralised monarchies appeared in western Europe from the sixteenth century, the relationship between the state and society differed from the modern one. These states were not involved in government or regulation in the modern sense.

Foucault drew an important distinction between sovereignty and government. He referred to the pre-modern state as trapped in a 'self-referring circularity of sovereignty' (1991: 95). Its object is simply its own survival, that is to say the survival of the ruling family. The feudal monarch rules in a patriarchal manner as head of the family, defending and reproducing his status. This contrasts with the modern notion of the state as governing, that is pursuing social and economic policies directed towards the management, reproduction, improvement, etc., of its own population. For feudal monarchs the main issue was the maintenance of the loyalty of their subjects, including of course the rest of the aristocracy. Although various serious crimes, often known as heinous crimes, were dealt with by the monarch or his judges, the issue was less that of crime control in the modern sense as governance and regulation of society, than the revenge of the monarch on those considered a threat to his sovereignty.

Foucault's approach is important in going beyond a notion of the feudal or absolutist monarchical state as simply inefficient. The mediaeval judicial system was undoubtedly inefficient from a modern standpoint. There were harsh and frequently barbaric penalties on the one hand and a very low chance of detection on the other. By contrast in modern criminal justice systems lower penalties are combined with relatively high rates of detection of crime, largely due to efficient police forces. This view is simplistic if it sees the pre-modern and modern states as engaged in the same sort of enterprise; namely the effective regulation of crime as part of the governance of society. The local community in mediaeval society was left to manage its own affairs not simply because the central state was inefficient, but because it was not seen as the role of the state to regulate the community, as long as the latter posed no threat to the sovereignty of the monarch, and paid its tithes and tributes to church, king and local seigneur, matters largely governed by local custom and tradition. The localism and particularism of other norms and their frequent violation was thus not at all dysfunctional from this standpoint. Foucault summarises the relation between illegality and sovereignty in this way:

> By placing on the side of the sovereign the additional burden of a spectacular, unlimited, personal, irregular and discontinuous power, the form of monarchical sovereignty left the subjects free to practise a constant illegality; this illegality was like the correlative of this type of power. So much so that in attacking the various prerogatives of the sovereign one was also attacking the functioning of the illegalities. The two objectives were in continuity. (Foucault 1977: 88)

The public theatres of royal vengeance were the exception rather than the rule. A host of everyday conflicts and problematic situations were settled informally. The majority were probably settled out of court and for most people 'taking a criminal grievance to court was often the ultimate step in a quarrel which had either become too important or too difficult for the parties to settle in any other way' (Lenman and Parker 1980: 125). These forms of self- regulation were not necessarily peaceful, and frequently, in the mediaeval period, took the form of feud and vendetta. 'The Middle Ages, from beginning to end, and particularly the feudal era, lived under the sign of private vengeance' (Bloch 1961: 125). Such '[f]amily vendettas ... not only existed among the noble born; the towns of the fifteenth century were no less filled with private wars between families and cliques. Even the little people – hat makers, tailors, shepherds – they all had the knife quickly to hand' (Elias 1978: 237).

In contrast to all this, the modern social relations of crime control are an aspect of government in the sense deployed by Foucault.[1] They involve the organisation of publics and communities into a particular functioning relationship with state agencies and with each other such as to secure the collaboration of population and state in the task of regulating society. They involve the 'birth of the social' or the discovery by the state of society as an object outside itself with its own dynamics which have to be understood scientifically and correctly manipulated. Crime control becomes one of a number of strategies of governance aimed at securing both the conditions for the profitable accumulation of capital and the assured sovereignty of the state. The task of securing the public peace and maintaining respect for property exists among other tasks of modern governance such as education, orderly habits of work discipline, health and the proper conduct of administration carried out through a variety of institutions and processes. This great task of governance goes well beyond the state. Private institutions play a role every bit as important as state bodies. It is the relationship between the parts and the whole that is important. In crime control the population becomes an instrument of the state in the guaranteeing of public tranquillity and respect for property. This development has to go through a number of difficult stages on the road to its modern form.

Early Capitalism

The transition from monarchical sovereignty to governance is an essential component of the transition to modernity. Society is no longer seen as consisting simply of subjects to be ruled by the sovereign as patriarch but as a population to be considered as the object of policy interventions to achieve certain ends. Sovereignty is not replaced but is democratised, finding its source in law and constitution. The emancipatory side of this transition is of course that the population comes to be seen as consisting of individuals (initially restricted to male members of the bourgeoisie) whose rights must be respected. Foucault identified the Mercantilist period of the sixteenth and seventeenth centuries as a transitional phase in which the focus is still the aggrandisement of the monarch, but more modern rational techniques of governance, in particular the accumulation of wealth through trade, are deployed to this end.

But to what end is the population to be governed? Philosophically speaking, God, to whom sovereignty of the monarch was linked by doctrines such as divine right, is replaced by Reason. The new objects of governance are, for Foucault, economy and population which are now external entities and objects of state policy rather than the sum of subjects within the 'household' of the state. Behind these new discourses lies of course the rise of the bourgeoisie and the accumulation of capital. During the Mercantilist period the nascent mercantile bourgeoisie could be assimilated to the old regime – through mechanisms such as the sale of offices by the Crown – whose object remained that of traditional sovereignty. It is, therefore, manufacture, requiring a socialised labour force and a revolution in social structure, which properly constitutes population and economy as the objects of governance. With the hegemony of the capitalist mode of production there now appears a new agent of social synthesis, capital accumulation, which is outside the state and the associated paraphernalia of feudal sovereignty. The modern state wishes to govern society and to do this it must relate to this new motor force.

The eighteenth century thus witnesses several transitions. Firstly, there is the decline of monarchical power in the face of democracy and the rule of law as a political system suited to the dominance of the bourgeoisie. This process is, secondly, accompanied by the development of disciplinary institutions such as prisons, asylums, schools, factories aimed at the production of 'docile bodies', fundamentally, that is, willing workers. The third transition involves the development of governance.[2] The concern with loyalty of the population remains but it is pursued through discipline and through strategies of governance concerned with understanding the dynamics of 'population', that is, social and economic relations outside the state. The aim is the encouragement of good habits of conduct, restraint, self-control and respect for bourgeois property in the population as a whole in order to facilitate and strengthen that which is already developing under its own laws and dynamics: the accumulation of capital. Crime control by the state takes on this characteristic. The significance of crime is less the affront to the legitimacy of rule, though it continues to take this form as long as the main response is through juridical institutions, and more the disruption of ordered processes of social and economic life. Crime control is a form of regulation rather than simply of retribution. It is not, as Foucault points out, a matter of criminal justice institutions or the law fading into the background or disappearing, 'but rather that the law operates more and more as a norm, and the judicial institution is increasingly incorporated into a continuum of apparatuses (medical, administrative and so on) whose functions are for the most part regulatory' (Foucault 1979: 144).

Foucault's account of the transition from sovereignty to governance has the virtue of enabling us to avoid any crude reduction of the state to the status of ancillary institution for capital. The practice of governance certainly is concerned with making a world safe for capital through the regulation of the working class. But it also becomes, in the hands of the enlightened and reforming sections of the bourgeoisie – the carriers of the modernising offensive – a vehicle for the regulation of the bourgeois class itself, as a whole, through the encouraging of habits of thrift, abstinence, deferred gratification, the compromise with aristocratic values of status and hierarchy and the rejection of traditions of expressive violence characteristic of the old warrior aristocracy (duelling, debauchery, etc.) in favour of sobriety and restraint (see also Elias 1982, 1994). It is important to understand that the transition involved struggle and conflict. The development of clear notions of crime and crime control are bound up with the development of modern notions of government. In what follows I shall mainly be concerned with the working class. The issue of the regulation of the bourgeoisie itself will be taken up in Chapter 3.

Communities and Police

The term police emerges in Europe as early as the thirteenth century but comes to prominence during the Mercantilist period of the sixteenth and seventeenth centuries. It functioned less as a particular institution than as a strategy combining aspects of both feudal sovereignty and modern governance. On the one hand, the security of the sovereign remains the overriding aim. But to achieve this, new strategies aimed at penetrating and managing the population are devised. In Continental Europe the growth of police was associated with the rise of the centralised absolutist monarchies. This new concentration of monarchial power was partly modern in that 'the stress is no longer put on his mere entitlement but above all on his obligation for the maintenance of order and "good police" within all domains of life' (Wettman-Jungblutt 1997: 32–3). The monarch will retain his sovereignty less by traditional intrigue and outwitting potential enemies and usurpers than by skilful penetration and control of his population alongside other, economic, factors such as the encouragement of trade. This notion of police went far beyond what would now be regarded as the control of crime and often involved the attempt to regulate the minutiae of everyday life such as dress and deportment. The impulse for this was, in the earliest forms of police, the weakening of traditional feudal relations of deference in towns and the need to encourage restraint and conduct conducive to trade under circumstances in which such behaviour had yet to be internalised and normalised (Elias 1982, 1994). But the prime objective remains that of the stability of the rule of the sovereign. Where police did take the form of an institutional structure it tended to have wide functions. Jean-Paul Brodeur quotes a commentator on the functions of the royal police established in 1667 under Louis XIV with the explicit aim of strengthening royal authority in all fields of life with functions including

> to repress the tyranny of the merchants against the public, while at the same time stirring up their trade ... to penetrate inside families through underground passages and to keep the secrets that they never imparted for as long as it is unnecessary to use them; to be everywhere without being seen; finally, to move or to check at will this vast and tempestuous multitude and to be the ever active and nearly unknown soul of this great body. (Brodeur 1983: 514)

The modernising revolutions of the eighteenth century are marked by changes in the nature of police. The strategy still covers a very wide ground but tends to become a form of governance in that the imposition of general social order through police is linked to the regulation of the economy. This was the intention of the eighteenth-century Italian jurist Cesare Beccaria when he spoke of police as an aspect of public economy:

> But neither the products of the earth, nor those of the work of the human hand, nor mutual commerce, nor public contributions can ever be obtained from men with perfection and constancy if they do not know the moral and physical laws of the things upon which they act, and if the increase of bodies is not proportionately accompanied by the change of social habits; if, among the multiplicity of individuals, works and products one does not at each step see shining the light of order, which renders all operations easy and sure. Thus, the sciences, education, good order, security and public tranquillity, objects all comprehended under the name of police, will constitute the fifth and last object of public economy. (Beccaria [1764]1996: 22–3)

Increasingly 'police is no longer an ideal to be sought by governance but one of its techniques' (Dean 1999: 95). Police emerge as a distinct institution in the eighteenth and early nineteenth centuries; a body dedicated to encouraging industrious habits in the (working-class) population, alongside other institutions of discipline, and the removal of obstacles to capital accumulation. The initial tasks of the police apparatus are neither restricted to, nor defined as, crime control in the modern sense. Police activity is rather directed against the masses as a whole. It is only when the more general tasks of regulation have been accomplished that a sharper focus on criminality as a marginal deviance can become the main preoccupation.

In an English context this perspective aids understanding of some key stages in the development of police as a state or public institution. Modernisation involves the transition from the old idea of police as a set of injunctions and rules concerning appropriate deference to the monarch to the 'new police' as a distinct institution mainly concerned with the regulation of marginal deviance. In between is a crucial transitional phase in which the police appear as a distinct institution but with their target as the working class as a whole who stand in need of habituation to a life of subservience to capital. At the beginning of the nineteenth century the merchant and magistrate Patrick Colquhoun established a new private police force, the Thames Marine Police, to protect his docks and warehouses from pilferage. Peter Linebaugh, in his study of criminality and class conflict in eighteenth-century London, summarises Colquhoun's view of the working class

> as an epidemic ... a military enemy whose 'various detachments and subdivisions ... [form] the general army of Delinquents'.... The London working class has spun a 'system', a 'monstrous System of Depredation', a 'General System of Pillage'. It is 'disciplined in acts of Criminal Warfare'.... The working class is also uncivilised, possessing 'unruly passions', 'rapacious desires', 'evil propensities', 'noxious qualities', 'vicious and bad habits', and its moral turpitude needs the 'human improvement' by police.... (Linebaugh 1991: 428)

What he found particularly irksome was the attempt by his dock workers to preserve traditional rights to a portion of the cargo of ships unloaded. He complained that they 'consider it as a kind of right which attaches to their situation to plunder whatever opportunity offers' (quoted in Emsley 1987: 113). Such habits, derived from forms of pre-capitalist social order, violated the sanctity of bourgeois property. It was the working-class population as a whole, rather than a criminal minority, that was to be characterised as delinquent and in need of policing. In this context the historian E.P. Thompson warned against any attempt to read back into the eighteenth century the criminological categories of the twentieth. He criticised attempts to read contemporary reports of the life of the poor as accounts of a 'criminal subculture' of gangs.

> What twentieth-century criminologists describe as subcultures eighteenth-century magistrates described as gangs. What is at issue is not whether there were any such gangs (there were) but the universality with which the authorities applied the term to any association of people, from a benefit society to a group of kin to a Fagin's den, which fell outside the law. (Thompson 1977: 194)

This generalised fear of the working class as a whole as dangerous or criminal continues well into the nineteenth century.

the indiscriminate equation of the 'criminal class', the 'poor' and the 'working classes', and the loose assumption that the terms were rhetorically inter-changeable, had become commonplace in the more sensational writings on the urban crisis which now began to proliferate. And it was not only the motley, vast and hitherto little regarded populace of paupers and pimps, vagrants and sharp practisers, pick-pockets and beggars, unemployed and derelict, thieves and robbers, who were now transformed into that collectivity which Frenchmen in the 1840s were to term the 'dangerous classes'. The whole world of the poor tended to be accommodated within a system of criminal labelling not only to express the social fear of the respectable, but also to justify a broader strategy of control to cope with that fear. (Gatrell 1980: 270)

Colquhoun's project for a private police force under his personal direction illustrates another feature peculiar to England at the time: the simultaneous weakness of the state authorities and the dependence upon law as the main instrument of policy. 'By the late seventeenth century the English State lacked the coercive capacity to exact a uniform compliance throughout its social structure' (McMullan 1995: 123; see also McMullan 1987). There were large areas of the rural periphery beyond the control of the state, or with only periodic visits by state officials such as revenue officers and soldiery to coastal smuggling communities. The expansion of trade both between towns and between continents exposed the weakness of the state in the face of the professional highwayman and pirate whose existence was dependent, much as in the Middle Ages, on the sanctuary of unguarded and uncharted territory. As towns rapidly expanded, a similar weakness of the state was highlighted by the *rookeries*, areas, usually a maze of narrow streets and alleyways navigable only by their inhabitants and safe from all except the episodic incursion of the authorities. In these areas underworlds, networks and a thriving criminal economy had been expanding, in London at least, since the middle of the sixteenth century (McMullan 1984).

In such circumstances the control strategies were heavily reliant on spies and informers.

Deviant populations could not be immediately controlled, and command over information conferred a power which could affect most court proceedings. Justice came to resemble a market place in which an elaborate trading eco-nomy developed. The moral and the immoral, the regulated and the regulators, came to be utterly entangled in one another. (Rock 1983: 203)

In the early eighteenth century thieftakers were frequently both criminal practitioners, which enhanced them as their information sources regarding criminal activity, and law enforcers. Often the latter furthered criminal interests. The notorious eighteenth-century thieftaker, Jonathan Wild, used his power to organise the criminal underworld and eliminate competitors.

'What distinguished Wild's organisation in the first decades of the eighteenth century was also to characterise the Sicilian mafiosi, the capacity to serve as an acknowledged and necessary intermediary between weak community and weak governance' (Rock 1983: 216).

The excessive reliance on law as the main instrument of rule – sovereignty as a cumbersome and primitive instrument of governance (see Brewer and Styles 1980: 20) – itself contributed to a response to the general recalcitrance of the masses in adapting to the new conditions of labour for capital as a problem of 'crime'. Thus '[u]p until the 1840s almost all the measures directed towards control over the labour force were ... penal and repressive ...' (Saville 1994: 28), an example being the notorious Combination Acts of 1799 and 1800 which defined attempts at trade union organisation as criminal conspiracy. This use of law and police as a crude modernising force, directed at the new working class as a whole, rather than mopping up a criminal residue, endures well into the nineteenth century. As the century progressed the police marched into the working-class districts with the quite explicit aim of enforcing the habits required by labour for capital.

> The imposition of the police brought the arm of municipal and state authority directly to bear upon key institutions of daily life in working class neighbourhoods, touching off a running battle with local custom and popular culture which lasted at least until the end of the century ... the monitoring and control of the streets, pubs, racecourses, wakes, and popular fetes was a daily function of the 'new police' ... [and must be viewed as] a direct complement to the attempts of urban middle class elites ... to mould a labouring class amenable to new disciplines of both work and leisure. (Storch 1976: 481; cf. also Brogden 1982: ch. 2)

Meanwhile the actual control of crime in the modern sense was, well into the century, primarily a matter for the older institutions such as privately funded Associations for the Prosecution of Felons and the hiring of private thieftakers, a system which remained well suited to the needs of property owners for whom these forms of private security never entirely disappeared during the nineteenth century (Johnston 1992). The masses meanwhile could be left to their own devices. Thus

> people who looked back on eighteenth-century law enforcement a century later would have ... been struck, for example, by the fact that eighteenth-century law remained for most people an expensive discipline of last resort; cheaper disciplines often did as well. Eighteenth-century society was cemented less by law than by informal sanctions neighbour wielded against neighbour, landlords against tenants, employers against labourers. Control was exercised face to face, not bureaucratically. Cheapness was a consideration too. Popular lawlessness cost eighteenth-century gentlemen little: it was farmers and tradesmen who bore the brunt of its costs – or the poor themselves. When it cost them so little, gentlemen were sensibly concerned that the business of curtailing it should cost less. And so (by later standards) the state kept a low profile. Detection and prosecution remained at the discretion and mainly at the

expense of victims or of associations of local farmers and businessmen. Sentencing was discretionary also, character and testimony deeply influenced an offender's fate. (Gatrell 1988: 247–8).

As the century progresses, the new institutions of police and magistrates' courts penetrate the working-class areas of the expanding cities and their activity focuses more precisely, though never exclusively, on criminality as a marginal phenomenon. But these developments reflect not simply a unilateral curtailing by the state of generalised governance of the masses by police, but also a decline in that which gave such generalised policing its rational kernel: the blurring by the masses themselves of certain forms of criminality and resistance to advancing capitalism.

Communities and Crime

The relationship between communities and crime in the transitional period of the eighteenth and early nineteenth centuries is a contradictory one. On the one hand,

> [b]y the middle of the [eighteenth] century ... 'crime' was beginning to take on something like the modern layperson's definition: murder, rape, the more serious property offences like theft, robbery and burglary, and the host of lesser offences which served as precursors to them. (Sharpe 1996: 106)

Likewise Foucault grasps the emergence of modern configurations of crime as a process whereby

> the diffuse, occasional, but frequent delinquency of the poorest classes was superseded by a limited, but 'skilled' delinquency.... A general movement shifted criminality from a 'mass criminality' to a 'marginal criminality' partly the preserve of professionals ... [and] a whole complex mechanism, embracing the development of production, the increase of wealth, a higher juridical and moral value placed on property relations, stricter methods of surveillance, a tighter partitioning of the population, more efficient techniques of locating and obtaining information.... (Foucault 1977: 75–7)

The 'popular illegalities' of the pre-modern period now needed to be eliminated in the interests of strict boundaries between legal and illegal. What was at stake now was not the sovereignty of monarch or seigneur, which could surmount and tolerate ambiguities, but the profitability of capital which could not. Under such pressure the concept of theft moves towards its modern form as a general category, interchangeable between properties and individuals. The criminalising abstraction becomes manifest in the figure of the 'criminal' as a general identity for the violators of these rights. It is the counterpart of the interchangeability of property as the embodiment of abstract labour analysed by Marx. What is crucial is no longer the sanctity of the property of this or that landowner but property in general; no longer violence against this or that person but violence in general. Edward Thompson, writing on the struggles around the eighteenth-century English game laws, pointed to 'an increasing impersonality in the mediation of class relations, and a change, not so much in the "facts" of crime as in the category – crime – itself, as it was defined by the propertied. What was now to be punished was not an offence between men ... but an offence against property ...' (Thompson 1977: 206–7).

However, on the other hand, the extension and consolidation of bourgeois property involved not only the increasing refusal to tolerate traditional illegalities but the criminalisation of activities many of which had been customary practices since time immemorial. These included such activities as the gathering of wood or hunting of game on common land, together with a whole host of traditional 'perks' like the entitlement of agricultural workers to a portion of the remains of the harvest, of coal miners to pick the waste coal from the pit heaps, and of dockers to a portion of the cargo: the practice which so outraged Colquhoun. The criminalisation of such customary activities produced a 'criminality' which functioned as working class opposition to the advance of capitalist social relations. In eighteenth-century England the state, with its expanding 'Bloody Code' of capital offences, followed in the footsteps of capitalist property relations.

This *social* crime has become a controversial topic amongst historians and criminologists.[3] The focus has been, firstly, on the extent to which such criminality can be seen as a form of collective resistance to the advance of capitalism and, secondly, on the question of the boundaries between social crime and 'ordinary' crime. Both these areas of argument are vulnerable to the danger of looking at the eighteenth and early nineteenth centuries from the standpoint of concepts and distinctions which did not become established until much later. The concept of social crime as proto-political resistance was originally developed by Eric Hobsbawm, in studies of 'social bandits' and peasant outlaws, to refer to 'a conscious, almost a political, challenge to the prevailing social and political order and its values' (Hobsbawm 1972: 5). The studies of eighteenth-century England are also partly concerned with active resistance. Douglas Hay, in his study of poaching, showed how local communities 'united solidly in defence of poaching. The keepers met with a wall of silence when they tried to make inquiries, but found that word spread like lightning when they obtained a search warrant, and that the suspects had escaped with "the apparatus" just before they arrived' (Hay 1975: 198).

Thus, for the rural masses of eighteenth-century England, excluded from political representation, not only poaching but food riots (see Thompson 1967; Randall and Charlesworth 1996) and machine-smashing can indeed be seen as active proto-political resistance. However, as regards other activities, there is a distinction between 'crimes which draw their collective legitimation from their explicit protest nature and actions which although against the law were not regarded as criminal by the large numbers who participated in them whether their purpose was to make a protest or not.... The most important characteristic of "social crimes" lies in positive popular sanction, not in the often present element of protest' (Rule 1979: 51–2). Thus organised illegal activity such as illicit distilling, pillaging ship-wrecks for cargo, various types of smuggling, etc., were less clearly forms of explicit social protest than they were continuities of older forms of 'popular illegalities'.[4]

The argument is not affected one way or the other by the recognition that activities such as poaching were participated in also by middle-class elements and organised gangs. Sections of the middle-class and small gentry were also engaged in violation of game laws that benefited large landowners (Fine 1984: 184–9), while much poaching was undertaken by professional criminal gangs (Archer 1989, 1999) who often sold illegally killed game to innkeepers and butchers, taking advantage, no doubt, of widespread tolerance of poaching, yet at the same time embracing the new capitalist market relations rather than resisting them (Emsley 1996: 4, 112). Such activity was nevertheless likely to be tolerated because it reduced prices rather than because it was a defence of traditional rights. Such gangs, in the form of smugglers, coiners and the pillagers of shipwrecks had been part of the life of the poor for centuries.

However, a debate as to whether or not such activities on the part of the poor were forms of protest can become fruitless when applied to a world in which the participation of the masses in institutionalised forms of politics had yet to be established. In the absence of political parties or organised trade unions linked to structures of negotiation and political compromise protest frequently took to the streets. Part of what enables the modern social relations of crime control to become clearly established is that the forms of legitimate conflict resolution are clearly demarcated. Where they are not, then the boundaries of criminality become blurred as a consequence.

Similar considerations apply to the issue of the distinction between social and 'ordinary' crime. It might be argued that a concentration on resistance results from a 'tendency to focus on the atypical instances where there was widespread collective opposition and ignore the vast majority of instances where no such resistance existed. Thus smugglers, costermongers, poachers, bootleggers, became the focus of attention, not thieves, rapists, burglars and murderers' (Young 1994: 87). The point, however, is not that all crime was *social* crime, nor that all social crime was in fact a variant of modern political struggle in all but name. Rather, the issue is that many elements were present, including resistance on the one hand and interpersonal harm on the other, but that the boundaries between them were indistinct and blurred. The masses during the eighteenth century still had, as Edward Thompson wrote, their own popular attitudes,

> amounting at times to an unwritten code, quite distinct from the laws of the land. Certain crimes were outlawed by both codes: a wife or child murderer would be pelted and execrated on the way to Tyburn. Highwaymen and pirates belonged to popular ballads, part heroic myth, part admonition to the young. But other crimes were actively condoned by whole communities – coining, poaching, the evasion of taxes (the window tax and tithes) or excise or the press gang. Smuggling communities lived in a state of constant war with authority, whose unwritten rules were understood by both sides.... On the other hand other crimes, which were easily committed and yet which struck at the livelihood of particular communities – sheep stealing or stealing cloth off the tenters in the open field – excited popular condemnation.... The law was hated, but it was also despised. Only the most hardened criminal was held in as much popular odium as the informer who brought men to the gallows. (Thompson 1968: 64–6)

These popular attitudes, safe to say, did not condone rapists, thieves and murderers. But their conceptions of these may have differed considerably both from those of the elite and from other communities in different parts of the country. Some cases would be taken to court – it was in most cases still up to the victim to initiate prosecution – others, probably the majority, would be dealt with by the community itself, and not necessarily by peaceful forms of mediation. The real issue is that of the lack of fixed categories of crime and criminality in the eyes of the masses. Just as the bourgeoisie tended to blur the distinction between workers and criminals so the masses blurred the distinction between criminals and resisters. Those who stole the sheep from the wealthy farmer may also have stolen from the poor, the poor from each other. Both may have ended up on the gallows together with those who engaged in neither. The historian researching the period and trying to distinguish social and ordinary crime finds it increasingly

> less possible to sustain any tidy notion of a distinction between these two kinds of crime. There is a real difference in emphasis at each pole: certainly the community (and its culture) was more likely to give shelter to some 'social' offenders (smugglers or rioters in popular causes) than to thieves or sheep stealers. Yet in many cases we found little evidence of a morally endorsed popular culture here and a deviant subculture there. (Hay et al. 1975: 14)

The difficulty of delineating the boundaries of social crime reflects, rather than its lack of coherence as a concept, the very fluidity of social relations in the nascent capitalist society of eighteenth-century England. The social relations of crime control are blurred, on the one hand by the role of criminal justice agencies in a general habituation of the working class to capital and, on the other, by various forms of active or passive resistance to capitalist property relations.

The Stabilisation of Modernity

The latter part of the nineteenth century and the first part of the twentieth is a period of institutionalisation of conflict. This is secured by the demo-cratisation of sovereignty through parliamentary control, at first restricted to the male bourgeois elite but then progressively expanded to include widening circles of the population through representation both in parlia-ment and in various organs of collective negotiation and compromise. These new mechanisms establish the aim of governance as the protection of autonomous social and economic processes; the freedom of capital and labour markets to operate within limits prescribed by the interests of profita-bility, on the one hand, and the health and reproduction of labour on the other. The habituation of the working class as a whole to capital through the blunt instrument of the criminal law and police is displaced by a more sophisticated plurality of agencies and knowledges, both state and private, aimed at securing the conditions of existence of a working-class population already socialised to the routines of living and working in modern capital-ist society. In the English experience in particular, the modernising offen-sive led by the enlightened sections of the bourgeoisie crosses the boundaries of public and private involving both the state and private action in many areas of urban reform (see Rose and Miller 1992). Capital under-stands the necessity to take steps to secure the reproduction of labour power. Modernisation pulls down the old rookeries to widen streets and make way for railways, it builds improved housing and urban environ-ments. Colquhoun's identification of the need of the working class for 'improvement by police' is translated into a host of philanthropic interven-tions from Sunday schools to sewers.

The reformers, it is important to understand, were working in tune with the spontaneous development of capitalism itself. True, capitalist develop-ment produced massive social inequality and periodic recessions or 'great thunderstorms which increasingly threaten ... the foundation of society and of production itself' (Marx 1973: 411). Nevertheless, these episodic com-motions did not interfere with capitalism's ability to develop the productive forces of society; to build cities rather than destroy them, draw workers into stable jobs rather than expel them, and lay the foundations for stable working-class communities rather than undermine them. David Harvey recently looked back on this epoch with an appropriate nostalgia.

> In the past ... urbanisation and the consequences of urbanisation were taken rather more seriously than they are today. In the late nineteenth century, the bourgeoisie at least had some notion that cities were important places and, therefore, that urban reform was necessary. This generated a bourgeois reform movement – from Birmingham to Chicago – which included such figures as Jane Addams, Octavia Hill, Charles Booth, Patrick Geddes, Ebenezer Howard and many others. All of these had some vision for the future and a clear grasp

of the need for reform. The nineteenth century faced the difficulties of the urban in a very positive and powerful way. It blended socialist sentiments, anarchist ideas, notions of bourgeois reformism and social responsibility into a programmatic attempt to clean up the cities. The 'gas and water socialism' of the late nineteenth and early twentieth centuries did a great deal to improve the conditions of urban life for the mass of the population.... Some of that concern would be helpful to have back in our cities right now. (Harvey 1997: 20)

The Expansion of Regulation

In this context crime control comes to assume its modern form as regulation of the margins of social relations and defence against episodic disruptions of their normal self-governing processes. As the bourgeoisie and the state abandon a view of the working class as generalised criminality and develop a more sophisticated view of a differentiated social stratum with a variety of needs requiring expert intervention and knowledge, so criminality becomes the pathology of the 'residual' elements.

> The concern of the authorities had shifted, by the 1850s from a fear of crime as part of a general social and political threat to the existing society and its institutions, to a view of crime as a normal problem inherent in industrial society, to be dealt with on a normal day to day basis by preventative, detective and penal measures. (Philips 1977: 284)

The weakness of the state authorities, evident in the eighteenth century, disappears with the opening up of the rookeries and peripheral rural areas, as criminal justice institutions, along with other agencies of regulation, penetrate into the working-class areas. Close behind the police constable comes the truancy officer and the public health inspector. The expansion of police is matched by the expansion of cheap, easily available summary jurisdiction. The percentage of offences in England and Wales tried in front of lay magistrates rose from 66 per cent in 1857 to 80 per cent by 1911 (see Gatrell 1980: 268). Today it is nearly 90 per cent. Much of this extension of regulation was, in the English case, directly administered locally by the bourgeoisie who both provided the lay magistrates and, through local government Watch Committees, supervised the new police forces which expanded in cities outside London (see for example Brogden 1982).

General policing of the perceived dangerous classes does not, however, disappear. It remains a key aspect of the police task (Bittner 1975). It rather becomes concentrated and focused on the poorest sections of the working class, those sections most likely to be in and out of crime as a mode of survival, on young people of criminal age. The key shift is the assumption that the sections of the working class in stable employment, having achieved an accommodation with the police, will support such policing. There is never a police focus purely on *criminals* but rather on those social strata perceived to be *likely* to commit crime. What behaviour and by whom is to be regarded as suspicious is, of course, a fertile ground for stereotypes and labels. The poor and immigrants – the Irish in particular during the nineteenth century – are candidates for criminalisation irrespective of actual behaviour.

The progressive extension of the agencies of criminal justice into working-class life undermined older traditions of autonomous community response. Louise Jackson (2000) in a recent study of reactions to child abuse in Victorian England reports a Bow Street (London) magistrate in 1830, unable to convict an alleged child molester for lack of evidence, encouraging in his closing speech the 'rough justice' of the mob waiting outside the courthouse, who acted accordingly. Similarly, older traditions of settling disputes within the community with monetary payment persisted. Jackson cites an example, as late as 1860 of a jury regarding a prior monetary payment as indication of the prior settlement of a case (of child molesting) and acquitted the defendant accordingly. Increasingly, however, the community withdrew. The crowd outside the courthouse came to be seen as disturbance and illegitimate public disorder while attempts to make compensation payments were seen as evidence of guilt and regarded as illegal (Jackson 2000: 38–40). Opposition to the presence of police in working-class areas, including physical resistance, continued well into the present century (White 1986). But an index of its overall decline is the substantial fall in the number of trials for assaults on police (in England and Wales) from an average annual rate of 67 per 100,000 of the population during 1856–60 to 24 during 1910–14 (Gatrell 1980; but see Davis 1989). Indeed, from around the middle of the century, recorded rates for most categories of offences fell steadily until well after the First World War (Gatrell and Hadden 1972; Gatrell 1980), reasonable indications of at least the beginnings of the consolidation of the social relations of crime control.

It would be a mistake, however, to see the increasing working-class accommodation to, and use of, the criminal justice agencies in preference to older methods as simply a result of the availability of the former, as if community-based regulation of conflicts and harms had only existed because of the expense and difficulty hitherto of making use of criminal justice. The process of accommodation to the state and the agencies of governance is also a result of profound changes in working-class life and in the nature and organisation of criminality during the nineteenth century. The extension of the governance of crime, as with other areas of governance, is part of the process of socialisation conducted jointly by capital and the state, the former drawing the masses into wage labour while the latter develops new forms of expert knowledge concerning the inner workings of the class – its family structure, educational problems, health and dietary habits, disorderliness. The result is that the working class comes to constitute a stable population whose cultural aspirations, forms of conduct, masculinity, femininity, cohere with the requirements of capital accumulation. An important part of this new stability is the marginalisation of crime as an aspect of the life of working-class communities.

The Marginalisation of Crime

The development of the stable working-class community was the result of a number of factors. The expansion of employment and the progressive decasualisation of the labour market led to the reduction of population turnover in working-class areas. By the 1880s in many areas 80 per cent of working-class marriages involved both bride and groom from the same locality (Savage and Miles 1994). Meanwhile the suburbanisation of the middle classes (in London after 1870) left working-class inner city areas with a degree of political control of local government. For the new working class generalised resistance to capitalism is displaced by reformist politics based on trade unions and political representation. The residues of resistance based on the defence of pre-capitalist values and habits – of which social crime was an important expression – vanish as the class is recomposed within the confines of the capitalist labour process and the monetisation of social needs around the family wage. The decriminalisation of working-class industrial and political organisation was the product of bitter struggles, but nevertheless formed the basis for reconciliation to capitalism and its culture and the consolidation of the appearance of the state as a neutral agency above the contending social classes.

The culture of the stabilised working class emphasised an orientation to family and consumption emulating the older labour aristocracy of craftsmen – what would later be referred to as *embourgeoisement*. There was a tendency towards 're-orientation of working class culture from being work centred to home centred ... generally shorter working hours and increased real wages eroded work-centred culture and increased the role of the home as the centre of life' (Daunton 1983: 220). The new family division of labour with its appropriate structures of masculinity and femininity, childhood and adolescence, ordered life transitions from school to work, marriage and new family formation, involved the withdrawal of women from the labour market and the idea of the male breadwinner as the provider of the family wage. A shift away from the street and communal life was reinforced by the development of elementary education which removed many juveniles from the streets and from potential recruitment to the criminal labour force, to organised sites of leisure and entertainment; pubs and music halls, parks and designated public spaces of leisure. The result as Phil Cohen (1979) shows in his study of North London at the turn of the century, was that the working class had begun to move away from the moral economies of street culture, and find in the institutions of public propriety a means, not just of respectability, but of material advancement. For them, involvement in trade unionism and local labour politics has been the great pathway to these twin goals.... [Labour movement institutions] not only organised the hitherto unorganised, but helped give them a stake in the new urban order that was taking shape. Unemployed men still gathered at the unofficial labour exchange ... but to talk politics or racing results rather than to jeer at passing toffs or spit at the police, as was their regular habit in the 1890s. (Cohen 1979: 125)

There was developing a new *moral economy of place and space* whereby:

a system of informal, tacitly negotiated and particularistic definitions of public order were evolved which accommodated certain working class usages of social space and time, and outlawed others. What were ratified were those practices which articulated the institutions of patriarchy and public propriety within the class habitat; what were outlawed were those practices of women and children which challenged the monopoly of those institutions over the working class city and its legitimate usage. The new norms in effect imposed a system of unofficial curfew, informal out-of-bounds, to define what were the wrong people, wrong age, wrong sex, in the wrong place and the wrong time. And 'wrong' was defined in the simultaneous terms of a moral ideology of deviance and the juridical ideology of crime. (Cohen 1979: 131)

The use of public space begins to follow predictable patterns: going to or returning from work, school, shopping, determinate places of entertainment and recreation, etc., at particular times of the day and in particular areas of the city.[5] People within these patterns are legitimately present; those outside these patterns stand out as suspicious either of likely criminality or various types of vagrancy. The surveillance of this public space, outside the tight housing communities, is yielded to the authorities. Mike Brogden quotes the Liverpool City Police *Instruction Book for New Constables* of 1878 which describes the task of the beat officer as 'Watching vigilantly the movements of all suspicious persons who pass through his beat.... If it be at an untimely hour, or if they fail to assign a proper reason for being in a place, he is to arrest them' (Brogden 1991: 87).

These developments have profound effects on the relation of the working class to crime. Those in stable employment, oriented to consumption and family, are distanced from the street economy of social crime and cheap goods of dubious origin. Consciousness of the value of property acquired from the wage, and from savings, assimilates the working class to definitions and attitudes to crime shared with the middle classes. The street thief, robbing workers of their pay packets as much as the middle classes of their wallets, or the stalking murderer, preying on the vulnerable of all social classes, becomes the paradigm of crime. During the second half of the nineteenth century the modern 'moral panic' about crime and violence becomes a feature of urban life, of which the two best known examples in

London are the garrotting panic of 1862 and the Jack the Ripper murders of 1888. The garrotting panic concerned violent street robbery. Several people were attacked, including a well known Member of Parliament, in the centre of London, and robbed while temporarily incapacitated by choking. The growing popular press played on public fears in a campaign for tougher legislation. As Sharpe comments:

> With the panic we find ourselves firmly in the world ... of the widespread acceptance of criminal stereotypes, and of crime and punishment as issues that were debated by newspapers, usually in terms of straightforward appeals to the instinctive reactions of potential readers. (Sharpe 1996: 138)

The growth in the popular press and media and their diffusion to a working-class readership was a potent vehicle for the dissemination of common notions of crime and stereotypes of the criminal as an essentially weak, pathological individual. The later part of the century sees the mushrooming of the crime thriller (Leps 1992), the authors of which gained a spurious objectivity about their subjects from the blossoming new science of criminology in its psycho-biological form. By the time of the Jack the Ripper murders of women in the East End of London, the popular media have assumed a considerable power of moral leadership and social integration.

> An analysis of the newspaper reports of the Ripper murders shows how effective the press could be as a tool of social integration: through various textual strategies ... [the press] not only united the public in its abhorrence of the crimes, but also reiterated all the truths about the 'lower orders' which supported established relations of power ... it authorised its readers to observe the world from a distance, as bystanders, a consensual community, united by a common 'shrill of horror', by an enjoyable, ironic perspective on bungling police officers and a sad but superior attitude toward the 'class of unfortunates' (who were the victims). (Leps 1992: 130)

The written word is reproduced in the increasingly prominent visual representations of the criminal. This, remember, is the epoch of Social Darwinism, of the classification of biological types and the survival of the fittest, of Cesare Lombroso's classification of the physical characteristics of the criminal type and of Alphonse Bertillon's invention of forensic police photography (Rhodes 1956). All these helped to fix a visual and biographical notion of the 'criminal' which focused the public mind and excluded as much as it included.

It would be a fundamental mistake to see the integration of the working class into a common view of crime as simply a product of the development of the popular media as an ideological force. The moral economy of place and space, with its firm injunctions of who could venture where, and under what circumstances, elaborated a complex imagery of threat and danger. The earlier bourgeois panic about the lower orders is displaced by a fear, shared across the social classes, of the criminal stranger which is elaborated into discrete sets of fears compartmentalised by gender, age and class – women's fear of men, old people's fear of the young, and the middle-class fear of the 'underclass'. Working-class communities use the police and magistrates' courts to enforce their own values as much as any imposed by the state (see Philips 1985; Davis 1989). The female victims of Jack the Ripper became the vehicles of moralising injunctions as to appropriate forms of behaviour for young women in public space (Walkowitz 1992), while police persistently moved on all those 'loitering' without obvious purpose. All these developments reinforce the role and image of the criminal as external threat to ordered life and morality and underline the role of the victim as symbolic injunction to conformity. On the other hand, the consolidation of the family as private sphere removes from community surveillance and intervention important sources of harm and violence which then, rather than being assimilated to official definitions of criminality, are both regulated by and assimilated to other forms of governance.

Social crime, meanwhile, declines and simply assimilates to petty criminality with various degrees of toleration, particularly in poorer working-class communities. Protest and resistance to the harsh effects of capitalism are increasingly conducted through struggles for trade union organisation, spreading from the skilled to the unskilled sections of the working class. The disappearance of memory of any alternative to capitalist property relations, particularly in urban settings, undermines the role of social crime as resistance to capitalism. It becomes rather a *form of* capitalism, a mechanism for lowering prices. It remains, however, part of life in the poorest sections of the working class, those in the casualised labour markets, dependent on the street economy to make ends meet and most likely to come into conflict with the police and local authorities. As Benson remarks:

> The evidence of working-class criminality remains elusive, difficult to interpret and impossible to quantify. Nevertheless some limited generalisation is possible. There seems little doubt that certain forms of popular crime declined in importance between 1850 and 1939. Poaching became less common towards the end of the nineteenth century.... On the other hand there seems little doubt that other, probably more common forms of popular crime persisted virtually unabated, with scavenging, pilfering and similar activities continuing to provide work and income for a large – though unknown – number of working-class families. (Benson 1989: 28–9)

However, the role of pilfering and theft is a complex and contradictory matter. On the one hand the victim of the unskilled petty thief is likely to be the local community itself, or its small shopkeepers. On the other, such offenders need support in their own immediate neighbourhoods, protection against police inquiries etc., in return for which some services must be rendered such as a supply of stolen property for sale at a nominal price.

Those communities cohesive enough to exercise control could ensure that theft was committed outside the locality. In more fragmented communities, crime could become a form of terrorisation, rather than tolerated illegality. Steven Humphries in his study of poor communities in the inter-war years uses the term social crime, but observes that life was 'prevented from deteriorating into a war of all against all by customary codes of honour and by the complex set of loyalties and obligations that developed within families, streets and the local working class community' (Humphries 1981: 172–3; see also Hood and Robins 1997). Liberal reformers might argue that poverty and need had to be grasped as the causes of much crime, but this was now quite distinct from any notion of the 'criminalisation of need' or the 'criminalisation of custom' which characterised earlier forms of social crime. The definition of activity as crime could be sustained irrespective of sympathy with the poverty and deprivation which had driven people to commit crime.

Alongside this shift of social crime into simple petty theft is the general decline, throughout the nineteenth century, in the organisation and power of many types of offenders. Traditional professional crime, from predatory robber bands, pirates, highwaymen, smugglers, coiners and urban pickpockets had relied on a mixture of toleration by poor communities – thus blurring into varieties of social banditry or social crime – to whom they brought cheap goods, and the sanctuary of areas beyond the frontiers of state power (see, for example, Hobsbawm 1969; McIntosh 1975; O'Malley 1981). In this respect the rookeries of the early Victorian cities fulfilled the same role as rural peripheries had since time immemorial. In the Victorian city, however, as urban reform and modernisation progressed, and the machinery of criminal justice improved, such sanctuary disappeared. Many of the old criminal fraternities were reduced to the status of petty criminals, easy prey for the new police forces. According to Gatrell 'the complex criminal hierarchies of the early Victorian city, each with its own specialisms, territories, status systems and underworlds had become obsolete and ... nothing comparable had replaced them'. The casualised criminality of the period was defenceless against the police, courts and Victorian moral reformers. 'Even early and random police forays into the back streets were to reap rich harvests of casual offenders who were waiting there for the picking ... who, unlike their present day counterparts had no cultural camouflages to protect them' (Gatrell 1980: 264).

There is also a general narrowing of the age range of offenders such that an increasing proportion of crime becomes part of adolescence rather than of the social division of labour. In Cohen's study the age and sexual composition of those involved in conflicts with the police gradually narrows around the turn of the century. Men, women and children figure in the pre-First World War reports, while by the 1920s and 1930s the accounts increasingly mention the predominance of male youths. This is also reflected in the details of those arrested, the age distribution progressively narrowing over time to the 14–18-year-old band, with a complement of slightly older, often unemployed youth (Cohen 1979).[6] Criminal offenders are decreasingly seen as members of a distinct caste or profession and increasingly as weak and pathetic individuals (Wiener 1990: 365). Youthful delinquency becomes a suitable target for the growing apparatus of welfare and educational intervention with the aim of assisting 'growing out of crime'.

The professional criminal survives, organised around particular families rather than communities. But the separation and distinction of the criminal from surrounding economic and social activity is clear. Modernisation brings, towards the turn of the century, new opportunities for economic crime, with rising incomes, property, organised leisure and commerce and, during the inter-war period, a new generation of skilled professional criminals will begin to make their impact. A measure of sanctuary may be achieved in areas where residual traditions of social crime persist and where villains are careful to commit harm mainly elsewhere, but the mode of operation of professional criminals begins to increase their distance from communal life. Skilled burglars for example begin to move to the suburbs where they rely on disguise rather than on social acceptance by a community (Chesney 1972; McIntosh 1975).

The Unfinished Project of Modernisation

A contrast, then, with the beginning of the century might stress the consolidation of the social relations of crime control, shared across the social classes within the territory of the nation state. The presence and acceptance of the police and the magistrates' courts in the working-class communities had been consolidated, older traditions of autonomous settlement of disputes and conflicts had been reduced to the ancillary role of informal social control, and the surveillance of public space had been significantly ceded to the authorities. Middle-class private policing and prosecutions were likewise ceded to the authorities. The power of the state *vis-à-vis* various types of offenders had increased. Its ability to criminalise in practice had been consolidated by the decline of the role of tolerated illegality as part of community life. The older dynamics of generalised control and surveillance of the working class remained for the poorest and weakest strata while a language of crime was increasingly shared between the more prosperous stable working class and the middle classes and reflected in the mass media and in the use of public space. The question of crime appeared increasingly a matter of the protection of all classes against dangerousness and deviance. The criminal justice agencies perfected their techniques and knowledges in the form of carefully collected and analysed crime statistics and forensic techniques. The wider issues of class relations entered only as background factors: that poverty could be expected to produce an environment conducive to crime and a suitable subject for intervention and social engineering. Criminality no longer made any sense as a form of class relations but only as an index of pathology. The social relations of crime control acted as a unifier across the class boundaries, locking the stable working-class communities into acceptance of the prevailing social and political system every bit as powerfully as the development of the labour movement oriented to parliamentary democracy and political compromise with capital. They were an established part of the governance of society.

Modern governance is not a negation of sovereignty but a more sophisticated variant. The aim of the governance of populations is to bring their activities into line with the requirements of the state as the embodiment of the coherent vision which transcends and reconciles the conflicts and particularities of civil society in the interests of capital accumulation. The social relations of crime control are an important component. They structure the actions of the population in accordance with the requirements of the criminal justice agencies. Their establishment requires the overcoming of numerous resistances, forms of counter-governance 'from below' (as in autonomous self-policing), and they involve a balance, not always a stable one, between their components: criminal justice agencies, communities, offenders and victims. Thus the role of the community and family as agencies of informal control, the moral economy of place and space, how the community uses public space in predictable organised ways, enables the gaze of the police officer to focus on those who are 'out of place' or 'acting suspiciously'. The police in turn gradually develop an occupational subculture of practical wisdom from which

> the officer learns who to expect to be doing what, where and when. Such learning equips the officer with sets of expectations of what will be demanded of him or her in different places at different times and what members of the public might be doing in those places at these times. (Brogden et al. 1988: 40)

But in addition, complex processes of judgement and skill are required as part of the development of techniques of governance. The police have to develop a new repertoire of skills, the 'delicate art of negotiated (or community) policing (i.e. how to turn a proverbial blind eye to certain infractions in the interests of the greater good of maintaining order or community acceptance)' (Brogden et al. 1988: 67). This of course is exaggerated and sanitised by propagandists as some sort of peculiar British genius of 'policing by consent' (see Reiner 1992 for a critique), but it is not without some basis in reality even though it is

> difficult to achieve as the police apparatus is pushed by contradictory forces: on the one hand, to eradicate those informal processes, because their very informality isolates them from the formal sphere and makes them 'dangerous': on the other hand, to utilise them for the positive benefits they might bring to

order maintenance. To a large extent, this contradiction corresponds to the difference between 'hard' and 'soft' policing styles. (Johnston 1992: 23)

Thus governance involves a complex two-way process. While a central dynamic of the social relations of crime control was the handing over of definitions and powers to the state, the situation is not one of passive acquiescence but rather of co-operation, compromise and conflict between the populations to be governed and the agencies of governance (see O'Malley et al. 1997; Stenson 1998).

On a more general level it is important to understand the constraints acting on any particular area of governance such as that of crime control by wider forces derived from the underlying conflict between capital and labour at the heart of capitalist society. The abandonment of the general criminalisation of working-class self-organisation in favour of negotiation and compromise is always relative and contingent on particular conditions such as stable expansion of the capitalist economy, the shortage of new sources of labour, etc. Despite overall expansion and consolidation, the nineteenth century was a period of intense class conflict between capital and the newly organising sections of the working class. Working-class self-organisation was still being fought for. The result was that the acceptance by the working class of the police in crime control was heavily qualified by a rejection of their role as agents of the employers in industrial relations. Working-class communities with a history of struggle and organisation consequently gave the police never more than a tentative acceptance. Brogden, describing relations between the police and the working class in Liverpool during the latter part of the nineteenth century, remarks that:

> In general, by the end of that period, the relations that had developed were not so much ones of consent but rather a grudging acceptance, a tentative approval that could be withdrawn instantly in the context of industrial conflict. (Brogden 1982: 184)

In addition, the poorest sections of the working class, those in and out of the legal labour market and criminality, still bore the brunt of generalised policing, and the label of the dangerous classes. Large parts of London were still, at the turn of the century, characterised by a 'bustling, potentially violent and effectively unpoliced street life' (Pearson 1983: 89). Attitudes to the police remained frequently those of 'fear and dislike' (Roberts 1973: 100). The extent of poverty and social inequality which remained despite urban reform and economic expansion reinforced the 'grudging' nature of any acceptance of police presence in the neighbourhood and stood in the way of any coherent general notion of social citizenship in which common attitudes to all forms of crime and policing would be firmly rooted across social classes. The *attempt* to consolidate and realise this project of a thoroughly *homogenised* society would be the task of the new welfare state.

Notes

1 Henceforward I will use the term 'governance'. As Alan Hunt has remarked, the term 'opens up a space that allows us to think of ... a process rather than ... an institution ... and to focus on the many dimensions of the experience and consequence of being governed' (1992: 305). 'Government' will refer to the state institutions.

2 There are of course other possible classifications of the great transitions involved in modernity. Stan Cohen (1985), for example, emphasises those of the centralisation of the state involved in crime control, the increasing differentiation and classification of types of deviance each with its body of scientific discourse, and the increased segregation of deviants into asylums, hospitals and prisons, etc.

3 For an overview of the debate see Lea 1999.

4 Peter Linebaugh argues that Foucault's notion of popular illegalities 'prejudges a relationship in which employers aggressively and systematically attacked, and in the end successfully expropriated, rights and usages that employees had customarily practised' (1991: 404). This is true of much of the conflict during the eighteenth century when the advance of capitalist class relations was in full swing. Foucault's concept may, however, be valid for an earlier, more stable feudal period.

5 Public space is, above all, the space of capital; the vital conduit through which the circuit of commodities and labour power takes place. It contrasts with the generalisation of private space characteristic of the present period.

6 David Greenberg (1965) in a North American study shows how peak offending age gradually declined during the nineteenth century as crime became more associated with youth and adolescence, of pre-socialisation rather than as a normal feature of mature adult life.

3

The Frontiers of Criminalisation

The previous chapter attempted an illustration of some of the factors involved in the development of the social relations of crime control during the nineteenth century. The example was limited: to one country, England, and was overwhelmingly concerned with the establishment of crime control in the working-class communities. These developments were nevertheless illustrative of the more general trend of the extension and consolidation of the social relations of governance during that period. The success of these developments was, it was argued, due to a confluence of the modernising offensive of the enlightened sections of the bourgeoisie and the predominant tendencies of capitalist development.

The process was not free of conflicts and contradictions. I have noted the two contrasting tendencies of liberation and disciplinisation involved in modernisation. On the one hand the rule of law, the extension of rights and due process were a general gain from the spread of criminal justice. But it involved, on the other hand, the handing over of the regulation of conflicts to the state and the associated dominance of criminal law at the expense of popular conceptions of conflicts and participation in their resolution. The extension of crime control was, moreover, part of a wider process of the regulation of social life and public space which reinforced class and gendered conceptions of behaviour. The persistent role of the criminal justice system as a direct agent of the repression of the working class on behalf of the bourgeoisie, of labour by capital, was a further dimension.

But crime control was not the only form of governance at work. It was, rather, one of a number of strategies of governance aimed at the disciplining and socialisation of the population. Others involved different principles and modes of operation. The welfare state, for example, was oriented to the management and treatment of social problems and pathologies and to some extent undermined the juridical notions of individual responsibility inherent in criminalisation. The two systems were able to reach an accommodation, particularly in areas such as youth crime where notions of individual responsibility could be substantially modified (see for example Wootton 1959). This facilitated the incorporation of the juridical into the spectrum of regulatory institutions of the state (see Foucault 1979: 144).

Other modes of governance and regulation placed more severe limitations on the deployment of criminalisation. In this chapter I shall focus on three examples. The first arose from the necessity to grant autonomy to private capital in the regulation of economic affairs. The result was a severe restriction on the penetration of the social relations of crime control into one of the key institutions of capital accumulation: the commercial enterprise. The second concerned the preservation of the family as an archaic institution of private authority and regulation. The third concerned the uneven development of capitalism as a global economic system with its resultant preservation and even intensification of various archaic forms of sovereignty at the geographical periphery of capitalist development. Modernisation has been a complex, precarious and contradictory process from the outset.

Conflicting Modes of Governance

The social relations of crime control constitute a mechanism of governance relying upon the autonomous actions and functioning of social groups: the reporting of crimes, the willingness of most sections of the population to give information to the police, appear in court as witnesses, etc. – in short directly to enable and support the functioning of the agencies of the criminal justice system. The actions of the population enable the functioning of legal discourses and state institutions. It is otherwise with those strategies of governance where the role of the state is to foster and support the autonomous functioning of systems of private authority as in the case of the commercial enterprise and the family. The company, and the issues which arise from its working, such as health and safety of workers, violation of legal property as in fraud, urban and environmental effects of production processes, etc., have to be regulated in such a way as to minimise interference with the processes of capital accumulation – the working of the market – and the autonomous authority of owners and managers to respond to its demands. Governance involves the setting in place of 'mechanisms of security' which establish the legal basis of a regime of self-regulation or 'government at a distance'. The importance of the private authority of capital is rooted in the nature of the capitalist production process itself. As Marx explained, the worker and the capitalist strike their bargain – wages for labour time – as juridically free individuals in the market place which is 'a very Eden of the innate rights of man. It is the exclusive realm of Freedom, Equality, Property and Bentham' (Marx 1976: 280). But having purchased the worker's labour time in return for wages, the capitalist puts his new possession to work. At this point bargaining between equals is replaced by the authority of master over servant. Capitalism thus requires the co-existence of the conflicting principles of freedom and subordination, liberation and disciplinisation (see Lea 1979).

The authority of the master to run his company as he will, and to direct his operatives, constitutes a counter to his appearance as a legal equal to the worker.

In a similar way the family as a cradle for the reproduction and learning of private authority, shielded from the legal equality of (and criminalisability of) citizens in the public sphere, thus makes sense in terms of the requirements of capital. As Ellen Meiksins Wood argues:

> the patriarchal conception of hierarchy and authority was conveniently adaptable to the requirements of capitalism, since it could sustain a substantive inequality without being incompatible in principle with formal juridical equality. It was particularly serviceable in defining the relationship between master and servant, where 'pre-modern' conceptions of authority, even when they were overtaken by 'liberal-democratic' ideas of political obligation, continued to underwrite the powers, and indeed the legal rights, of capitalist employers. (Wood 1991: 138)

The family functions as a place where equality and citizenship is heavily moderated by inequality and subordination. The functionality of the family for capitalism has frequently been stated in these terms, stressing its role in learning the acceptance of personal authority (Jackson 1999). However, capital has contradictory needs; it also regards all family members as potential sources of labour power. Capital has no 'group mind' which can balance such conflicts. In the earlier part of the nineteenth century social reformers were concerned that long hours of work for men, women and children in factories and mines would destroy the family. This is the starting point for state intervention through welfare, social work and philanthropy to sustain the family and check tendencies to breakdown and malfunctioning. In a similar way, under pressure from the working class, the state intervenes in the company through factory legislation which regulates the intensity of exploitation of labour. The actual development of governance is always a process of balancing conflicting demands. The aims of reformers may be the straightforward amelioration of poverty, or constraints on the autonomous power of capital. But the successful reforms were those that secured the more effective functioning of these systems of private authority distinct from the state.

Thus crime control develops alongside other modes of governance; the market mechanism, the internal authority of private institutions and state intervention aimed at their maintenance, all of which have distinct dynamics. Criminalisation of child abuse or domestic violence in the family, of unsafe working conditions or low pay involves a reconstruction of relations between members of these institutions as relations between offenders and victims which may compromise the preservation of private authority. These forms of governance are not meant to be mutually exclusive; crime control only impinges when the proper exercise of authority breaks down. The family itself as part of the community helps to reproduce the mechanisms of informal social control which filter the problems that must be encountered as crime. Nevertheless the *social relations* of crime control as such clash with those of private authority. The possibility of criminalisation is based on the formal equality of individuals before the law. Substantive inequalities, in both the commercial company and the family obstruct this. A closer look at both these arenas will show the constraints and boundaries such forms of authority have placed on the extension of the social relations of crime control.

Business crime

In the last chapter I focused on the great changes to the urban working class during the nineteenth and early twentieth centuries that facilitated the growth of the social relations of crime control. Those changes were partly the result of a modernising offensive led by enlightened sections of the bourgeoisie. It is easy to forget, however, that the latter does not come upon the face of the earth ready formed as a class. If the working class required 'improvement', then so did large sections of the bourgeoisie. The birth of capitalism is, after all, an affair bloodied with violence. Criminal expropriations through violation of land rights, privateering, piracy and straightforward robbery, what in modern parlance might be called 'gangster capitalism' (see Chapter 6), all played their part in what Marx termed the process of the 'primitive accumulation' of capital (Marx 1976: 915; Jachcel 1983), while the affinity between the entrepreneurial spirit of the capitalist and that of the colonial adventurer and the criminal has not passed without comment by historians and sociologists (see Sombart 1967). In a similar way the 'robber baron' entrepreneurs celebrated as pioneers of American capitalism were men who became symbols of respectability and business shrewdness but whose business methods were those of gangsters and thugs (see Abadinsky 1994: 60).

These characteristics are reinforced by the nature of the bourgeoisie as a class. Money capital is the only criteria for membership, underlying unity of economic interest is moderated by aggressive competition between companies as well as conflicts between various types of capital – finance and manufacturing, agricultural and industrial, small and large. The idea that aggression and deception, even violence, will not feature as a significant aspect of behaviour, not only towards the working class, but between members of the bourgeoisie as well, is absurd. In many ways the early bourgeoisie has a better claim to the title of the *dangerous class* than any section of the poor. Constraints on criminality and violence come from a variety of sources and, as with the stabilisation and habituation of the working class, there is a combination of the effects of capitalist development itself and the specific efforts and achievement of reformers.

A long-run tendency towards restraint and temperate behaviour has been noted by Norbert Elias (1982, 1994). He saw it as a result of the emergence of the strong state at the end of the mediaeval period and also of the growing complexity of the economic division of labour which, by increasing the interdependence of entrepreneurs, placed a premium on trust and prudence in choosing business partners rather than short-termism and aggression. The need for reform was recognised by the great liberal theorists of the new society. For example, Adam Smith,

> [a]fter his better-known early social optimism of the 'hidden hand' … came to worry about the moral basis of a commercial society. In his 1790 revision of the *Theory of Moral Sentiments*, Smith reverted towards a more theological position, placing greater emphasis on the need to reinforce weakening moral influences. (Wiener 1990: 17, n. 24)

The moralisation of the bourgeoisie became centred on notions of respectability and family life, of the bourgeois gentleman as provider and protector of his wife and children, from which calm oasis of an almost feudal patriarchy he ventured out into the public world of commerce and competition (Zaretsky 1976). Meanwhile, pressures for constraints on the freedom of capital came both from enlightened sections of the bourgeoisie, concerned about the health of the labour force as a whole and the state of the working-class family, and the increasingly organised working class itself. The result was the wide spectrum of state intervention covering areas of housing, public health and the regulation of working conditions. A legal framework for the governance of the company gradually developed. Factory legislation regulated working conditions while the principle of limited liability aimed to protect a widening circle of middle-class investors. Meanwhile the development of auditing and accountancy, the growth of the financial press and the legalisation of trade union organisation would lay the institutional foundation for key sources of information and their communication between investors, customers and workers, and would thus establish at least some of the preconditions for the development of social relations of crime control in this area.

However, important counteracting forces to practical criminalisation in the business world were evident. The entrepreneur with his social status and legitimate authority is, in practice, harder to criminalise than the propertyless worker. The authority relation between master and servant constrains the ability of employees to act, for example, as 'whistleblowers' and to publicise information concerning illegal action by management. The necessity to protect company secrets from competitors, the loyalty of personnel, client confidentiality, all were, and are, obstacles to simple assimilation of commercial life to the social relations of crime control.

Other obstacles were to be found in the growing complexity of business and commerce. The complexity of business crime was (and indeed is today) seen as weakening the effectiveness of criminal justice intervention. The business offender does not stand out as does the household burglar leaving his fingerprints and other tell-tale signs in a place where his very presence – someone else's house – signifies his criminality, but is rather, in Michael Clarke's (1990) phrase, 'legitimately present' at the scene of the crime; working away at his desk, behaving apparently normally as he falsifies the accounts. By analogy with street crime, the offender is the normal user of public space rather than the identifiable intruder. The crime may be discovered only later when the accounts are audited. The growth in size and complexity of business operations meant that business offenders were growing in power and their activities were becoming increasingly inaccessible both to criminal justice detection methods and to public surveillance, notwithstanding the developments mentioned. Company audits only became compulsory in the United Kingdom in 1900. This trend to complexity contrasts with that of street crime where, as noted in the previous chapter, offenders were becoming progressively weaker as the century wore on. Finally, victims themselves, particularly if they are institutions such as banks or other deposit takers, have understandable motives for reluctance to report crime to the authorities. No bank wants to discourage deposits by it becoming known that it has been a victim of successful fraud.

Thus business illegality remained rife in the nineteenth century. During the period 1866–83, 17 per cent of all new companies formed in the United Kingdom failed. The economist Henry Shannon, attempting to calculate the levels of fraudulent company formation, reckoned that about one-sixth of all new promotions during that period were fraudulent (Robb 1992: 142). The amount of reported white collar crime – mainly fraud, embezzlement and false pretence – increased during the second half of the nineteenth century in contrast to a general fall in crime.[1]

Complexity acted as an important rationalisation for the failure of criminalisation effectively to penetrate the business world. The elaboration of a framework of governance involving the march of criminal justice agencies into the working-class communities and the dismantling of the old criminal rookeries can be contrasted with the absence of such penetration into the financial centre of the City of London and the boardrooms of major companies. These remained, in effect, bourgeois rookeries, places where criminals could fraternise and plan, relatively secure from the surveillance of the state authorities. A framework of governance of the company developed which was to a great extent seen as a substitute for the criminal justice system. The strengthening of criminal justice in the working-class areas of the city was predominantly a hegemonisation of *public space* – through the moral economy of place and space – against communities that had lost not only control over the means of production but also over a large part of the means of conflict resolution. This progressive loss of working-class autonomy in the resolution and regulation of internal conflicts contrasted with the deliberate celebration of the principle of internal self-regulation for the bourgeoisie. It is not that fraud and embezzlement were legitimised but rather that the company comes to be seen as an institution in which self-regulation is more appropriate than criminalisation as the mechanism of first resort. This is quite different from the informal social control exercised by local working-class community functioning as an *adjunct* to crime control.

While police surveillance in no way obstructs – indeed it might be seen to encourage – the productivity of workers, the activities of capitalists were understood to require shielding from the obstructions of too much external surveillance and legal regulation which might stifle enterprise and weaken the company in the face of competitors. The state consequently feared to move effectively in such areas. When it did penetrate into the world of business and financial activities its aim was mostly to deal with the white collar crime of lower-ranking managers and 'embezzling clerks'.

Alongside the feebleness of state action and the opaque and complex nature of much business crime, a further missing element of the social relations of crime control was the reluctance of the business community itself to practically criminalise and marginalise the offender. Partly this was a simple matter of class culture which united the upper ranks of the bourgeoisie with that of the legal profession with the result that 'Victorian class prejudice permeated the criminal justice system, which directed its greatest wrath against the lower classes and treated upper-class criminal capitalists with relative leniency' (Robb 1992: 182). Thus where the marginalisation of the business offender did occur, it was seen simply as punishment; as a *substitute* for judicial punishment, rather than as the criminalising abstraction which makes judicial punishment possible.[2] Hence the widespread idea that the shaming and social disgrace consequent upon being discovered as fraudulent were more effective punishments for respectable members of the bourgeoisie than anything the criminal justice system could inflict. 'Exclusion from polite society was viewed as a more serious penalty than imprisonment.... For white collar criminals prison was seen as ancillary to their personal sense of shame and loss of social status' (Robb 1992: 165). Shaming refers to the loss of status and authority of the bourgeois as the autonomous regulator of his company and confirms the importance of that role.[3]

Finally, the cultural legitimisation of capital accumulation as the overriding goal shifted the blame for crime on to the victim: those who invest in fraudulent enterprise have only themselves to blame. Even in clearly established cases of fraud and deception the victims whose investments had been plundered were held ultimately responsible for their misfortunes and 'chastised for failing to exercise proper judgement or for being blinded by their own greed. Legislation, it was argued, could not protect a fool from his folly' (Robb 1992: 148). Robb concludes his discussion of the regulation of business crime during the nineteenth century by noting how

[t]he depressing history of fraud and chicanery detailed before Parliamentary committees in 1867, 1875, 1877 and 1878 had little influence on resulting legislation. Despite an alarming incidence of fraud, legislators feared alienating the business community or hindering trade through the imposition of tougher company law. (1992: 150)

Violence in the family

The modern family ceases to play a role as a productive unit, as in pre-modern society, but becomes rather the site of reproduction – of labour power and of the respect for authority and hierarchy which are central in putting labour power to work for capital. The family thus resembles in some respects the commercial enterprise. The employer as master of his employees is paralleled by the husband as master of his wife and children. The family, like the company, functions as a self-regulating system of private authority and governance. The domestic sphere of family life is insulated from the development of the social relations of crime control in similar ways: the state agencies are reluctant to enforce criminalisation as a strategy of regulation for fear of undermining the family and its functions, while the social role and status of the husband, like that of the entrepreneur, is insulated against the criminalising abstraction and marginalisation. The object of state intervention during the nineteenth century is that of the reform and strengthening of the family as a self-regulating institution rather than as a terrain for regulation by criminalisation.

Violence by husbands to wives and children in nineteenth-century working-class communities was

> not random but was subject to legitimating rites and rules. The distinction between 'legitimate' and 'illegitimate' violence was sharp.... If the man wasn't 'boss' of the home he wasn't considered to be a man. Equally, however, excessive violence dragged down everyone's reputation. Rules about 'legitimate' violence set the tone of a neighbourhood and it did no one any good to break them. (Bourke 1994: 73)

Such violence seemed to fall during the second half of the nineteenth century along with the general trend in crime. In London the number of aggravated assaults recorded in the police courts dropped from 800 in 1853 to 200 in 1889 and continued falling throughout the twentieth century (Bourke 1994: 72). Historians have, however, questioned how far this decline reflects changes in the actual level of violence. There is evidence that it rather reflects both a weakening of those elements of communal regulation which could then form a basis for the social relations of crime control combined with a conscious attempt by state intervention to shield the family from criminalisation in the interests of its consolidation as a self-regulating institution of hierarchy and personal authority.

Thus Nancy Tomes (1978) argues that in the earlier part of the nineteenth century, although levels of violence were probably higher, the working-class community exercised higher degrees of surveillance and autonomous regulation of conflict. The traditional community lived much of its life on the streets with less of the distinction between public and private which later came to characterise the 'moral economy of place and space' mentioned in the last chapter. Thus 'tensions culminating in conflict as well as the actual beating were highly visible ... it is clear that neighbours regularly watched and even participated in each other's personal quarrels' (Tomes 1978: 329). They also frequently intervened to

> prevent or moderate a wife-beating by a combination of surveillance and reproach. When a fight seemed likely they watched a couple closely.... Surveillance was usually accompanied by reproaches for the husband.... The most common community response to a wife-beating was simply to help the wife, either by nursing her or offering her shelter. (Tomes 1978: 336)

Generally falling rates of street crime in the later nineteenth century have been explained in terms of a combination of social changes relating to stabilisation and privatisation of working-class life together with the hegemonisation of public order and public space by the criminal justice agencies. As regards domestic violence the first tendency is certainly evident; part of privatisation and increasing family orientation was an increasing censure of domestic violence. Tomes, on the basis of a study of the views of the London magistracy, identified a displacement of the traditional idea of the 'unruly wife' as deservedly provoking a violent reaction, in favour of a view, originating in the Victorian bourgeoisie and moving down to the working class, of violence against women as cowardly and unmanly, with women as the suffering victims and the wife-abuser as a ruffian and a brute. From an earlier period of communal 'unruliness' in which the relations between the sexes were more combative, the development was towards a new stable patriarchal family centred on a less aggressive 'domesticated manliness' (Davidoff and Hall 1987), emphasising the husband as protector and provider. The wife, following her middle-class counterpart in steadily withdrawing, after marriage and childbirth, from the world of work, found her position weak. The price paid by women for a decline in violence was a new definition of femininity in terms of dependence and submissiveness. 'Having repudiated the idea that women were aggressive, fit partners for combat, they [working class men and women] had no alternative but to embrace the middle-class view of women as weak, fragile, passive creatures who needed "natural protectors"' (Tomes 1978: 342). Thus violence is delegitimised but less by virtue of its coming to be seen as a relationship between victims and offenders with the associated ideas of legal equality, than as a violation of the principles of hierarchy and inequality upon which the family is based. As with the high-status business offender, the family patriarch is seen as sufficiently deterred by the shame and disgrace of failing to effectively govern his domain without losing his temper rather than through his reconstruction as criminal offender.

A second important obstacle to the development of the social relations of crime control is the reduction in the flow of information about domestic violence. Whereas in the case of business criminality some of the elements of the social relations of crime control can be seen to develop, albeit weakly, in the form of new sources of financial information and communication, in the case of family violence sources of information and public surveillance progressively weaken during the nineteenth century. The issues around which the social relations of crime control consolidate in the working-class communities are those of publicly visible 'street' crime. As family life moves away from this public visibility, a process led by the suburbanisation of the better-off sections of the working class, it moves away not simply from communal self-regulation but also from a public availability of information about violence which may be transmitted to the criminal justice agencies. Increasingly the only person in a position to report the violence is the victim. The community as a key component of the social relations of crime control is displaced through the privatisation of violence. This is accomplished by the status of the family as private space into which the intervention of outsiders is a violation of privacy and 'none of their business', and by the consolidation of the bourgeois model of female passivity which entails the victim, increasingly isolated from support networks, being encouraged both by fear of her husband and by affection to take on the belief that she is the perpetrator and provocateur by failing in her duties as a 'good wife'. Domestic violence comes, therefore, to take on some of the same characteristics as business crime. It takes place behind closed doors, the offender is 'legitimately present' at the scene of the crime and the victim will have motives for not reporting the crime as it may reflect badly on her character.

Meanwhile the aim of state action, as in the case of the commercial enterprise, increasingly becomes that of fostering the process of self-regulation. Where violence occurs the question of criminalisation is increasingly displaced by that of sustaining and preserving the family. In his study of nineteenth-century family conflict in both middle- and working-class families, James Hammerton (1992) counsels against too much reliance on magistrates' court statistics showing a decline in domestic violence,

> for the simple reason that during the period of statistical decline these courts increasingly became courts of conciliation as well as summary conviction. With the Matrimonial Causes Act of 1878, which provided for separation and maintenance allowances for wives of husbands convicted of aggravated assaults, local magistrates courts increasingly took on a more paternalistic role, eager to intervene in an attempt to make the wife forgive, the husband reform and the family reunite, and thus avoid the fragile division of slender

economic resources. Magistrates, together with a growing army of police court missionaries, probation officers and clerks of the court came to see themselves as marriage menders. (1992: 39)

Criminalisation was becoming displaced by a body of social policy oriented to strengthening the family as an autonomous institution with the criminal justice agencies themselves becoming assimilated to this task. During the Great Depression of the 1880s and 1890s middle-class fear of the habits of criminal classes spreading back into the ranks of the respectable working class, whence they had been so successfully expunged, led to further interventions of criminal law into the family. But most of this legislation, such as the Criminal Law Amendment Act 1885 and the Punishment of Incest Act of 1908 were aimed at criminalising *departures* from family norms, such as incest and sex with under-age girls, rather than the violence that lay within the family (Zedner 1995). The family as such when functioning properly was, like the company, considered best left to regulate itself. Criminalisation, with its potential for the reconstruction of conjugal relations as relations between legal equals, victim and offender, threatened that process. Just as in business crime the full force of criminalisation is reserved for the weak and marginal; it is only the poorest and most unstable families which the welfare agencies will hand over to criminal justice.

Modernisation and power

Business crime and family violence illustrate one aspect of the process whereby crime control was established within the boundaries of, and in negotiation with, other forms and strategies of governance. Individuals and their actions falling outside these boundaries, while not escaping criminalisation altogether, find shelter behind a number of obstacles: the hierarchical authority of the company and the family as obstacles to the reconstruction of the participants as victims and offenders, the reluctance of the state to impose the criminalising abstraction as a disruption of the proper functioning of these institutions, and the complexity and lack of 'visibility' of their workings. Other examples, such as the development of youth justice, would have revealed different emphases and different compromises between forms of governance – crime control and welfare – occupying the same terrain. Both family violence and business crime are areas where those concerned with justice and human rights have generally called for greater criminal justice intervention. Socialists demand the more intensive prosecution of criminal corporations and fraudulent capitalists while feminists denounce the inactivity of the criminal justice system against sexual assault and domestic violence. The progressive aspects of crime control as the carrier of the rule of law and equal rights are emphasised in these struggles to penetrate sites of private hierarchical authority.

It might be supposed that further modernisation would work in favour of an extension of legal relations into these spheres. Greater social mobility into and out of the business elite might break down the exclusivity which sustains the cultural obstacles to criminalisation, while an expanding middle class with interests in consumption, investment, pensions and insurance, and having every interest in defending itself against fraud and deception, could force the principle of legality to make serious inroads into the independent authority and status of the capitalist enterprise without compromising the principle of capital accumulation as such. Meanwhile rising levels of education would sustain demands from women for the breaking down of the exclusivity of family relations, an entry into the public sphere of work and career which would act to publicise family relations, restructure the family as a relationship between equal partners and so lay a firmer basis for criminalisation as a response to family violence. This view is part of a wider assumption that modernisation would continue to reduce the power of the offenders in relation to both victims and the state and facilitate the extension of the social relations of crime control into new areas. The accuracy of such a view will be discussed later.

The Periphery of Modernisation

So far I have looked at some examples of the boundaries to crime control within urban capitalism as it developed during the nineteenth century. I have been concerned with the relations between crime control and adjacent forms of urban governance. A second, and equally important, set of limitations to the social relations of crime control is to be found at the geographical periphery of the modernisation process.

The notion of periphery can be highly misleading if taken to imply that those areas which lie outside the core urban areas of capitalist modernisation are somehow untouched by its dynamic: that they remain areas as yet to be assimilated to the modernising process. This can then be further elaborated as the claim that the lack of development in such areas is due, not to the contradictory dynamics of modernisation itself, but rather to obstacles and resistances located in the peripheral areas. Such assumptions lie behind a number of key discourses on social dynamics and governance (see Ryan 1976). The theme of the culture of poverty as the main obstacle to poor communities taking advantage of the opportunities presented by modernisation occurs both in the context of underdeveloped regions within the modernising countries and on an international scale in the guise of analyses of 'backwardness', lack of governance, etc., as the main reasons why poor countries have been unable to participate in an otherwise smooth and beneficial process of global modernisation.

From such a standpoint the dynamics of crime control in peripheral areas would have little interest in an explanation of the relationship between criminalisation and modernisation. However, once it is understood that backwardness is an aspect of the modernisation process itself; that the industrialisation and urbanisation of northern Europe and North America was predicated on the enforced underdevelopment of other areas of the world, then things appear in a different light. Indeed, when the under-developed areas within the modernising countries themselves are taken into account, any rigid separation between 'development' and 'underdevelopment' becomes increasingly problematic. The features of both appear within one another. The archaic forms of sovereignty and power character-istic of backwardness are seen both to be variants of those formerly exist-ing in the modernising countries and, as we shall see later, tending to recur and revive in the later stages of modernisation.

Colonialism and crime control

One important periphery of the modernisation process during the nineteenth and early twentieth centuries was constituted by colonialism and imperial-ism. Colonies, rather than following in the footsteps of the colonising powers, were kept in subjection as a prerequisite of the latter's modernisa-tion. The production of cheap raw materials was a central requirement of the industrialising and modernising states. Not all colonies were economi-cally productive and not all areas which produced cheap raw materials were political colonies. Nevertheless the general suppression of the masses was a key aim of the colonising powers. While the working class in the modernising states was integrated, albeit precariously, into structures of reformist politi-cal compromise, the bulk of the population in the colonial areas was main-tained for as long as possible in a state of disenfranchised servitude as cheap and semi-slave labour. The forms of colonial oppression varied but an important aspect was the combination of a partial destruction of traditional communities with a form of authoritarian sovereignty imposed by the colonisers. Indigenous systems of political authority and subsistence eco-nomy were often maintained in an atrophied form with traditional author-ity figures, such as tribal chiefs, being co-opted into the colonial structures of 'indirect rule' which allocated to them some low-level political func-tions. Economically, the *partial* destruction of traditional subsistence agri-cultural economies forced able-bodied workers from rural areas to offer themselves for work in the colonial money economy, usually in extractive industries or settler agriculture, located on forcibly enclosed land. These mechanisms were frequently supplemented by more direct ones of forced labour. The preservation of traditional subsistence agriculture meant that wages in the money economy could be at below subsistence levels since part of the reproduction cost of the labour force was met by traditional agriculture.

These conditions were fertile soil for social crime as a form of resistance to colonial rule. The defence of traditional subsistence economy and social structure against colonial encroachments has some analogy with social crime in eighteenth-century England. For example, British colonial rule in southern Africa was resisted through such activities as cattle raids on settler farms and hunting on land enclosed as game reserves for the exclusive use of Europeans. The latter were obvious targets for poachers who, like their eighteenth-century English counterparts, saw themselves as continuing activities sanctioned by their own custom and tradition in the face of illegitimate repression by alien colonisers (Ranger 1986). Likewise, wage workers in colonial extractive industries exhibited strong support for pilferage and theft of raw materials as part of a refusal to recognise the legitimacy of colonial property laws. Such pilferage can be the basis of a parallel economy consisting of a 'lumpen-capitalism' of petty commodity production, based on stolen resources, existing alongside colonial and international capital (Freund 1986). Again, there is some analogy with the commercially oriented poaching gangs of eighteenth-century England.

There are, of course, also differences. In eighteenth-century England the blurring of criminality and social resistance occurred in the absence of clearly formed political ideologies and movements. Colonial resistance movements generally took the form of organised political movements and armed guerrilla struggle demanding national independence and forms of political representation analogous to those existing in the colonising countries. This posed much more sharply the distinction between criminality on the one hand and political struggle on the other and, consequently, the dynamics of transformation of the one into the other; of the bandit into the guerrilla (Hobsbawm 1959). Some 'social bandits', or even straightforward robbers were temporarily recruited to the cause of national liberation – out of the need for sanctuary and sustenance from the masses – even at the same time as some of the less disciplined members of the guerrilla armies engaged in predatory crime (Ranger 1986). Meanwhile liberation movements usually attempted to establish some rudimentary variant of crime control in the territory liberated from the control of the colonial state. Such experiments in 'people's justice' tend to be, as I shall note presently, heavily influenced by their relationship to the political struggle.

Policing by the colonial authorities, meanwhile, was heavily overdetermined by its role in the general suppression of the population at large. Colonial states were authoritarian regimes devoted to the general task of the maintenance of cheap labour and the exclusion of the mass of the population from effective political organisation and representation of interests, a crude system of rule frozen in the transition from sovereignty to governance characteristic of the early stages of modernisation. But they were often weak structures in that they not only lacked legitimacy in the eyes of the majority of the population but also depended upon the surviving atrophied structures of pre-colonial traditional authority. Colonial police forces were predominantly thinly disguised paramilitary repressive agencies (Marenin 1982; Deflem 1994). Features of police–community relations which undermined crime control in the cities of the industrialising states and which therefore were contained, became key features of colonial policing. The 'grudging acceptance', noted previously, of the police by urban working-class communities in the imperialist metropolis depended on an element of trust which could be periodically disrupted by factors such as the importation of a large body of police from another area for strike-breaking purposes. In the colonial situation this was a permanent and normal feature of policing. The alienation of the police from the community was not so much an impediment to *crime* control as a key aspect of *political* repression. Thus in the British colonies in Africa

> [r]arely did the colonial police or military receive the fundamental assent of those they ruled, or ever approached the ideal that 'the police are the public and the public are the police'. The employment of uniformed aliens housed in barracks and police lines emphasised the coercive nature of the forces of law and order and their foreign-ness from the ordinary people. (Killingray 1986: 424. See also Alemika 1993; Ahire 1991)

The pattern of colonial development was not entirely one of blocked modernisation. Local agriculture and industry required a working class with the consequence that similar pressures for trade union and other civil rights built up in the urban sections of the colonial peoples. Yet this process was often met by a repressive state determined to retain the benefits of cheap labour and to obstruct any repetition of the process of political inclusion of the working class that had occurred in the colonising countries themselves.

South Africa under the apartheid regime, lasting well into the last third of the twentieth century, stands as an example of these contradictions at their most acute. The development of an industrial base resulted in an urban working class rapidly developing a sophisticated class and political consciousness. The continued exclusion of this class from the forms of political integration and compromise developed in the colonising countries required an intensifying level of repression rivalling that of the inter-war European fascist regimes. State strategy involved an attempt to delay artificially permanent urban residence for as long as possible (Posel 1991) and the erection of a battery of restrictions, surveillance and daily repression which obstructed and negated the ordinary concerns of crime control and access to law.

> Black people conducting activities reserved for whites were criminals until proven otherwise. A conception of 'law and order' informed by dominant

South African values prevailed over other considerations of legal and social justice. (Brogden and Shearing 1993: 61–2; see also Brewer 1994)

The main activity of the police and other South African criminal justice agencies was that of the enforcement of regulations criminalising whole communities. By the late 1960s a million black South Africans were being prosecuted annually for infringement of regulations which did not apply to the whites (Cawthra 1993: 15). In 1972 it was calculated that one in four black people was arrested each year by the police for such violations which were officially defined as criminal (Brogden and Shearing 1993: 66). These activities cannot of course be considered as crimes, not simply from considerations of morality and natural justice, or of the widespread use of torture by police and security forces (Steytler 1993), but also by virtue of the fact that their interdiction was in no way based on the social relations of crime control. They were largely dependent on a network of spies and informers and their basis of support lay entirely outside the policed communities in the white bourgeoisie and labour aristocracy. There was also a tacit acceptance from sections of international capital which, despite certain inflexibilities of a racially segregated labour market, benefited from the restrictions on working-class political and trade union organisation. The white minority was the source of funding for various groups of vigilantes, auxiliary or private police forces which operated in support of the state in the general task of repression (Brogden and Shearing 1993: 71–3, 80–9).

To the extent that the state attempted to operate as a component of the social relations of crime control in the black community its repressive role seriously compromised its ability to do so. There was little confidence in the criminal justice agencies impartially resolving disputes and harms which arose within the community, and victims of harm turned in greater numbers to alternative popular institutions (McCall 1995).[4] The relationship between the police and the community also affected that between the offender and the community. When faced with a police force whose very existence implied an alien oppression and which was more interested in general oppression of the masses than with protecting them against theft, violence and other harms, the oppressed communities were less able, and less inclined, to distinguish rebels from criminals among those from their own ranks who fell into the hands of the 'criminal justice system'. There was a tendency to see the treatment of the ordinary offender by the state as a symbolic attack on the whole community. In such situations petty offenders take on something of the status of social criminals irrespective of the actual targets of their offending. Thus even attempts at ordinary crime control on the part of the police may provoke widespread resistance and disturbance.

Conversely, preoccupied as it was with general repression, the state police adopted an instrumental attitude towards petty offenders, regarding them, for example, as potential informers and spies in return for leniency.

The process of 'turning' criminals into informers is a feature of police work in most societies. However, in liberal democracies it may be oriented to gathering intelligence about more serious offending of the type which the community itself criminalises. By contrast in authoritarian states, the petty criminal as informer is more geared to the gathering of intelligence about general opposition to the regime. The informer becomes a spy against the community as a whole rather than against other offenders. In apartheid South Africa police frequently cynically made use of any available resources to terrorise the population, including the use of criminal gangs to 'counter-organise' the black working-class communities (Cawthra 1993: 33).

Such circumstances provided fertile ground for the development of alternative structures of popular justice. Such structures had two sources which in the long run conflicted with each other. The first lay in the remaining structures of traditional society which persisted usually in the rural hinterland, and upon which the colonial state relied for some measure of political stabilisation. Thus traditional forms of tribal-based dispute resolution were tolerated by the South African apartheid state as they tended to enhance the position of traditionalist and conservative forces. The second source lay in the anti-colonial struggle itself out of which emerged dispute-resolution structures as part of the infrastructure of mass mobilisation for political opposition. In the black townships of South Africa the development of self-defence units, people's courts, street committees and other alternative dispute-resolution systems became a major feature of community life (Burman and Scharf 1990; Pavlich 1992; Brogden and Shearing 1993: 135–65; Cawthra 1993: 199–202).

It would be a mistake to see such counter-institutions, however, simply as a subterranean alternative making up for the deficiencies of the authoritarian colonial state and covering the activities undertaken in liberal democracies within the social relations of crime control. The alternatives themselves are influenced by the fact that they are *alternatives* and in no way isolated from the prevailing political situation. Their goals and mode of operation are heavily influenced by their oppositional nature to the existing regime. Firstly, unlike the traditional tribal structures, they operated for the most part in clandestine conditions. This necessitated that processing of cases and implementation of decisions be undertaken swiftly, usually without much in the way of due process, and with sudden and often disproportionately brutal punishments.

Secondly, the concepts of criminality with which such structures operate are themselves partly a product of the political struggle itself rather than simply an attempt to enforce some neutral notion of crime control. Political crimes–aiding the oppressor in various ways – are the object of swift vengeance. Furthermore, a certain pragmatism is usually adopted towards petty crimes committed by members of resistance groups actively opposing the state and placing their own lives at risk. On the one hand, if the members of such organisations are allowed to get away with petty crime they will lose the respect of the communities on whose behalf they are fighting. If, on the other hand, they are unmasked and dealt with openly as criminals in the community then this may compromise the security of the armed organisations. Likewise those who approach the alternative institutions for redress may find themselves drawn into hazardous political tasks as a form of *quid pro quo*, for the redress of their grievances, a fact that may induce hesitation in approaching the alternative institutions rather than the state authorities. The justice of the oppressed is bound up with and infected by the rule of the oppressors. Of course, such situations may be found in the heartlands of the imperialist nations themselves. The following contribution from a victim of domestic violence in Northern Ireland is eloquent testimony.

> When women decide not to use the policing services of the RUC they instead can turn to the respective paramilitaries within their communities. In some cases the response has been effective, with the abusive partner being removed from the home and sometimes the country. Yet many women remain reluctant to involve paramilitary organisations. In part this may be because some women feel they may then be unwillingly drawn indirectly into paramilitary activity such as through storing weapons. Some women believe that paramilitaries use incidents of domestic violence as a pretence to punish an offender for other criminal activities, and as such the women can be seen to be informing and therefore open to retaliation and abuse from her partner and others. Such problems highlight why women are reluctant to involve local paramilitaries – even when a man has abused his partner any retaliation by others upon him can also be construed as her fault.
>
> For those women whose abusive partners are involved in paramilitary and state security activity, access to help is seriously problematic. Women whose husbands are politically involved cannot – for obvious reasons – contact the police and often calls for help from the paramilitary organisation itself falls on deaf ears. Similarly, women whose husbands are soldiers or police officers find themselves in a comparable situation as these official institutions are often ignorant and unwilling to censure the violent behaviour of some of its officers towards their partners. (McWilliams and Cullen 1994: 15)

The location of colonialism and imperialism as a set of boundaries and obstacles to the social relations of crime control is thus of more than historical interest. It provides a model for many aspects of the situation pertaining in more recent liberation struggles against authoritarian regimes. But it also serves to pose the key questions of modernisation in yet another guise. Is the overall tendency of development one of weakening and undermining such structures and enabling a completion of the transitions, made earlier in Europe, from generalised repression, social crime, and alternative structures of self-regulation to the social relations of crime control? Or is it rather a matter of the eventual exhaustion of modernisation itself such that these peripheral features return to haunt its heartlands?

Crime as governance

The final example from the geographical periphery of modernisation concerns the role of criminality itself as a form of governance. Elements of this have been noted in the preceding discussion as in the role of criminal gangs and petty criminals as spies and agents for the authoritarian state. In the previous chapter I noted that the weakness of the eighteenth-century English state resulted in the use of thieves and criminals themselves as rudimentary forms of crime control agents. It is worth repeating Paul Rock's analogy between the role of characters such as the eighteenth-century Englishman Jonathan Wild who combined the roles of thief and thieftaker, with the Sicilian mafia as regards 'the capacity to serve as an acknowledged and necessary intermediary between weak community and weak governance' (Rock 1983: 216). The most significant European example of criminal organisation itself serving as a surrogate for crime control is indeed the traditional Sicilian mafia. Again, the importance of a brief familiarity with its mode of rule is not simply to understand it as a peripheral idiosyncrasy, a form of retarded development awaiting modernisation, but as exemplary of a form of 'backwardness' destined to reappear in new forms as the modernisation process becomes exhausted and which will infuse itself in new ways into the dynamics of crime control far beyond its original location.

The Mafia may be compared in some respects to the activities of social criminals or bandits, with the crucial difference that the role played is not that of supporting communal resistance to oppression or finding sanctuary in the communal toleration of a beneficial illegality but rather that of consolidating the power of rulers. In his account of the development of the Sicilian mafia, Anton Blok (1974) criticised what he detected as an overemphasis in Hobsbawm's work on the connection between the bandit and the masses. Bandits, as predatory criminals, need protection and sanctuary, but, underlining again their unpredictability as a social group, it is not necessarily the peasants and working people who are in the best position to provide this.

> Protectors of bandits may range from a close narrow circle of kinsmen and affiliated friends to powerful politicians: those who held formal office as well as grass-roots politicians.... Of all categories, the peasants were weakest ... bandits served to prevent and suppress peasant mobilisation in two ways: first, by putting down collective peasant action through terror; and, second, by carving out avenues of upward mobility which, like many other vertical bonds in this society, tended to weaken class tensions. These courses to 'respectability' are institutionalised in *mafia*. (Blok 1974: 99–102)

The roots of the mafia lay in a process of aborted modernisation involving the collapse of feudalism in Sicily combined with the failure to establish strong modern state institutions of criminal justice (Pezzino 1991). The weakness of these institutions in Sicily produced a vacuum in which strong violent families were able to substitute themselves for the state and pursue some of its functions – protection of property, repression of petty crime and deviance, and mediation of disputes and conflicts – through the medium of private violence. Mafia families were able to usurp de facto the functions of the state, without any pretence at justice and the rule of law, while at the same time never breaking their own connections with criminality and the arbitrary use of violence (Hess 1973; Blok 1974; Catanzaro 1992; Gambetta 1993). This is what distinguished mafia from simple banditry. Whereas bandits survived by placing themselves as often as possible beyond the reach of the state, and perhaps seeking protection from poor communities to whom they provided some benefits, *mafiosi* not only protected the interests of the rich but did so through collaboration with the state. As Blok notes, '[b]andits are in open conflict with the law and the State. *Mafiosi* disregard both and act in connivance with those who represent formal law, thus validating their private control of the community's public life' (1974: 94–5).

The undermining of the social relations of crime control consists, then, in their *partial* appropriation by a competing form of legitimacy. This is the basis of an ideological accommodation to the presence of mafia as a normal feature of Sicilian life through its mythologisation as a force for social stability and justice and characterisation as a 'parallel legal order', rather than as a form of criminality.[5] Such a view, as Gambetta notes, has been influential in conservative Italian political and legal thought in the form of the proposition that

> the state cannot justifiably claim a monopoly over the law. The state is only one institution among many, and there is no reason why its legal order should be regarded as superior. (Gambetta 1993: 5)

Mafia thus appears as a form of 'governance from below' (see O'Malley et al. 1997; Stenson 1998, 1999). The strategy of governance pursued by strong modernising states such as Britain recognised the importance of retaining the autonomy of the individual family as a sphere of private authority. Nevertheless this authority was directed internally, to other family members. By contrast the older feudal notion of sovereignty (as described by Foucault) refers to the rule of society as an extension of the family with the sovereign as patriarch. Mafia presents a hybrid version in which the individual extended family, led by powerful men prepared to use ruthless violence, is directed outward towards the pacification of other elements in society, notably the working class and peasantry. Its strategy is less that of governance than a crude form of sovereignty aimed simply at the pacification of the masses. There is no developed notion of governing society as a complex entity with its own dynamics. Any 'social policy' or philanthropy on the part of mafia families, such as lending money or resources, is strictly subordinated to the production of acquiescence through fear (see Paoli 1998). Mafia intervenes in and neutralises modernising mechanisms such as the market and organised welfare through the deployment of older traditions of clientalism and personal service in return for loyalty. For this reason it might be thought of as an essentially pre-modern phenomenon, locked into the older techniques of sovereignty albeit in a decentralised and overtly violent form. However, as I shall note later, the potential for a very rapid transition to modern and indeed 'postmodern' forms of governance is present in the very decentralised nature of mafia organisation.

Other forms of traditional organised crime, notably the American mafia, played an analogous role. A connection with the geographical periphery of modernisation is retained in that one of the conditions for the growth of this variety of organised crime was large-scale immigration as an aspect of the growth of urban centres under conditions of rapid industrialisation. A certain similarity to the Sicilian variant was the result of ethnic linkages through immigration from Italy to America. But more important was the fact that the rapidly expanding cities of North America in the early decades of the twentieth century created localised power vacuums into which ethnically based organisations could insert themselves as traders of votes for welfare resources and jobs in the local economy (Ianni and Ianni 1972). Ethnically based political 'machines' (Merton 1957: 128) sustained a structure of clientalism in which ordinary people would be helped with welfare, employment, and assisted if in trouble with the police, in return for their votes. From the standpoint of business, particularly those sectors involved in urban services, building construction, etc., a corrupt relation with local political machines was a useful stabilising mechanism which avoided excess competition for public contracts, gave favourable tax concessions, and helped to secure a compliant labour force. The mafia, together with other ethnically based criminal organisations, acted as the brokers in this process of exchange.

Although hegemonising the *local* state apparatus, weak under conditions of rapid urbanisation, and to some extent escaping criminalisation in local communities by virtue of a rival legitimacy, in a manner analogous to the traditional Sicilian version, the American mafia negated the social relations of crime control more by its command of sufficient resources to bribe and corrupt the state or intimidate any members of the public willing to give evidence against it. This contrasts with the element of legitimacy and respect secured by traditional Sicilian *mafiosi* (Hess 1998). As the modern state apparatus consolidates itself, corruption *of* rather than substitution *for* the state becomes the predominant mode of operation of organised crime.

Thus to a greater extent than the rural Sicilian variant, the American mafia from the 1920s onwards enhanced its economic role. The use of criminal violence developed as a mode of 'forced entry' from the periphery into the modernisation process by short-circuiting upward social mobility from largely unskilled immigrant status, a process notably accelerated by the role of organised crime in illegal alcohol manufacture and distribution during the Prohibition era of the 1920s (Haller 1989; Abadinsky 1994; Bergreen 1994; Behr 1997) famously described by Daniel Bell (1961) as the 'queer ladder of social mobility'. The changed relationship to the community of a purely economic gangsterism compared to that of the traditional Sicilian mafia, means that the gangster begins to lose status and legitimacy in the local community:

> [B]ecause he has no necessary protective or mediatory function to fulfil within the social system he also possesses no legitimacy in popular morality; that is, he is no longer a *mafioso* but a criminal.... He grants no audiences and nobody calls on him. He is ... to the general public an anonymous big-city criminal, with no resemblance to the universally known and respected *mafioso* of the Sicilian village. (Hess 1998: 172–3)

The move is in the direction of the type of economic criminality more characteristic of northern Europe. Britain, for example, largely escaped the mafia variety of criminality except on a minuscule highly localised scale. Early industrialisation, the consolidation of a strong centralised state and ruling class (notwithstanding the transitional weaknesses noted earlier), the early development of an organised working-class movement left little space for the 'Sicilianisation' of social and political relations. Likewise nineteenth-century British urban expansion, though it involved some immigration, never developed the conditions of ethnic competition and clientalism characteristic of the American city. On the contrary, strong, well organised local government was the cradle of the modernising bourgeoisie and the 'gas and water socialism' of the later nineteenth century. It was paralleled by the organs of local working-class power, the trades councils and Labour clubs. While forms of criminality were present which could have matured into a more organised syndicate form, they remained localised and relatively weak, without linkage to either national, state or local government or the organs of working-class politics.[6]

Thus in Britain and northern Europe generally many of the main economic activities associated with organised crime such as trafficking in illegal commodities, loansharking, protection racketeering, were assimilated to looser forms of professional criminal organisation or white collar criminality (Mack 1964, 1975; McIntosh 1975; see also Taylor 1999, ch. 5). The activity of modern professional criminals, emerging in the last decades of the nineteenth century following the dismembering of the older criminal fraternities, discussed in the previous chapter, forms a continuity with the predatory bandit rather than with mafia. Such criminality is oriented to simple accumulation of money. It adopts flexible and temporary organisation based on a loose-knit underworld, with some role for family structure but with few if any links to the state or political system. Its capacity to corrupt is limited to low-level police agencies, and small tight-knit local communities. This form of criminality could be seen as posing quite different types of threat to the social relations of crime control than traditional mafia organisations.

Conclusion

In this chapter I have considered, albeit briefly and schematically, various scenarios which might seem at first impression unrelated. What they have in common is that they illustrate boundaries and limitations to the development of the social relations of crime control.

These boundaries, to summarise the discussion, are of a number of types. Firstly, there is the preservation of older forms of hierarchical regulation and authority which obstruct recourse to the modern legal and criminal justice apparatus and the various aspects of the social relations of crime control. These forms of authority are co-opted by modernisation, as illustrated by the reconstruction of the family and the constitution of the commercial enterprise as key forms of governance. Secondly, at the geographical periphery forms of authoritarian sovereignty aimed at the generalised pacification of colonial populations impeded the growth of modern relations of crime control. Thirdly, criminality as a form of 'governance from below' appeared in two forms: the persistence of social crime and mafia as forms of mediation between the masses and ruling elites under conditions of a weak or absent state authority. The usefulness of mapping out something of the diversity and variety of these obstacles to crime control will, I hope, become obvious as we turn to the later stages of modernisation in which such phenomena are partially overcome and weakened but subsequently reappear in new forms and as core rather than peripheral features of contemporary governance.

Notes

1 From 5.3 offences per 100,000 population in 1840 to 11.8 in 1910 (Gatrell 1988).

2 See the discussion of the criminalising abstraction in Chapter 1.

3 Shaming and disgrace presuppose of course some of the ingredients of the social relations of crime control in the sense that even if the action is not criminalised, there is still moral opprobrium from the surrounding (business) community. This contrasts with the bourgeois as the amoral 'robber baron' which is characteristic of early capitalism and also, as will be argued later, the criminogenic business culture of the present period. For an attempt to appropriate the positive elements of shaming in the context of business crime as a general alternative to criminalisation and punishment see Braithwaite 1989.

4 Though McCall's research shows an increasing willingness to refer disputes to state agencies towards the end of the apartheid regime.

5 This has resulted also in an idealist or cultural theory of the Sicilian mafia as a state of mind or morality rather than an organisation; 'a kind of exaggeration of the presumed aspects of the Sicilian character' (Catanzaro 1992: 7).

6 For a comparative analysis of organised crime in Britain and the United States see Jenkins and Potter 1986.

4

The Contradictions
of Modernisation

During the period between the two world wars, the dynamic of capitalist modernisation, particularly in Europe, appeared either to have exhausted itself or taken new authoritarian forms represented by fascism and Stalinism. In fact the authoritarian systems shared with the liberal democratic innovations of the New Deal in the United States and the Keynesian welfare state in western Europe a strategy of state intervention aimed at sustaining economic expansion and stabilising the relations between capital and organised labour. After the defeat of fascism in Europe it could be plausibly maintained that in western Europe and North America repressive versions of modernisation had been overcome and the 'modernising offensive' could now resume its course as a form of 'organised modernity' (Wagner 1994) led by the interventionist liberal democratic state.

Other themes such as sexuality, family and culture were present and were drawn upon in the elaboration of the authoritarian regimes of both fascism (Theweleit 1987; Koonz 1988) and Stalinism (Buckley 1985) and in the new model family of the welfare state (McDowell 1991). Nevertheless, the overriding problem which these regimes set out to solve was that of sustained economic growth and the stabilisation of class relations. In the liberal democratic Keynesian welfare state – the form of organised modernity which concerns us here – the means of establishing peaceful class relations was a form of democratic corporatism or 'social contract'. Other issues, however important as policy areas, were essentially ancillary to this project.

The question of criminality occupied a subordinate status. Its eclipse by matters of class and even family relations testifies to the progress of the social relations of crime control. The socialisation of the working class as a whole was no longer an issue. Class relations now took the form of corporate compromise between well organised labour and capital. The issues which preoccupied the Keynesian welfare state were not those of the general insubordination or criminality of the working class but the new forms of political and industrial organisation which it had devised and the necessity of confronting the problems of poverty and social inequality to which it demanded solutions. In this context, issues of crime and crime control become marginal to the main issues of social and political planning.

Crime consolidates its modern status as the clearly defined deviant and exceptional, the episodic disruption of normality and the concern of a specialist body of legal professionals and criminologists.

This state of affairs is, however, essentially an interregnum. The achievements of organised modernity in its Keynesian democratic form, from the end of the Second World War to the late 1960s, can in retrospect be easily exaggerated and should be seen rather to constitute 'an interim configuration that, while it displayed a certain internal coherence, also bore the seed of its own demise' (Wagner 1994: 77). From the perspective of crime control this interregnum of the 1950s and 1960s stands between two periods in which crime control and criminalisation are major, if not dominant, discourses and instruments of social control: the nineteenth-century discourses of police, discipline and moral socialisation of the working class, and the new discourses, emerging in the 1970s and 1980s of ubiquitous crime and risk as central preoccupations of new forms of governance in advanced capitalist societies.

The self-image of the period of organised modernity was anything but that of an interregnum – rather a completion of, and elimination of the residual obstacles to modernisation. Social science and social engineering would enable the mastery of society and the elimination of residual social problems in the same way that the physical sciences and technology enabled the mastery of nature. In this scenario, notwithstanding the relatively low profile given to the question of crime there were a number of unresolved problems left by the first phase of modernisation. The consensus around the social relations of crime control was fragile in working-class communities. Despite increasingly common definitions of criminality there was still widespread acceptance of petty social crime and the acceptance of police and criminal justice agencies was still precarious. The use of criminal justice as a general mechanism of class control, though more narrowly focused on periodic industrial disputes than in the previous century, remained a significant feature of working-class life and underlined the difficulty of isolating and neutralising the social relations of crime control from contamination by more overt political conflict.

Less prominent in debate, but still unresolved issues, were the boundaries of practical criminality constituted by the relative autonomy of the commercial organisation and the family as institutions of private governance. The boundaries which they represented to the social relations of crime control were inherently unstable. Precisely because of the formal universality of the criminal law, demands for its practical reinforcement in spheres such as domestic violence or serious commercial fraud could be expected to develop. Finally, from a more global perspective, the various obstacles to the social relations of crime control constituted by colonial repression or varieties of criminal governance were likely to become increasingly unstable as modernisation progressed. In view of the character of the present period it is important to understand the various ways in which the structures of organised modernity envisaged a solution to these 'residual' problems. Beginning with the development of the advanced capitalist countries, I shall argue – again focusing mainly on the British case – that the two main perceived axes of stabilisation of the social relations of crime control were the consolidation of the relations between state and the community, and the progressive weakening of the criminal offender.

The Affluent Society

The underlying force for change was the prolonged economic boom of the 1950s and 1960s, seen by many contemporary commentators as the reflection of a process whereby capitalism had apparently been, in the words of leading Labour politician and social theorist, Anthony Crosland, 'reformed out of all recognition' (Crosland 1956: 517). The agent of this transformation was seen as the Keynesian welfare state; state fiscal and monetary policy combined with the expansion of public utilities, schools, housing, health care, would stabilise the economy and create a regime of near full employment and rising incomes which would both provide funds for welfare and, by reducing poverty, minimise the demands on state welfare guarantees. The character of the economy during this period has been subsequently described as a 'Fordist' regime of mass production of standardised commodities by a well-paid, stable, labour force for an expanding consumption market fuelled by rising incomes and the expansion of demand for consumer goods through mass media and advertising (see Aglietta 1979; Harvey 1989; Lea 1997).

Keynesian economic theory provided an account of class compromise in terms of which labour–capital conflict could be overcome by sharing the results of productivity increases between wages and profits and by positing wages as less a cost to capital than a source of buoyant 'effective demand'. Likewise, state spending on public utilities was seen as a source of economic stability through the creation of further demand for goods and services produced by the private sector. The state, the working class and capital were now seen to be mutually involved in a virtuous circle, or at the very least a system of equally distributed 'countervailing power', replacing outdated ideas of class conflict. Economic regulation, the importance of state spending and public contracts with the obligations they impose on private companies, and entrenched trade union consultation rights, extended economic governance from that of 'mechanisms of security' defending the autonomy of the private company towards a more elaborate relationship of negotiation and compromise between the company, the state and the organised and socialised working class.

This was being accompanied, it was argued, by profound changes in the economic and social structure of capital accumulation itself, heralded by the growth in the size of commercial companies. At the level of economic theory it was suggested that aggressive competition was being replaced by market-stabilising agreements between these large corporations aimed at stability, predictability and risk avoidance (Galbraith 1967). The social effect of these changes was seen to be the decline of the aggressive capitalist entrepreneur in favour of a management bureaucracy characterised by an ethic of security, stability and organisational loyalty (Whyte 1956; Sampson 1995). The working class was similarly affected by the new stability. A Fordist working class of high-wage, secure production-line jobs combined with membership of trade unions led by conservative bureaucrats would moderate the old combativeness of class conflict. These two groups, together with the Keynesian state bureaucracy, dedicated to tweaking the economy to secure stable growth and near full employment, would sustain the neutralisation of class conflict.

The welfare state meanwhile aimed at what today would be called 'social inclusion', displacing and removing the sources of social conflict, criminality included, by policy interventions designed to reduce and minimise the effects of socio-economic inequality. This would be achieved, firstly, by a combination of progressive taxation and rights to housing, education, health care, social insurance and minimum income guarantees which would constitute a new system of social citizenship (Marshall 1950). Richard Titmuss, a leading social policy theorist, commenting on the political mood of the 1950s, wrote:

> Inequality, as a subject of political discourse, was less in evidence everywhere, and what remained of poverty in Britain was thought to be either eradicable through the natural process of growth or as constituting a permanent residue of the unfortunate and irresponsible. (Titmuss 1964: 11)

The British variant of the welfare state, inspired by William Beveridge, emphasised 'universalism' or the right of all social groups, irrespective of original income, to welfare benefits, as a strategy to bind the social classes together in common interest and identification with social rights.

A second focus was on urban renewal and slum clearance, a process that had begun during the inter-war years. The proportion of the housing stock in Britain owned by local authorities and New Town Corporations rose from 1 per cent in 1938 to 25 per cent in 1969 (Power 1987: 44). New housing estates and 'new towns' built on the periphery of existing conurbations involved a strategy of the uprooting and relocation of the poorest sections of the working class in new housing estates, often of high-rise flats (see Young and Willmott 1957). The aim was the breakdown of class ghettoisation and the creation of a common, 'classless' living space.

For the majority of the population rising incomes and social mobility were seen as underpinning a cultural revolution based on mass consumption. 'Mass production meant standardisation of the product as well as mass consumption; and that meant a whole new aesthetic and a commodification of culture' (Harvey 1989: 135–6), leading to a homogenisation of the lifestyles of the middle and working classes around what the French sociologist Raymond Aron (1967) called 'a more middle class mode of life', an orientation to leisure and family displacing older identities based on work, class conflict and community. The latter were fading away as the technical solution of social and economic problems heralded the 'end of ideology', while work was simply a means of income for individuals to 'maintain their relatively prosperous and rising standard of living and ... their inclination towards a family centred style of living' (Goldthorpe et al. 1968: 150).[1]

This orientation to family and leisure and away from work and politics was seen as an important basis for a theory of the stability of organised modernity in terms of a *civic culture* characterised by the depoliticisation of the mass of the population which then acted as a filter preventing an overload of demands on the political system (Almond and Verba 1963; see also Wagner 1994: 115). This dynamic of *civic privatism* or 'political abstinence combined with an orientation to career, leisure and consumption' (Habermas 1976: 37) formed the basis of a depoliticised relationship between citizens and state agencies as one between client and expert in which social problems were handed over to professionals with their respective knowledges and discourses. The vehicle of the diffusion of this passivity to widening layers of the working class was the demolition of traditional oppositional working-class communities through relocation and social mobility combined with the spread of a mass culture. One was less an active member of a political community than a passive consumer of culture (Clarke and Jefferson 1976). This view clashed considerably not only with the image of the 'active citizen' of the initial period of enthusiastic post-war reconstruction but, as critical theorists such as Habermas (1976) noted, with some of the long-term effects of mass secondary and higher education.

In such conditions criminality could hardly function as anything but a highly dysfunctional deviance, a disruption of otherwise integrative stable normality. Organised modernity would complete the consolidation of those stabilising forces already at work during the later nineteenth century. The main axes would be a continuation in falling crime rates due to the reduction in criminogenic poverty and inequality, a strengthening of the relations between the state and community through an unambiguous acceptance of the role of the police and criminal justice agencies by all social classes, a further weakening of criminal offenders as marginal individuals or small groups without significant power or social support, and a removal of ambiguous areas of practical criminalisation through clear consensual definitions of, and reactions to, crime. A closer look at each of these areas, even without considering the countervailing forces at work, will reveal a slightly more complex set of relations.

State and Community

The combination of harmonious relations between the social classes and the state and the cultural homogenisation of the population would, it could be supposed, lay the basis of a new regime of consensus on crime control. A 'grudging' acceptance of criminal justice by the working class would crumble into a cross-class consensus based on common standards of criminalisation and a faith in the ultimate accountability of criminal justice agencies to a democratic system in which all interests were represented. Both the language of the criminal law and the activities of the criminal justice agencies would be brought into closer correspondence with popular ideas governing the dynamics of practical criminalisation. A fully democratic citizenship, and a consequent widening public sphere in which all social groups could participate and be heard, would ensure the legislative process reflected popular concerns, while increasing social mobility and social homogenisation would standardise conceptions of, and sensitivities to, criminality. The elimination of the old isolated working-class communities, and the last residues of social criminality, would complete the latter process. Meanwhile the strengthening of a sense of the common good, and common membership of the social community implied in the rights of social citizenship would in turn strengthen the foundations of progressive penal policy as the reclamation of the offender and his reintegration into the social collectivity.

There was indeed evidence of consensus. Debates on punishment, such as those which ended the death penalty for murder in Britain in 1957, and the decriminalisation of homosexual acts between consenting adults in 1967, were not conducted on class lines. In the meantime the passive consensus was reflected in the largely depoliticised status of criminal justice in the 1950s and 1960s, at least by today's standards (Downes and Morgan 1994). Robert Reiner sees evidence of a cross-class consensus around policing revealed in the social survey conducted for the 1962 *Royal Commission on the Police* which signified what he calls the 'high point of police legitimacy', and confirmed

> those contemporary opinions which stressed the widespread acceptance of the police *throughout the class structure*.... By the 1950s 'policing by consent' *was* achieved in Britain to the maximal degree it is ever attainable.... Police *power*, that is, the capacity to inflict legal sanctions including force, had been transmuted into *authority*. (Reiner 1992: 59–60)

The idea of consensus can embrace, of course, a number of quite different dynamics. Radical social democrats, particularly in the immediate post-war years, emphasised a positive consensus presupposing a politically active working class making strong demands on the state. But as the enthusiasm for post-war reconstruction subsided it was clear that fundamental changes in the political and economic structure would be moderated by a combination of civic privatism, a conservative trade union and Labour politicians who wanted to become part of the system rather than change it. As the civic privatism thesis implied, the precondition of stability, given that the major institutions of capitalism remained intact and unchallenged, was a passivity on the part of the working class in the face of a depoliticisation and technicisation of social problems rather than the active assertion of citizenship rights. Indeed, the growing militancy of organised labour, together with increasingly articulate new social movements such as feminism from the early 1970s onwards, were components of the *breakdown* of the post-war consensus, and growing legitimation problems and 'demand overload'.

Policing the middle-class neighbourhood

The dynamics of this passive consensus around criminal justice, and its manifestation in the social relations of crime control, were exemplified in the relationship between police and the middle-class neighbourhood as a form of the expert–client relationship mentioned above. This relationship in which the police are viewed as expert professionals to be willingly invited in to the neighbourhood to provide a service and solve problems has been aptly termed 'Keynesian policing' (O'Malley and Palmer 1996). It contrasts with the situation in the traditional working-class community. The latter has a strong sense of place and the ownership of territory within which operate networks of solidarity and mutual aid. As David Harvey puts it: 'Exchange values are scarce, and so the pursuit of use values for daily survival is central to social action.... The result is an often intense attachment to place and "turf" and an exact sense of boundaries' (Harvey 1994: 371). The control over space is crucial where people are engaged in direct material exchanges and the appropriation and distribution of non-market goods and services some of which may be of illegal origin. These networks – which include elements of social crime – have to be defended against outsiders concerned to tax, criminalise or otherwise disrupt their operation. 'Successful control presumes a power to exclude unwanted elements.... The state is largely experienced as an agency of repressive control (in police, education etc.) rather than as an agency that can be controlled by and bring benefits to them' (Harvey 1994: 371).

Furthermore, in the traditional community, crimes such as theft and violence are part of a more complex economy of disorder in which locally based problematic situations will be widely known and understood. Who is 'out of order', why, and with what consequences for whom, will be judged in their many-sided concreteness rather than in terms of the criminalising abstraction. The ability of the community to take sanctions upon those who violate its norms, and without the interference of police or the transformation of those involved into criminals, is the other side of the coin of the toleration of all sorts of 'bother' or 'trouble' regarded as less threatening because understood, and is also a crucial aspect of the mechanisms of control over the local economy of mixed legality and illegality.

Middle-class neighbourhoods, by contrast, are

> [A]lready blessed with abundant exchange values with which to sustain life, ... [and] are in no way dependent upon community-provided use values for survival. The construction of community is then mainly geared to the preservation or enhancement of exchange values.... Interpersonal relations are unnecessary at the street level and the command over space does not have to be assured though continuous appropriation.... Community associations form to take care of externality effects and maintain the 'tone' of the community space. The state is seen as basically beneficial and controllable, assuring security and helping keep undesirables out, except in unusual circumstances (the location of 'noxious' facilities, the construction of highways etc.). (Harvey 1994: 371–2)

Such a neighbourhood does not have to defend its ground, its moral economy of mutual aid, against outsiders. A majority of its consumption activities take place outside the locality and may be shared with others who live elsewhere, being linked as part of what sociologists during the 1960s were calling 'distance' or 'telephone' communities (Young and Willmott 1960; Willmott and Young 1973). The locality is viewed similarly as part of individual consumption. The collective local interest is that between all property owners to maintain the 'tone' and 'upkeep' of the area and hence the exchange value of their property. Thus the external threats that concern the middle-class neighbourhood are not police intrusions upon local collectivities but immigrants, burglars, and any other group whose presence would have the perceived effect of reducing property values and increasing insecurity. Police are welcome as experts who will defend property values.

In a more general sense the values of the middle-class neighbourhood replicate those of the police and the criminal law. Linked to the locality only by roots which may be opportunistically broken as social and geographical mobility require, the middle class has a more universal concept of property. The closed, traditional multi-generational working-class community in which theft may be less serious if committed against targets elsewhere is replaced by a generalised conception that theft is wrong. Other areas are those to which one may conceivably move, other property is that which one may conceivably wish to appropriate at some stage. The middle-class consciousness assimilates to the concept of universal property and general categories of criminalisation which are the basis of the modern criminal law.

There are yet further dimensions to the expert–client relation between police and the middle-class community in Keynesian policing which are important to spell out, particularly in the light of more recent developments. In the middle-class community the type of concrete knowledge of local interactions which would enable autonomous communal control is largely absent. Little may be known about what is going on next door, let alone down the street. As noted previously, some working-class communities began to develop in this direction in the later nineteenth century. The police task is not, therefore, that of prising the identity of offenders out of a community reluctant to co-operate, but to sift carefully through a mass of willingly given but *fragmented* information. Under such conditions the approximation of descriptions of troublesome events to the language of the criminal law is a natural result, as part of the handing over of the management of problems to experts. Meanwhile in the central city an egalitarian society of consumers encounters forms of criminality – shoplifting, snatch thefts – committed by outsiders with no connections to any moral economy of social crime or other forms of tolerance. In both cases the task of governance – of the expert responding to the needs of the client – is to link the latter to the sovereignty of the state: the requirements of social order expressed in the criminal law. The more the working class assimilates to this model and makes its purchases, and seeks its entertainments in the city centre rather than locally, the more it loses affinity with and control over local criminals and criminal economies.

From the standpoint of the police, the response to requests for intervention from the public continually displaces the struggle to impose a continuous regime of control characteristic of the earlier stages of incursions into working-class communities. In the more tension-ridden relationship between police and the traditional working-class community, the police have continually to decide whether and to which minor crimes they are to turn a blind eye in return for a manageable existence and hope of co-operation on criminal activities considered to be more pressing. Often there are quite complex forms of co-existence to be established even with serious villains in the area who will only attract police attention if they move seriously 'out of order'. In addition, the tasks of generalised policing – capturing, occupying, patrolling and securing the control of a particular terrain or ground, 'moving on' troublesome and recalcitrant populations, etc. – are never far away. But to the extent that social homogenisation around the values and structure of the middle-class community proceeds, the dominant mode of operation of Keynesian policing becomes precisely that of effective response to public requests for intervention. Thus,

> one of the most prominent features of post-war police policy has been the concern to reduce the amount of time taken to respond to calls for assistance from the public. As a result, less emphasis is placed upon the general duties of 'guard, watch and patrol', and relatively little time is given over to investigation. (Baldwin and Kinsey 1982: 28–9)

The decline of 'guard, watch and patrol' in particular signifies a further move away from policing as sovereignty (in Foucault's sense) and in the direction of governance involving the self-activity of the public as a key component taking the form of episodic intervention triggered by public response and involving the deployment of expert knowledge and technique in the solution of problems. The police concentrate on effective response to calls by a community whose co-operation and willingness to impart information can be assumed. The police thus *administrate* a neighbourhood rather than *rule* it. The general tendency of criminal justice to withdraw from residual tasks of general social control is a key feature of governance in organised modernity. The partial displacement of disciplinary power and sovereignty by administration and deployment of techniques and knowledges aimed at maximising the *internal* forces of cohesion and order in a community is central to the expert–client relationship.[2]

It need hardly be added that such developments were simply a tendency. There remained large numbers of poorer working-class communities in the older industrial regions as yet unclaimed by the modernising institutions of the Keynesian welfare state and where policing represented something closer to the struggle for sovereignty over the population. Crime in these deprived areas still echoed many of the characteristics of the nineteenth century. Studies of criminal subcultures noted the survival of strong elements of social crime. John Mays (1954), in his studies of the Liverpool dockland communities, was most concerned to find that young delinquents still retained the older moral economy of legitimate and illegitimate victims.

> It is nearly always abhorrent to rob members of the family or personal friends. To a much lesser extent it is not done to steal from small one-man shops or elderly people. But with strangers inhibitions are weaker and fellow sympathy reduced to a minimum. They are therefore the natural victims on whom to prey. Such would seem to constitute the ethics of shoplifting! (Mays 1954: 118)

The legitimate victims, in this case shops in the city centre, were basically outside the community. Moreover, such behaviour was part of the traditional working-class culture of the area and still being transmitted from father to son.

> The amount of theft from the Liverpool docks is considerable ... and the effect on children who see their fathers and elder brothers bringing home goods stolen at work must be considerable. (Mays 1954: 117–18)

This lack of 'correct attitudes' towards crime in such communities was seen as a symptom of a backwardness rooted in traditional working-class culture. Mays' interpretation was followed in other British studies. David Downes, in the first systematic appropriation of American subcultural theory into the British context, noted the popularity of the approach taken by

Walter Miller (1958) for whom delinquency was, in Downes' words, simply 'the direct, intensified expression of the dominant culture pattern of the lower class community' (Downes 1966: 69). It was Miller's approach that fitted the situation. 'The evidence of all the English studies appears strongly supportive of Walter Miller's theory that the bulk of delinquency represents straightforward adolescent conformity to the expectations of lower class culture' (Downes 1966: 113).

The modernisation of such areas was a major task for welfare, education, community development and social planning agencies. The issue was how to secure their integration into the processes of social mobility and homogenisation at work in mainstream society. Rehousing was a major aspect of policy. It would allow the forces of modernisation to penetrate into the heart of the community itself and restructure its interpersonal relations. Nineteenth-century modernisation had established the moral economy of place and space in public areas; now the residual backwaters of the housing estates themselves needed to be tackled. Relocation to new housing estates would break down the old community norms through new forms of living space in flats based on the nuclear family rather than the collective community. Meanwhile communities would be broken up and segments relocated to different areas. Young people, with more money in their pockets, would seek entertainment and leisure in the city centre rather than in the localities, and would assimilate to the type of middle-class view of their neighbourhoods outlined above (see Cohen 1972; Clarke and Jefferson 1976).

Residual Criminality

Besides the drawing into the modernisation process of residual populations, the second main axis along which the social relations of crime control would be strengthened, concerned the weakening power and increased social marginalisation of criminal offenders. The power to subvert state criminal justice agencies or to hegemonise communities and institutions would be further whittled away. The pathological petty criminal would continue to become the paradigm for the vast bulk of criminality. It was widely expected that the rate of crime would resume the downward tendency it had exhibited in the latter part of the nineteenth century. Crime had risen during the war but this was seen as largely the result of disruption, economic shortages and family break-ups. Post-war reconstruction would remedy such matters.

Again, the argument appeared in both radical and conservative variants. From the left the criminologist Herman Mannheim spoke in glowing terms of the link between a reduction in crime and a programme of widespread public ownership of the economy:

In countries which are expected to undergo, in the future, a process of gradual nationalisation of 'a limited number of key industries or services' supplemented by a system of state supervision of privately owned industries and by growing equalisation of incomes, the resulting 'we'-feeling may also eventually lead to a considerable decline of crimes of acquisitiveness, especially theft. (Mannheim 1946: 114)

He emphasised that

for nationalisation and those other parts of the socialist plan for social recon-struction to have any substantial effect on petty crime it is essential not only that the programme should not be too much watered down, but also that the masses should know what is being done to reduce the present inequality in the distribution of wealth. (Mannheim 1946: 114–15)

This thesis linking public ownership and social cohesion echoed the opti-mistic view of the Soviet Union as a 'new civilisation'. Official Soviet pro-paganda had certainly linked the abolition of private property in the means of production to social cohesion and low crime rates (Handelman 1995: 276) and, during the 1960s wave of colonial emancipation, it was fre-quently assumed that political independence and the end of colonial oppres-sion would reduce crime rates.

From a more conservative standpoint, the key factors in falling crime lay along lines more consistent with the civic privatism thesis, such as the strengthening of the family after the period of wartime disruption:

In the period of social reconstruction after the war the family would be restored and strengthened, and the sense of community experienced temporarily in the wartime period would be institutionalised as a permanent feature of social and economic relationships. Crime and delinquency, the expression of inconsistent family control and socialisation brought about by the war, would decline and lose significance in proportion to the success of social reconstruc-tion. (Taylor 1982: 51–2)

Again, from a conservative standpoint the main way in which reductions in poverty and inequality would reduce motivation for criminality lay less in any collective 'we'-feeling than in the elimination of the residual patho-logy of the deprived areas which would reduce (a mainly juvenile) delin-quency to an aspect of the traumas of adolescence. Its supervision could be appropriately placed under the direction and supervision of the expanding welfare and educational agencies for whom the criminal justice agencies could be subordinated as a trawling mechanism in the new relationships of governance (see Wootton 1959). Appropriate therapeutic regimes to assist the process of 'growing out of crime' could be imaginatively devised. Petty crime did indeed remain low until the mid 1950s but even as it began to rise during the subsequent period this did not lead to any new assumptions about its nature and social function.

But falling crime rates were by no means the only possible result of rising living standards and the mass consumption society. It could be pointed out that modernisation and affluence, even if they reduced the supply of criminal *offenders*, certainly increased the amount of criminal *opportunities*. The Keynesian welfare state itself provided opportunities for fraud and corrupt relations between business and the state in the area of public contracts. Affluence, meanwhile, meant more people on the streets with money in their pockets, more money in bank branches and more consumer goods in the shops. Affluence might also have a 'dark side' reflected in an increased demand for illegal services such as drugs, vice and gambling. Daniel Bell, commenting on the activities of the American mafia in the post-war period, referred to a temporary obsession with gambling (illegal in most states of the USA) on the part of the newly rich middle classes as a result of the 'first flush of exuberance of rising incomes' (Bell 1961: 149). On a more global scale the modernisation process allegedly taking place in the underdeveloped countries during the 1960s was understood to presage rising crime rates due to rising incomes and rapid urbanisation (see Clinard and Abbott 1973; Shelley 1981; Heiland and Shelley 1992; Findlay 1999).

But none of this meant that the street robber, shoplifter, long-firm fraudster, vice-merchant or pimp was anything other than a marginal excrescence on the face of society; a predatory parasite pure and simple with little political or economic power and little or no public support or tolerance. Elaborate criminal economies and forms of criminal governance could be expected to continue a process of steady decline and marginalisation of their activities and participants even if they continued to accumulate sizeable incomes.

A supposed decline in the supply of serious criminal offenders seems a logical outcome of increasing social mobility, rising education levels and near full employment in the legitimate economy backed up by comprehensive social insurance. These sources of income, in particular with the rising affluence of young people, would marginalise crime as a source of status or route to advancement. The destruction and relocation of many traditional communities through rehousing and outward migration to employment opportunities elsewhere would break up the family networks, the criminal fraternities and their sanctuaries. The streets would belong to the police and the other agencies of local governance. Ageing villains known to the community would move out to the suburbs to retire, or remain as comic characters deserving of a certain respect but no longer more than icons to be exploited by T-shirt manufacturers, movie-makers and biographers. Those who remained in criminal activities under such circumstances would appear for what they were: misfits, deviants and unambiguous inflictors of harm.

Furthermore, even if the opportunities for criminal activity increased it would be increasingly disconnected from any community-based economies of social crime as modes of collective survival. Criminals who robbed banks, stole merchandise, etc., would be doing it largely for themselves and laundering goods and stolen money through increasingly dispersed networks. The proceeds of a robbery would be more likely to be spirited out of the country and into the expanding world financial system than to find their way back into local communities who, in return, would provide a measure of sanctuary for the offenders. Likewise, semi-permanent criminal economies of service provision would cater to segregated markets in perversions such as pornography, drugs, and illegal gambling, having little relation to ordinary upwardly mobile working-class and middle-class communities. Such economies, besides becoming segregated, would also become globalised in scope – as with sexual tourism – and the power of criminal groups within local communities would diminish. Looking back from the mid-1990s, Duncan Campbell surveyed the changing shape of British professional crime:

> In a way, what has happened to British crime parallels what has happened to British Industry. The old family firms ... have been replaced by multinationals of uncertain ownership, branches throughout the world, profits dispersed through myriad outlets.... (Campbell 1990: 8; see also Hobbs 1995, 1998)[3]

The disconnection from localised communities in the mode of operation and the dynamics of criminal markets is reflected in the forms by which professional criminals attempt to maintain their security. Older traditions of sanctuary and community protection are replaced by strategies of disguise, mobility and fluidity of organisation. This tendency, again, is not new – it was noted during the nineteenth century – but post-war modernisation might be thought to make it an increasingly predominant characteristic. The reliance on disguise, the ad hoc group of experts with the requisite technical skills for the job (safe-breaking, driving fast get-away cars, fencing the proceeds of crime) drawn from a wider network of contacts, the rapid sharing out of the proceeds and 'lying low' for a period, or even permanent migration (southern Spain became a favoured retreat for post-war British robbers), would further distance the professional criminal from any community roots. The old underworld decays in the face of more opaque networks and chains of contacts. Describing London in the 1960s Mary McIntosh wrote:

> Traditional criminal areas in London have declined and, increasingly, criminals live scattered about the various boroughs. The 'underworld' is no longer a residential area in which neighbours work together and children are brought up with a knowledge of crime and with possible criminal contacts. The underworld is now much more of a social network and if it has a geographical location it is in the centre of London and in the pubs and clubs that various sorts of criminals frequent. (McIntosh 1975: 23)

In a similar way evasion rather than corruption could be expected as the main method whereby such ad hoc and flexible forms of criminal organisation attempted to neutralise the police. The provider of illegal goods and services to clients would lurk in the 'red light' districts of large cities behind a front of legitimate business activity. Attempts to corrupt the police could be expected to continue, but again these would be most likely fairly low-level exchanges with street detectives, and partly subsumable under the normal relationships between police and criminals of turning a blind eye to certain activities in return for co-operation and information on more serious crimes. Of course, as with other types of crime, a residual pathology of criminal areas temporarily resistant to, or skirted by, modernisation could continue to sustain a more traditional criminal habitus. The East End of London could sustain the Kray twins, south London the Richardsons, well into the 1960s and beyond (Hobbs 1988: 54; Foster 1990; Robson 1997).

Peripheral modernisation and the decline of the mafia

But this particular national experience was part of a much wider global dynamic affecting not only the advanced capitalist countries. The modernisation process was held up as the image of development for the rest of the world – the newly independent colonies, the backward areas of Mediterranean Europe, the 'underdeveloped countries' as a whole. Modernisation theory laid out a strategy of transformation from 'traditional' to 'modern' society and sociologists and political scientists went in search of 'modernising elites' and strategies to overcome 'obstacles to modernisation' (see Harrison 1988 for an overview). In contrast to the present period when globalisation is understood as resulting in the weakening and displacing of nation states by multinational corporations, at that time globalisation (though the term was hardly used) was seen as a process whereby the advanced societies, within their national terrain, set the model of development and were in a position to provide assistance to developing countries to follow the same path.

From such a standpoint authoritarian states in various parts of the world, including the USSR and South Africa, appeared highly dysfunctional systems.[4] Whatever advantages early capitalism had gained from the ruthless exploitation of raw materials by slave and forced labour, it now required expanding markets and skilled, socially mobile workers, while rising wages could benefit both capital and labour, as in the advanced countries, if they were accompanied by productivity increases. Hence apartheid and oppressive police regimes sustaining a brutalised sovereignty through criminalisation of the masses, could be seen as a dysfunctional anachronism which simply held back capitalism (see Horwitz 1967). Meanwhile, to the extent that industrialisation did proceed, the increased urbanisation of the working class would create an unstoppable demand for democratic rights by the masses which would in turn result in the removal of generalised policing in favour of the social relations of crime control.

These forces of modernisation would, it was frequently assumed, lead also to the decline of traditional systems of organised criminality. The changes at work in the social relations between professional crime and communities in Britain could also be seen at work in the more dramatic environments of elaborate systems of organised crime in the Sicilian and North American contexts. Taking the three examples together we have three different ways in which powerful offenders subvert the social relations of crime control. First, the traditional Sicilian mafia which partially *appropriates* the social relations of crime control by substituting itself for a debilitated modern state apparatus and by securing a mixture of fear and respect in the community. Second, the American model of mafia as gangsterism or predominantly economic organised crime that *neutralises* crime control by intimidation of opponents and corruption of otherwise well functioning state organs, predominantly at a local level. Third, the model, discussed in the British context, though it is of course universal, of a professional criminality that deals with a well organised state and a largely unsympathetic community by *evading* them both, through disguise, invisibility and flexible organisation.[5] Modernisation, it might be argued, tends to push criminal organisation towards the third model which, as noted above, neither benefits nor seeks hegemony over local communities.

In the case of the Sicilian mafia it was widely believed during the postwar period that modernisation of the region was dispossessing the mafia of its status and power. Its role in governance was declining and it was being reduced to a simple gangsterism either along the lines of the American mafia (Hess 1998: 172) or even to more loosely organised variants of petty criminality. Agricultural modernisation from the late 1940s onwards led to the disintegration of the large landed estates and land redistribution which reduced the mediating role of the traditional mafia between the big landowners and their tenants (Blok 1974: 216–17). Secondly, large-scale migration, particularly of young men, to the expanding industries of northern Italy together with the expansion of public sector construction activity in Sicily itself weakened traditional sources of mafia recruits and enforcers (Arlacchi 1988: 57). Modern forms of employment in southern Italy fostered the growth of trade unions and workers' parties, in particular the Italian Communist Party which strengthened modern democratic corporatist forms of representation and interest mediation in complete conflict with traditional mafia methods. Likewise, employers bidding for contracts in public sector construction, or in any other area of economic expansion, would have an interest in rational, open and free competition and would constitute a growing force not only against the mafia itself but the entire system of bureaucratic clientelism and favouritism which characterised traditional Sicilian society and within which the mafia flourished. Increased economic activity and public investment meanwhile would bring a strengthening of the state apparatus and a withdrawal of toleration of any rivals to the state in the sphere of public order maintenance. Finally, at the level of popular culture these changes were believed to be undermining the traditional symbols of social prestige and status. The old virtues of the mafia 'man of honour', in particular the social prestige and respect flowing from the willingness to use violence, were being undermined by the values of the accumulation of wealth and conspicuous consumption as symbols of social status. The old mafia was, during the 1950s and 1960s, believed to be undergoing a profound crisis.

> During the 'fifties, and still more during the 'sixties the men of honour underwent a deep crisis: what was their identity, where did they fit in, if they were no longer official proxies in the mediation of conflicts and the repression of non-conformist behaviour, and if public praise and flattery from the authorities had given way to speeches at meetings and sentences in courts that denounced them as enemies of order and progress? (Arlacchi 1988: 64)

The old mafia, it appeared, was becoming weakened and marginalised from the central dynamics of power in Sicilian society. It was failing to reproduce itself as a social group as evidenced by the ageing of the mafia population appearing in court trials during the 1960s. The status of the *mafioso* was 'becoming more and more nearly that of a mere common criminal, a modern urban gangster who had neither popular roots nor popular backing' (Arlacchi 1988: 65).

The weakening of the Sicilian mafia was apparently being accompanied by a similar decline of its North American variant. The argument of sociologists such as Robert Merton and Daniel Bell was that after the Second World War traditional organised crime was in decline under the impact of Roosevelt's New Deal and the expansion of the welfare state, which precipitated the decay of the old urban political machines through which the Mob had secured its local bases of power. Although less all-embracing than the British system, it was the welfare system which, in Merton's opinion, weakened the power of the urban political machine.

> ironically, in view of the close connection of Roosevelt with the large urban political machines, it is a basic structural change in the form of providing services, through the rationalised procedures of what some call 'the welfare state,' that largely spelled the decline of the political machine ... it was the system of 'social security' and the growth of more-or-less bureaucratically administered scholarships which, more than the direct assaults of reformers, have so greatly reduced the power of the political machine. (Merton 1957: 194)

The enforcement of rationalised norms of distribution by the federally administered welfare system was seen as displacing the personalised clientalism of the political machine with instrumental universalistic norms. In doing so, it undermined the role of the Mob as fixers and mediators, trading votes for jobs and resources. Meanwhile, rising incomes and the diffusion of middle-class lifestyles undermined both the demand for the services of organised crime and the attraction of criminality itself as a form of social mobility. Bell lamented the passing of an era:

> With the rationalisation and absorption of some illicit activities into the structure of the economy, the passing of an older generation that had established a hegemony over crime, the rise of minority groups to social position, and the break-up of the urban boss system, the pattern of crime we have discussed is passing as well. Crime, of course, remains as long as passion and the desire for gain remain. But big, organised city crime, as we have known it for the last seventy five years ... is at an end. (Bell 1961: 149–50)

While crime would indeed remain, it was no part of this scenario that mafia organisations would be pushed off American streets by a new type of globalised entrepreneurial crime with far more resources at its disposal than the old mobsters ever had (Bourgois 1996; Schneider 1999). But that is to move ahead a few years. In the meantime it seemed that in a diversity of contexts the impact of modernisation, fuelled by a capitalism seemingly freed from crisis tendencies, appeared to be in the same direction: towards the consolidation of the social relations of crime control as a form of governance. This consolidation, essentially a continuation and completion of processes which had begun in the previous century, was based on the one hand in the close and stable relationship between an increasingly 'middle-class' society and the welfare state and on the other by the increasing weakness and social marginality of criminal offenders. At the same time, the expectation that crime rates would remain generally low would complete the essentially peripheral nature of the criminal question in modern societies. The management of crime could be consolidated as an essentially technical, specialist and, above all, apolitical form of governance.

Stable Boundaries

It is equally important to understand features apparently resistant to the impact of modernisation. Earlier I noted the family and the commercial company as two areas from which, while not formally excluded from the sphere of criminal law, secured a relative autonomy from the social relations of crime control. The impact of modernisation on these areas is important to assess. What is clear in the British case is the absence of any significant shift of the boundaries of the social relations of crime control into these key areas of governance.

Many of the developments which were held to characterise the Keynesian welfare state and post-war social change might appear to have created conditions conducive to a stronger practical criminalisation in the areas of corporate crime. Yet what is striking is the lack of movement. The integration of the working class, through the trade union bureaucracy, into corporatist structures of political negotiation and compromise might also have been expected to lead to increased pressure to firmly criminalise violations of hard-won regulations governing health and safety at work. Yet studies of the work of factory inspectors showed the predominance of a 'compliance' approach directed to assistance and persuasion rather than criminal prosecution of violations, a strategy which resulted in a lax attitude to observance by many employers (Carson 1970, 1982).

Mannheim certainly anticipated that wartime social cohesion and its continuation through the extension of state planning and public enterprise as part of the Keynesian mixed economy would give rise to pressure for new initiatives against corporate crime. His particular concern was the widespread fraud and racketeering which had become evident during the war. Rationing continued for several years after the end of the war and this served to heighten public consciousness about white collar crime. In this context the police obtained a good deal of public support. Ian Taylor noted the doubling of prosecutions for fraud in the immediate post-war years and referred to a popular conception of the detective as 'the hard-working defender of the new social democratic community burrowing away in pursuit of the predatory crimes of the powerful' (Taylor 1982: 70). A publicly demonstrated determination to deal with powerful offenders helped sustain the discourse of criminalisation as a democratic and consensual process. However, in practice the focus of increasing police activity was on mainly small-time racketeers and businesses, particular crimes such as long-firm fraud committed by groups of professional criminals *against* legitimate business, rather than criminality internal to the business world (Levi 1981).

As a consequence of limited liability, state surveillance of companies by the Department of Trade and Industry had increased since the late nineteenth century, before which responsibility for fraud prosecution was entirely in the hands of the victim. But again the approach was hardly that of a determination to secure the criminal conviction of law violators. As affluence and upward social mobility developed, the growth of savings and investment by an expanding middle class could be expected to provide additional pressure for effective criminalisation in this area. However, the forms of saving in an organised welfare state society (state guaranteed pensions and savings funds, building societies, etc.) tended to be risk-spreading, and shielded victims from the direct impact of fraud. Social mobility might also be expected to lead to the breakdown of social exclusivity of the business and financial elites and so weaken resistance to stronger supervision. It was paradoxically not until the 1980s when both the Keynesian welfare state and the prospect of sustained economic growth were in considerable disarray, that a pressure towards greater regulation of business gathered pace. The realisation of the precariousness of an affluence dependent on unprotected private investments and pension funds enhanced middle-class feelings of insecurity about the credentials of the large numbers of new entrants into the business and financial worlds. But, as we shall see, by then it was far too late.

In the meantime the City of London 'old boy' network of informalism reigned supreme, much as it had during the nineteenth century. In the United States conditions favoured somewhat stronger surveillance. The American financial world, by comparison with Britain, 'has never been subject to the same degree of restriction of access and social exclusiveness' (Clarke 1986: 8–9). Meanwhile, widespread suspicion of fraudulent activities surrounding the Wall Street crash of 1929 combined with the perceived penetration of organised crime into the business world led to the establishment of the Securities and Exchange Commission, during the New Deal of the 1930s. However these are marginal differences. The key issue is the power of modern large corporations and banks. The philosophy of self-regulation is ultimately a rationalisation of the power of capital which steers ideas of criminality away from the notion that the corporation may be 'inherently criminogenic for it necessarily operates in an uncertain and unpredictable environment such that its purely legitimate opportunities for goal attainment are sometimes limited and constrained' (Box 1983: 35).

Analogous considerations apply to the family. The Keynesian welfare state gave a further impetus to intervention within the family by welfare and education agencies. The happy integrated middle-class home, the housewife aided by a new technological revolution in labour-saving domestic machinery, would rear the next generation of socially and geographically mobile workers. The return of women to traditional roles following the disruption of social relations during the war could be given a progressive gloss through the family as the focus of the new Keynesian emphasis on mass consumption. The welfare state would pay close attention to the health of the nuclear family as a functioning unit. A major task of social workers and child psychiatrists would be to ensure the effectiveness of the family in its role as primary socialiser and educator of the next generation. This emphasis was reinforced by the theory of self-perpetuating culture of poverty or pathology perspective as the predominant account of residual criminality or poverty, the family being the locus of primary socialisation into these dysfunctional motivations. The 'problem family' as a criminogenic environment for the rearing of delinquents would become a major research theme (Bowlby 1953).

It might be thought that this new emphasis on the internal workings of the family, in the context of a regime of social rights and new claims to social citizenship, would lead to increased criminalisation of family violence. However, if violence is read as a sign of institutional dysfunctionality, criminalisation is not a necessary outcome. Rather, there was a consolidation of the alliance between criminal justice and welfare agencies begun during the later nineteenth century in which family violence appears as a breakdown in family functioning and at the most a dispute between two parties, rather than as a relation between victim and offender. Police intervention is then, as in minor public disorder, limited to calming the disputants and contacting the welfare agencies who then act in terms of a parallel concept of pathology in which all participants, including the recipient of violence herself, are seen to play a part in causing. The subordination of the police to concepts of pathology is illustrated by a memorandum, during the mid-1970s, from the Association of Chief Police Officers to the House of Commons Select Committee on Violence in Marriage which explained police reluctance to act in 'domestic' cases on the grounds that 'we are, after all, dealing with persons "bound in marriage", and it is important, for a host of reasons, to maintain the unity of the spouses' (quoted in Atkins and Hoggett 1984: 134). Such developments were of course a continuation of trends noted in the later nineteenth century, as was the impact of housing renewal and relocation in increasing the isolation of individual family units and hence the invisibility of domestic violence.

The stability of the boundaries of the company and the family as semi-autonomous institutions of governance in which the social relations of crime control had little foothold, is central to the relationship between crime and modernity, in particular to the stability of the concept of crime and the identity of the criminal offender. Too strong an emphasis upon criminalisation in both commercial deviance and family violence would reveal the blurred boundaries of criminalisation, between fraud and the normal conduct of business and between violence and the normal dynamics of family life, in a way that the actions of the lone murderer, the petty juvenile thief, or the bank robber, do not. In other areas of private life the *withdrawal* of formal criminalisation during the 1960s – as with the legalisation of homosexuality – was part of a progressive extension of human rights and a recognition that the boundaries of popular morality and practical criminality had already been redrawn. The effect was to consolidate the view of private life as an area of governance based on moral and economic self-regulation and to concentrate the focus of crime control on public space. To have the company and the family, the core social institutions for the production of capital and the production of subservience, revealed as *inherently* criminogenic *as well as* being key institutions of governance would have introduced fractures not simply into the social relations of crime control but cast doubt on the entire discourse of modernity and progress.

Emerging contradictions

Thus far, the focus has been on the optimistic side of post-war development: optimistic, that is, from the standpoint of the stabilisation of modernity, the strengthening of forces of social cohesion and the regulation and marginalisation of conflicts. An attempt has been made to see the social relations of crime control as a component of this process of consolidation. Sometime during the 1960s, gradually, and at differing paces in different areas, it became clear that organised modernity had run into the sand: that the forces of expansion had become exhausted and that unforeseen counter-tendencies were now making themselves felt. The main lines of development will be familiar enough and can be briefly discussed.

Economic growth and social fragmentation

At the level of economic development, the declining performance of the British, relative to other capitalist economies, during the 1960s is well known (Overbeek 1990). Needless to say there was a superfluity of explanations for poor economic performance in Britain. These turned out to be variants of the pathology thesis in which reference to the inadequate motivation and socialisation of those poor communities which failed to engage with modernisation was echoed in references to the backwardness and outdated attitudes of the City of London in providing inadequate funds for industrial expansion (see Gamble 1994). The exhaustion of economic growth was accompanied by a reversal of trends towards income equality and social homogenisation. New statistical studies showed these to have been in any case exaggerated (Titmuss 1962), while other researchers noted how a slight income equalisation within the top 5 per cent of the population was matched by a reduction in the share of the total by the bottom third of the population (Nicholson 1967). It was becoming increasingly clear that even the economic expansion which did occur was having socially disruptive consequences by drawing both investment resources and the skilled and better educated sections of the working class away from older industrial and inner city areas. The result was a gathering crisis of the Keynesian welfare state manifested both in the breakdown of the social contract between capital and organised labour and in the increasing failure to achieve progress towards social homogenisation.

Social planning in crisis

During the 1970s a new resurgence of right wing neo-liberalism began to argue that the mounting problems of inner city poverty and slow economic growth were a product of the very state intervention designed to ameliorate them. The New Right developed a threefold critique. Keynesian deficit financing and subsidies enabled inefficient and unviable companies to survive, taking resources from more dynamic ones. The integration of trade unions into structures of corporatist compromise led to a permanent regime of inflationary rising wages and the protection of outdated working practices. Finally, social benefits created a poverty trap and a dependency culture in which the poor had little motivation to go and seek work at economic wages (see Gamble 1994: ch. 5). What was, in effect, being argued was that the expansion of capital and the social rights defended by the welfare state, even if in a bureaucratic and authoritarian manner, were now becoming mutually incompatible such that the continuation of the former required the demolition of the latter. To the extent that the state sought to defend social rights, or ameliorate social problems through resource redistribution, it increasingly found itself working against the grain of economic development.

There was plenty of evidence of a gathering crisis of social policy. There was increasing talk of a fiscal crisis of the state (O'Connor 1973) and an intensifying pressure, from capital, to reduce state spending. The happy coalition of public spending and buoyant markets celebrated by Keynesian economics was turning into its opposite: public spending as an inflationary burden on capital. At the same time, the consequences of major areas of social policy were wildly different from their original intentions. Much rehousing and slum clearance had the effect of weakening rather than strengthening communities. An obsession with alleged criminogenic features of older communities glossed over the fact that while they may have sanctioned forms of social crime such as pilferage from work or shoplifting, they also exercised control over many forms of interpersonal violence and victimisation. They had been based on work, kinship and solidarity. Newly rehoused communities, far from experiencing a new democratic citizenship, experienced isolation, lack of social support networks, lack of collective space and, with the increasing move of skilled workers out of old city centre and industrial areas, lack of work (see Cohen 1972). The departing skilled working class took with it much of the tradition of working-class cohesion: large local Labour Party and trade union branches, trades councils, etc., which had been the main forms of political integration and community stability in traditional working-class communities and which were the basis of the new structures of compromise and negotiation. Social and geographical mobility was taking place, but it was leading, not to social homogenisation around middle-class lifestyles but to a spatial and social fragmentation of the working-class, with poor communities simply dropping out of both the consumer society and the new Keynesian structures of political compromise.

Resurgent delinquency

An obvious result was rising crime. By the end of the 1950s one of the largest housing estates in Dagenham to which families had been moved from the East End of London had a higher delinquency rate than the area from which most residents had come (Fyvel 1961: 213). Residents in such areas often demanded, unlike in the traditional communities, an increased police presence (Taylor 1982). But this was hardly an indication of the consolidation of the middle-class neighbourhood discussed earlier. In many places it was more a demand for the 'direct rule' of police sovereignty. Community networks of support for victims were being undermined, as was the ability to withstand intimidation by offenders. This collapse of crime control was most evident in areas into which immigrants had moved to take on low-wage jobs in older industries and in the service and welfare sectors left behind by the outmigrating skilled working class. The stratification of the working class took an ethnic form in which immigrants concentrated in low-wage jobs in the inner cities, and the combination of racial discrimination and lack of sufficient demand elsewhere in the economy kept them there (see Castles and Kosack 1973; Rex and Tomlinson 1979; Lea 1980). The breakdown of crime control in immigrant areas was evident as these communities became victims of overt racial violence. The targeting of immigrants by gangs of white youths with a surrounding white community either colluding or too intimidated and fragmented to impose an alternative, and a police force infused with at best indifference and at worst overt racism, symbolised the collapse of the social relations of crime control as part of a more general weakening of governance.

It was becoming clear that social homogenisation had indeed taken place but on the level of cultural values and aspirations in contrast to the reinforcement of material differences in income and life chances. Just as an obsession with the pathology of traditional cohesive working-class communities had steered attention away from the breakdown of controls in newer locations, so the focus on supposed criminogenic tendencies in traditional working-class culture had diverted attention from the consequences of a new cultural homogenisation co-existing with growing material inequalities. The criminogenic consequences of this co-existence had already been studied in some detail by American subcultural theorists (Merton 1957; Cloward and Ohlin 1960; Cohen 1955) who saw one of the major sources of delinquency in the conflict between the generalised goals of the American Dream – upward social mobility, wealth and social status – and the restricted distribution of the means of legitimately attaining them. Thus David Downes, while supporting Miller's analysis that youth delinquency was a matter of conformity to traditional working-class culture, perceptively saw that the breakdown of this culture and the integration of working-class communities into a new mass culture may not reduce crime but simply change its dynamics. Those at the bottom of the ladder of income and social mobility may feel an even greater sense of *relative* deprivation than they had in the closed world of the traditional community and so 'the very measures proposed to cut down on delinquency might seem to aim at promoting status-consciousness and ... status frustration, thus providing the necessary base for the emergence of delinquent motivations on "American" lines' (Downes 1966: 268).

During the mid-1970s a new cultural sociology, emanating from the Centre for Contemporary Cultural Studies at Birmingham University, had studied the emerging subcultures of working-class youth, including deviancy and criminality, as various ways of coping both with the decline of traditional working-class communities and values and with the lack of resources for success in the new consumer society (Cohen 1972; Hall and Jefferson 1976; Willis 1977). Racism was an aspect of this dynamic, partly an empiricist reasoning which correlated the presence of the immigrant with the decline of a traditional economy and way of life (Pearson 1976), and partly a deflection into race of a growing sense of unease as the long economic boom slacked and the Keynesian consensus began to fall apart at the seams (Hall et al. 1978).[6]

But none of this yet signalled a generalised disruption of the main dynamics of crime control. We were still dealing with petty crime at the margins. Despite a wave of moral panics about the criminality of various youth cultures (Cohen 1980), the middle- and upwardly mobile working-class coalition with the police held firm. Offenders were mainly weak and youthful delinquents who could still be relied upon to grow out of crime as they reconciled themselves to dead-end low-paid jobs. As yet there was no significant change in the ability of the majority communities to deal with the petty crime and disorderliness of young people (and this for the majority of the population was what crime *was*). The problems were still at the periphery.

This can be contrasted to the situation in the United States where the 'periphery' was much larger. There were the same dynamics of migration of skilled (white) working-class jobs outside the old cities and industrial areas and large (black) ghetto populations facing high prices and high unemployment. The overwhelmingly black population of these areas meant that racial violence came predominantly from white police. The wave of inner city rebellions which began in Watts (Los Angeles) in 1965 and then repeated in Detroit and other cities across the country in 1967 was about entrenched racism and widening economic disparities between black and white. These were not riots of criminals but rebellions by citizens among whose grievances was the breakdown in the social relations of crime control through the return by racist police to older strategies of containment of entire populations surplus to capital accumulation. From now on the issues of social polarisation either as resentment (by the poor) or fear (by the middle classes and the rich) would not be far away.

Government response was to attempt a redirection of resources to inner cities in various programmes such as the US 'War on Poverty' of the 1960s. Similar themes emerged in Britain. The dilemma that all these programmes faced, and still face, is the relative powerlessness of government in the face of the logic of capital. During the nineteenth century, urban reform and capitalist modernisation were generally working in the same direction. What became clear in the 1960s, though only in retrospect since it was not formulated as such, was that the reform necessary to stabilise urban unrest, reduce crime, and ameliorate poverty involved a social policy which worked against the grain of capitalist development. For the neo-liberals the response to this dilemma was the demolition of the welfare state in favour of the market – the untrammelled freedom of capital; while for the Keynesian liberals and social democrats the dilemma was increasingly how to tax capital for welfare funds without creating inflation or precipitating the flight of capital abroad. If capital could not be taxed then the problem was how to avoid a middle-class tax revolt.

The form of state intervention became that of attempting to 'plug the holes' by special programmes to transfer resources to deprived areas, accompanied by appeals and incentives to capital to reinvest in deprived areas. This was initially accompanied by an analysis which located a major cause of the outflow of capital in the cultural pathology ('culture of poverty' or 'transmitted deprivation') of the working-class populations of these areas who were enjoined to re-activate or motivate their enthusiasm for a lifetime of servitude to capital through various 'community development projects'. What began in the 1950s as symptoms of backwardness which would be overcome by being drawn into modernisation and economic growth now appeared as its own self-perpetuating cause. Both in the USA and in Britain such projects frequently ran up against the fact that even some of their practitioners came to realise that the issues lay elsewhere than in the motivations of the local community (Piven and Cloward 1971; CDP 1977). Despite changes of terminology over the years, such programmes continued since they were really the only framework available in which the state, still seeking in a modernist sense to co-ordinate society as a whole and rescue a measure of citizenship and social integration for the entire population, could establish a working relationship with a globalised capitalism that increasingly had its mind, and its investment, elsewhere.

Civic privatism undermined

A final set of issues concerned the effects of Keynesian state planning and welfare intervention on consciousness. Critical theorists such as Jürgen Habermas (1976, 1987) and Claus Offe (1984) developed an analysis of the welfare state in which social policy has simultaneously a stabilising and destabilising effect on social relations. This is because 'while the welfare state guarantees are intended to serve the goal of social integration, they nevertheless promote the disintegration of life-relations when these are separated, through legalised social intervention, from the consensual mechanisms that co-ordinate action and are transferred over to media such as power and money' (Habermas 1987: 364).

An illustration can be taken from the effect of the welfare state on family relations. Social policy is aimed at social integration through the granting of social rights. Even where these rights are directed towards the preservation of traditional family structures through, for example, welfare payments to families with children, the very fact of state intervention sets up a pressure for the transformation of 'taken for granted' patriarchal family values into issues of rights. Who should receive the payments for dependent children, who should control how they are spent and why? Policy intervention in the family, of which welfare payments for children are simply one example, thus enables the politicisation and critical questioning of values previously taken for granted. They become de-traditionalised. If these developments are combined with the effects of larger numbers of, mainly middle-class, women being drawn into higher education, then the resurgence of the feminist movement during the 1960s can be seen as a variant of what Habermas called 'legitimation crises'. The de-traditionalisation of family relations and a growing feminist critique of both family structure and wider aspects of gender relations, precipitated severe strains for civic privatism. The slogan, 'the personal is political', was valid in two senses: firstly, in the sense intended by feminists, that personal relations between men and women could now be subject to critique; secondly, in the Habermasian sense that, once de-traditionalised, such values as patriarchy could only be reasserted as political ideology. Thus the rise of an 'offensive' feminist critical movement was accompanied by a 'defensive' movement from the conservative right, reasserting family values as political ideology (Ray 1993).

Of course social policy did not directly produce the resurgence of the feminist movement, but rather provided a de-traditionalising mechanism that could make its critique of patriarchal family life immediately communicable and translatable into a political programme. Part of this programme became something that the dominant traditions of modern governance had hitherto avoided, namely the extension of the social relations of crime control into the family: the pressure to supplement the formal criminalisation of family violence with its practical criminalisation. Thus contradiction in the public sphere between a homogenisation of cultural expectations and aspirations through the images and symbols of the consumer society and an increasing differentiation of abilities to attain them was accompanied by the contradictory effects of increasing state intervention aimed at the preservation of the private sphere, simultaneously expanding opportunities for its critique.

To agree that Habermas had identified a contradiction in the dynamics of the welfare state does not involve following his argument (during the 1970s and 1980s) that the modern welfare state would face a growing legitimation crisis taking the form of radical demands for the 'discursive justification of values'. How, precisely, the latter would concretise itself was never spelled out. Delegitimation could lead to cynicism and a return to civic privatism (Ray 1993). The ambiguity was further illustrated by the appeal of the theme of legitimation crisis to the New Right who observed 'a breakdown of traditional means of social control' (Crozier et al. 1975), and the need for a reassertion of authority by mobilising new bases of conservative support through a politicised variant of the civic privatism stressing 'family values'. Fear of crime, of the 'underclass', and of a criminogenic potential of any departure from traditional forms of socialisation was of course a key theme in such mobilisation. Meanwhile, attempts on the left to articulate a more precise concept of *hegemonic crisis* (Hall et al. 1978) tended both to read crisis symptoms too widely – as in the simple fact of increased class struggle in the early 1970s – and to misread strategies of consolidation – as with *moral panic* about crime – as evidence of the exhaustion of hegemony. As it happened, developments took a rather different and more complex turn.

Inequality and underdevelopment

Finally, the contradictory nature of modernisation was evident also on a global scale in the continued and widening gap between the advanced and poor countries. As with the social fragmentation beginning to develop in the advanced countries, the issue was not simply that of the slow pace of progress of modernisation, but of its very nature. Modernisation theory was increasingly challenged by theorists who stressed dependency and neo-colonialism, and pointed out that the expansion of the industrialised world was still dependent upon the forcing of Third World countries into the status of cheap raw material producers rather than independent modernising states. Thus, the relation between the centre and periphery of capitalist development remained in direct continuity with that of nineteenth-century colonialism (see Gunder Frank 1967a, 1967b). In this context it became necessary to re-evaluate the effects of modernisation on crime rates and on undermining traditional structures of organised crime. Rising crime rates in post-colonial societies had less to do with rising incomes and rapid urbanisation *per se* than with the structural inequalities resulting from continued dependency (Sumner 1982).

Finally, new studies of the post-war Sicilian mafia as it continued into the 1970s concluded that the issue was less the effect of modernisation in eliminating organised crime, but rather that of the modernisation of organised crime. It seemed clear that the mafia, far from being undermined by economic and political modernisation, had succeeded in inserting itself at the core of the modernisation process itself. This was a variant of the relation between the production of offenders and the production of opportunities mentioned above. Rapid and sustained modernisation might, for example, by drawing the labour supply for organised crime rapidly into secure and well-paid jobs and well organised trade unions, have continued the decay of organised crime. But that remains a hypothetical proposition of modernisation theory. In reality there is a complex balance between the forces undermining traditional social structures and their capacity to adapt and find ways of managing the new forces. Modernisation was proceeding sufficiently slowly to enable the mafia to succeed in the latter endeavour. It was able to insert itself into the management structures of the welfare state and the associated expansion of the construction industry, and to develop structures of political compromise and alliance with decisive sections of the Italian political elite who oriented to it rather than to organised labour, as in northern Europe, as a source of political control and manipulation (Arlacchi 1988; Catanzaro 1992).[7] Of course, modernisation theory could still rescue its core orientation by simply denoting the entire Italian political and social structure as characterised by 'backwardness' (see della Porta and Vannucci 1999: 4–25).

Conclusion

We are now at a watershed. Up to this point I have described the modernisation process driven by expanding capitalism as conducive, in a variety of different ways and in different contexts, to the emergence and strengthening of what I have called the social relations of crime control which form the basis of modern construction of, and responses to, criminality. In this chapter we have seen 'organised modernity' as a transitional period, on the one hand a culmination of the consolidation of crime control but, on the other, containing growing counter-tendencies which undermined it. Henceforth, as we move into the present period – from the mid-1970s onwards – it is these latter forces which come increasingly to predominate. Our task, therefore, in the remaining chapters, is to trace the gathering crisis of crime control.

Notes

1 For changes in family and social networks see e.g. Young and Willmott 1957, 1960. Class relations and the workplace were the subject of classic studies by Zweig 1961, Goldthorpe et al. 1968, Goldthorpe and Lockwood 1963. By no means was this literature an expression of consensus. Thus, whereas Zweig stressed 'embourgeoisification' or assimilation of the working class to middle-class patterns, Goldthorpe and his collaborators criticised this thesis in favour of a notion of convergence. For an overview of this debate see Devine 1992.

2 Anthony Bottoms (1983) made a similar point in the context of the development of penal policy during the period of the Keynesian welfare state. He attempted to explain the growing proportion of offences punished by fines and non-custodial, non-supervisory surveillance in the following terms: 'The implication would be that the penal project of the classical reformers failed at the end of the eighteenth century because it did not in itself produce order ... and there was insufficient social control exercised elsewhere in society to make the classical juridical project possible. In modern states, however, such power does exist, and so the schemes of

classical penality render themselves as more realistic possibilities, at least for some crimes and some offenders' (1983: 195–6).

3 But as Campbell continued: 'The 1990s is seen as a boom time for them, with the exploitation of a recreational western culture that wants its luxuries and its drugs. The legitimate businesses will run alongside the illegitimate ones.' (Campbell 1990: 8). There is in fact a double process: on the one hand a trend to the disconnection of criminality from the old localised family and community structures, and on the other increasing power and resources combined with an integration into the global legal economy which blurs the boundaries of criminality in new ways. This theme will be taken up in Chapter 6.

4 It is still an article of faith among the ruling elite that capitalism somehow 'leads to' democracy as it did in the bourgeois revolutions of the eighteenth century. See Street 2000.

5 Obviously the evasion of the social relations of crime control carried to its extreme renders them useless as a form of governance of crime. People have less and less information to provide the police, however willing they may be to do so. This problem will be considered in more detail in Chapter 7.

6 There was an attempt to connect these cultures of resistance to the earlier notions of social crime (see in particular Hall et al. 1978). Pearson (1976) saw racial violence against immigrants in a Yorkshire town as analogous to the Luddite machine-smashing of the early nineteenth century, thus reinforcing Edward Thompson's point that social crime is not necessarily progressive. There was, perhaps, a tendency to read too readily a proto-political consciousness into youth culture at this time (for an overview see Lea 1999).

7 The question of to what extent this involved a fundamental change in the nature of the mafia, for example a turn to an innovatory, entrepreneurial form of capitalism, is a question we shall leave until later.

5

The Disintegrating Society

By the end of the 1970s a whole epoch, perhaps even modernity itself, appeared to be drawing to a close. It was becoming increasingly clear that fundamental changes were occurring in the direction of development of capitalism. From the middle of the nineteenth century onwards it had appeared that, despite periodic economic recessions, massive poverty and social inequality, war and violence, capitalist development acted as a force for social consolidation. It sustained the spread of the ideas of the Enlightenment, individual liberty and human rights. It created the conditions in which the masses could demand inclusion into those rights. It built cities and stable communities. It created the conditions for the emergence of forms of integration which reduced social and political conflict to a minimum compatible with the survival of the system. Even if that stability had eventually required a growing state intervention, a transition to the *organised* modernity of the Keynesian welfare state, it had appeared capable of sustaining itself. More specifically, it consolidated the social relations of crime control as a mechanism for the governance of a wide variety of conflicts and harms.

This is no longer the case. It is reasonably clear in the first years of the twenty-first century that the direction of development has fundamentally altered. Tendencies to social cohesion, integration and cultural homogenisation are now displaced by counter-tendencies toward social fragmentation and polarisation, inequality, pluralisation and diversification. On a larger scale modernisation as a process of global assimilation to the social structure of the advanced capitalist countries, a weak tendency at best, has been displaced by the accentuation of differences and inequalities between states and regions. Such tendencies were discernible, as I have noted, even during the heyday of the Keynesian welfare state, but they are now in the ascendancy, the defining character of the system.

We are, in short, in the midst of what Peter Wagner (1994) has termed the *second* crisis of modernity – the first being the crisis which produced the Keynesian welfare state – in which the coherent structures of organised modernity dissipate in the face of the decline of the Fordist mass production economy, the weakening of the nation state under the impact of globalisation, the pluralisation and fragmentation of social identities and values and the decline of civic privatism and restraint in individual conduct.

Destructive Reproduction

The changed dynamic of capitalist development has been articulated by István Mészáros (1995) in the following terms. During the nineteenth century, when Marx produced his classic analysis of capitalism, periodic economic and social crises manifested themselves as 'great thunderstorms' (Marx 1973: 411). These *episodic* disruptions, severe as they were, did not interfere with 'the predominantly productive social articulation of capital in Marx's lifetime' (Mészáros 1995: 559). In capitalism today crisis and dislocation are manifest in a variety of ways as a permanent feature of the system rather than as sudden episodic or cyclical disruption. Crises are *'spread out*, both in a *temporal* sense and with regard to their *structural location'*. What we have now is rather a *'depressed continuum*, exhibiting the characteristics of a *cumulative, endemic*, more or less *permanent* and *chronic* crisis, with the ultimate perspectives of an ever-deepening *structural crisis'* (Mészáros 1995: 597–8).

This depressed continuum combines the intensification of classic symptoms of crisis such as the falling rate of profit (Brenner 1998, 2000) and massive industrial overcapacity in relation to profit opportunities (Greider 1997) with the steady destruction of the social and economic infrastructure, and increasingly of the physical environment also. Growing structural unemployment, rising levels of global poverty, below-poverty wage levels, the increasing production of environmental pollution and waste, and the generation of enormous funds of 'fictitious capital' which, unable to find profitable investment in the production of commodities and the stable employment of labour, deploy purely monetary methods of profit-taking such as speculation in currency and bond markets, are increasingly prominent features.[1]

The combination of intensifying competition for profitable outlets in global markets and the dominance of speculative financial capital produces an increasing orientation to short-term profitability and insecurity of employment in a regime dominated by what the American economist Bennett Harrison has called 'impatient capital' (Harrison 1994; see also Sennett 1998: 22–3). This regime contrasts with the economic stability and long-term predictability of the post-war Keynesian period. The structural location of crises spreads out to wider spheres including the disorganisation of social structure, decimation of communities, the weakening of the state and politics as steering mechanisms, culture, and the entire spectrum of the organisation of urban life. Capitalism as a world system is now characterised by growing instability, uncertainty and risk. Capitalism is now tearing apart the old structures of organised modernity that it once sustained.

The root of this lies in the transformed relation between capital and labour. Capital is increasingly relinquishing a dependence on the traditional mass working class composed of 'Fordist' blue collar workers in high-wage stable jobs and a vast white collar salariat of 'organisation men'. The driving force for this change is the drive to retain the profitability of an increasing mass of capital. However, not only can profitability decreasingly afford a strong, stable, well-paid working class with which it has to compromise socially and politically but, more importantly, it decreasingly needs it. As a consequence it is losing interest in the modernist institutions of political compromise with these strata and with high levels of welfare and citizenship rights designed to secure their reproduction and to ameliorate class conflict.

Social fragmentation

While capital cannot ultimately dispense with labour as the source of profit on capital, the relation between these two great classes takes progressively disconnected forms. In the increasingly important sector of finance capital – of money capital attempting to enlarge itself directly through speculative means without the mediation of the production of actual commodities – the relation of capital to labour is in any case indirect. But also in manufacturing the impact of labour-saving technology and global communications is to enable the recomposition both of capitalist production and of the working class. With redesigned labour processes emphasising cheap unskilled labour, capital is able to substitute global mobility in search of new sources of labour for investment in the socialisation and integration of the working class characteristic of the Keynesian period. Increased mobility of operations means that the most powerful corporations are able, on threat of moving elsewhere, to secure significant reductions in taxes destined for the welfare rights and education of such a workforce (Martin and Schumann 1997: 200–206; Hertz 2001). The costs of socialisation and reproduction can be shifted back on to the working class itself in a process which increasingly equalises labour conditions in Third World and advanced capitalist countries. This new relationship between capital and labour has been captured by the Spanish sociologist, Manuel Castells as one in which

> capital and labour increasingly tend to exist in different spaces and times: the space of flows and the space of places ... [T]hus they live by each other, but do not relate to each other ... the social relations of production have been disconnected in their actual existence. Capital tends to escape in its hyperspace of pure circulation, while labour dissolves its collective entity into an infinite variation of individual instances ... capital is globally co-ordinated, labour is individualised. (Castells 1996: 475–6)

Capital accumulation thus no longer sustains social cohesion and integration. Instead it produces polarisation and fragmentation. The long-run trend is now towards a polarisation between the very rich and the very poor

(Sassen 1991). This process has social, political and spatial dimensions. The social dynamics of fragmentation are well known. At one extreme of the social structure are expanding numbers of the very rich, the owners and managers of capital, particularly finance capital, the latter becoming an increasingly dominant section of the capitalist class (Sampson 1995: 151). These top managers and CEOs are becoming a global class, no longer tied to any particular society. Below them the supporting professions of lawyers, accountants, systems managers, technical 'knowledge workers', 'informational service' workers and lower managers combine high salaries with long hours and job insecurity (Reich 1992). At the other end of the social structure we are witnessing, as Ulrich Beck puts it, '[t]he uncoupling of economic growth and corporate profits from better working and living conditions for employees' (Beck 2000: 97). The fastest growing sections of working-class jobs are now in low-wage, part-time and temporary employment, especially in services (Gray 1995). These jobs, epitomised by employment in such areas as the fast food industry, are no longer a means of escaping poverty and are vulnerable to replacement by automation or supplies of even cheaper labour elsewhere to which production can be easily shifted. Large factories, of course, remain but their employment conditions are concerned less with the negotiated working conditions characteristic of Fordism and more with Third World conditions of long hours and low wages and a compliant replaceable workforce (Head 1996). At the very bottom of the social structure increasing numbers of people are virtually outside the legal labour market and, concentrated in ghettos, inner cities and decaying older industrial areas, they function as labour supply for a growing informal and shadow economy of untaxed and criminalised activities.

This polarisation is reflected in growing income inequality in most advanced capitalist societies upon which falling levels of welfare services have a declining ameliorative effect. Recent studies in the UK, such as those by the Commission on Social Justice (1994) and the Joseph Rowntree Foundation (Barclay 1995; Hills 1995), have shown that the bottom tenth of the population failed to participate at all in economic expansion over the decade to the mid-1990s and that class differences in health and life expectancy are widening steadily. The share of total income (after housing costs) of the poorest tenth of the population fell from 4 per cent in 1979 to 2 per cent in 1991/2 while that of the richest tenth rose from 20.9 to 27 per cent over the same period (Hills 1995: 25). This trend has continued in recent years (Harris 2000). Growing inequality has been particularly acute in the United States where the percentage share of the poorest fifth of the population in total aggregate household income fell from 4.3 per cent in 1974 to 3.6 per cent in 1994 while the share of the richest fifth rose from 16.5 per cent to 21.2 per cent over the same period (US Census Bureau 2000; see also Freeman 1996).

Social inequality does not of itself signal social fragmentation. Poor communities can be cohesive and the rich remain sensitive to the need to secure overall social stability and integration through a measure of redistribution of wealth and the sharing of certain entitlements to social citizenship. What the new inequality represents is a growing gap between the life chances of rich and poor, increasing fragmentation within social classes as well as the decline of communication between them, and the abandonment by the ruling class of effective concern with social integration.

The fragmentation of working-class communities results from the decline of steady employment and relative wage levels. Lack of work weakens the family. Fewer two-parent families are formed because young couples find the costs of new household formation insuperable and young women are less inclined to marry men with no prospects of employment (Wilson 1987, 1993). Existing families become increasingly dependent upon women's dual role as wage-earners and housewives, leading to increased conflicts, domestic violence and family breakdown (Campbell 1993). The proportion of female single parents increases. Young women have benefited from the decline in the 'deviant' status of single parenthood, a change which characterises the life of all classes as part of a general decomposition in the *gender order* of modernity (Connell 1995; see also McDowell 1991), involving the decline in the centrality of the family as reproducer of hierarchy, and increased participation of women in work. But under conditions of grinding poverty such a status often means isolation, difficulty in finding work and in participating in community life. Communities are further weakened by the declining respect for adults. It is not that children reared in families without fathers somehow turn into deviants, but rather under conditions of lack of communal support and where adults of either sex are not in work or are in dead-end jobs unable to cope, the latter no longer provide an image for young people of their own future development in terms of work or success. Many adults appear simply as examples of failure and the hopelessness of life. There is a decline in the role of the school for similar reasons. Truancy rates increase, schools in poor areas suffer declining resources and increasing difficulty in offering young people a clear image of access to skills which will make a difference in life (see Pitts 1998). The process of social inclusion through the transition from school to work and family formation is replaced by the process of social exclusion through the transition to unemployment, dead-end jobs and the criminal economy as sources of both opportunity and victimisation.

Meanwhile the middle class and residual Fordist working class still remain the largest single group but they are being continually squeezed. Here the process of social fragmentation presents itself in the form of increasing economic insecurity. The 'downsizing' of layers of middle management, under the impact of information technology and the rise of short-term consultancy contracts replacing permanent careers, has proceeded apace in middle management as much as on the shop floor, and as a result of the same processes of outsourcing, computerisation, post-Fordist-style 'just in time' production. As Anthony Sampson noted, the 'traditional company man with his confidence in annual increments and a growing pension is as extinct as an eighteenth century clergyman. His decline ... is causing one of the biggest social upheavals of the twentieth century and its repercussions are still spreading' (Sampson 1995: 307). John Gray, who in recent writings has focused on the insecurities of the middle class, talks of the 'de-bourgeoisification of what remains of the former middle classes.... Whole strata of former middle-management employees have been dispensed with in corporate downsizings which have an immediate beneficial effect on profit statements' (Gray 1998: 72; see also Luttwak 1998). Gray points out that throughout the Anglo-Saxon world companies are offloading responsibilities for such items as pension provision, housing costs and health insurance to their short-term contracted employees as individuals. If company welfare did for the middle classes what much of the welfare state did for the poor, then both groups are in positions of growing insecurity. The social exclusion of the poor from effective welfare state citizenship is paralleled by the transformation of the middle classes from citizens to customers as they purchase their pensions, health care and their children's education in the private market.

But of most consequence is the process of social exclusion, or rather self-exclusion, of the very rich. Leading sections of capital no longer need to invest in the socialisation and political stabilisation of a mass working class. It is easy to move operations globally in search of pools of cheap labour, or even skilled professionals such as information technology workers, while important sections of financial capital have minimal need of a traditional blue collar labour force. The global mobility of capital and the reach of transnational corporations has fostered the growth of a 'transnational capitalist class' (Sklair 2001; see also Reich 1992), which decreasingly identifies with a particular location or country and retains little interest in the provision of public welfare goods by national states since these can easily be provided privately, while global communication networks widen location choices. There is in a real sense no longer a need to be a member of society defined as a particular national terrain and political system. As Christopher Lasch wrote of the American ruling elite:

> To an alarming extent the privileged classes by an expansive definition, the top 20 per cent have made themselves independent not only of crumbling industrial cities but of public services in general. They send their children to private schools, insure themselves against medical emergencies by enrolling in company supported plans, and hire private security guards to protect themselves against the mounting violence against them. In effect, they have removed themselves from the common life. It is not just that they see no point in paying for public services they no longer use. Many of them have ceased to think of themselves as Americans in any important sense. (Lasch 1995: 45–6)

There is an important difference between the social exclusion of the poor and the self-exclusion of the rich. The growing exclusion of the poor – from the welfare and citizenship rights of the Keynesian welfare state and the secure jobs of Fordist capitalism – is simultaneously a process of the internal weakening and dismembering of community and the capacity to mobilise against capital and to defend traditional rights. For the very rich, however, self-exclusion from the welfare state is a celebration of strength, the ability to provide private services and increasingly to dispense with a concern for negotiation and compromise with the working class. This process of political and institutional fragmentation is of crucial importance.

These tendencies to inequality and fragmentation are reproduced on a global scale. In 1960 the average income of the richest fifth of the world's population, living mainly in the industrialised countries, was 30 times greater than that of the poorest fifth, living predominantly in the Third World. By 1990 it was 60 times greater and has continued to widen (Watkins 1995: 3; see also Cornia 1999). Thus the global mobility of capital in search of cheap labour has no equalisation effect, but rather destroys indigenous economies without replacing them with equivalent income sources. Globalisation and free trade are associated with rising inequality within poor countries (Lundberg and Squire 1999) while indigenous sustainable agriculture is being destroyed in the interests of the domination of multinational agri-business (Shiva 2000). Structural adjustment programmes unleashed by the World Bank and International Monetary Fund on these countries have the effect of substituting much domestic production with imports, raising unemployment and keeping the working class in the Third World as a pool of extremely cheap labour (Bello 1994; Chossudovsky 1997). Despite the shift of many unskilled manufacturing processes to cheap labour states, an increasing number of developing countries are 'helpless in a world economic system that has lost interest in the competitive resources that once made them viable, such as plentiful supplies of raw materials and labour power' (de Rivero 1999). There has been a decline in demand for both labour and raw materials relative to surging population growth.

The inability of capitalism to develop the Third World, despite massive investment programmes and the freedom of capital to roam the world, is one of the key symptoms of its deepening crisis (Mészáros 2001). The modernisation perspective has been largely abandoned as a theory of global development. At the beginning of the 1980s US governments abandoned the key tenets of modernisation theory as exemplified in the 'Rostow doctrine' (Rostow 1962) according to which poor countries would follow the capitalist road, in favour of a view of the tasks of Third World governments as simply that of maintaining solvency and management of mounting debts (Arrighi 1991). The institutions which secure the interests of global capital (the World Bank, International Monetary Fund, etc.) now speak of the need for 'good governance' in Third World states. Modernisation as a process of large-scale institutional and social change has been replaced by a concern for efficient administration to secure debt repayments. There is no process of 'catching up' and the 'modernisation of backward areas' but rather a single global process of economic and social fragmentation and growing inequality. The meaningless rhetoric of modernisation functions simply as an ideological smokescreen for domination by the institutions of global capital.

Political fragmentation

Alongside *social* exclusion as a matter of poverty and insecurity, exclusion from living standards and life chances regarded as normal entitlements, a parallel process is under way of *institutional* exclusion from the mechanisms and conduits of political negotiation and communication within which compromise between the social classes occurred. The Keynesian welfare state characterised a society in which the ruling class saw the need for compromise with the working and middle classes because it understood that ultimately production is a *social* process. Footloose global capital and financial speculative capital see production increasingly as a process of short-term profit-taking in which the stability of society as a whole is no longer an agenda item. It is important to understand that institutional exclusion occurs at both ends of the social structure.

For the working class, stable communities underlay the formation of trade unions, the most important institutions of compromise. Negotiations with employers could take place both within the framework of the individual company or industry and, under organised modernity, through an organised corporate framework sustained by the state. With the decline of both national and local labour movement institutions, the representation and organisation of working-class interests at the level of the state has been fatally weakened. The exclusion of increasing numbers of the poor from organs of political representation, negotiation and compromise is of little interest to capital which no longer needs to enter into a dialogue with an increasingly fragmented, unskilled, high-turnover, easily replaced labour supply. Where worker loyalty is required, as in the remaining large productive plants, then it is orchestrated increasingly by the company itself rather than through negotiation with trade unions. Otherwise it is the replaceability of low-wage workers which is the main disciplining mechanism. Capital demands not the incorporation but the destruction of trade union organisation. For the poor, some substitutes may be found, for example in ethnic political organisations, particularly in America. However, such organisations may not reach the very poor, and membership of ethnically based community groups, unlike class organisation, does not necessarily lead to command over significant economic or political resources.

Capital, as a consequence, is able simply to walk away from its traditional responsibilities, derived from 'enlightened self-interest'. The bourgeois elite becomes, in Zygmunt Bauman's characterisation, a new variety of absentee landlord whose global mobility

> means the new, indeed unprecedented in its radical unconditionality, discon-nection of power from obligations: duties towards employees, but also towards the younger and weaker, towards yet unborn generations and towards the self-reproduction of the living conditions of all; in short, freedom from the duty to contribute to daily life and the perpetuation of the community. (Bauman 1998: 9)

Again the strongest contrast between old and new is epitomised by finance capital. In the Victorian industrial town the farsighted traditional manu-facturing capitalist, surveying the workers' tenements from his office win-dow, understood not only that he needed to employ their inhabitants in a reasonably healthy state, but that he would also eventually have to meet the representatives of their trade unions. In twenty-first-century London, by contrast, the financial executive looks out of his Canary Wharf skyscraper on to the desolation of the East End. But his gaze turns rapidly back to his bank of computer terminals which link him to Frankfurt, Tokyo, New York – places which are much *nearer* than the slums half a mile away and which have much more effect on his salary and the future of his business activities. The trend is for major urban centres to become more connected to each other than to their local economies and social structures. This is the basis of the social and spatial polarisation of the 'global city' as argued by writ-ers such as Saskia Sassen (1991, 1994, 1998), in which the poor appear continually less as workers to be employed and subjected to a basic mini-mum of education and socialisation, let alone trade unions to be negotiated with, and increasingly as a group to be managed and kept at bay and from which a casualised low-skill, low-wage labour force will be drawn. The language of class relations undergoes a subtle change: from active social groups whose interests are to be, even if grudgingly, accommodated through representation and negotiation, to risky populations to be managed by designing them out with high walkways and closed precincts, closed-circuit television cameras and access control manned by the burgeoning private security industry (see Davis 1990, 1992).

The urban crisis

All these developments come together in a spatial form in the growing crisis of urban living. The city has, throughout the history of capitalism, been the key form of spatial organisation for bringing together capital and labour and organising the circulation of commodities. The impact of economic fragmentation on the city is succinctly summed up by Peter Hall as a scenario in which

> the larger cities are characterised by an increasing dispersion of real income between rich and poor city-dwellers, with a 'disappearing middle' representing the jobs that are exported to other places. This is a result partly of economic shifts which produce relatively large numbers of highly-qualified and highly-paid 'informational services' jobs and of low-paid, casualised 'MacJobs', and partly of long-term structural unemployment among large sections of the population who formerly found employment in the manufacturing and goods-handling sector. This produces an increasingly polarised society, with upper-income high-consumption enclaves next door to low-income ghettos dependent on casual service work and welfare payments. The quality of life of these citizens clearly demonstrates extreme contrasts, even though they occupy the same geographical space.
>
> Typically, such a situation was characteristic of major cities in countries undergoing rapid development (e.g. 19th-century Europe and North America; 20th-century Latin America). Now, however, it seems to have returned to the cities of the advanced world, which earlier [in the 'welfare state' era of the 1950s and 1960s] appeared to have passed through this phase and out of it. A new wave of immigration is one contributory factor in many such cities; but economic restructuring, in particular the decline of well-paid unionised jobs in traditional manufacturing and goods-handling occupations, is another element that impacts on old blue-collar workers and new immigrants alike. (Hall and Pfeiffer 2000: 9)

Meanwhile the declining concern of the wealthy with the city as an essential public good contrasts with the nineteenth and early twentieth centuries during which period, as I noted earlier, the general developmental tendencies of capitalism complemented the activities of social reformers in building stable working-class communities and an ordered public space. David Harvey, having noted the achievements of bourgeois philanthropy during the nineteenth century (see Chapter 2 above) continues:

> In the past, capital regarded cities as important places which had to be efficiently organised and where social controls needed to operate in some sort of meaningful way. We now find that capital is no longer concerned about cities. Capital needs fewer workers and much of it can move all over the world, deserting problematic places and populations at will. As a result, the coalition between big capital and bourgeois reformism has disappeared. Moreover, the bourgeoisie itself seems to have lost much of its guilty conscience about cities. It has, I think, concluded there is little to fear from socialist revolution, and so has attenuated its engagement with reformism. Increasingly the wealthy seal themselves off in those fanciful 'gated communities' which are being built all over the United States that enable the bourgeoisie to cut themselves off from what their representatives call by the hateful term 'the underclass'. The underclass is left inside the ghetto, along with drugs, Aids, epidemics of tuberculosis and much else. In this new politics, the poor no longer matter. The marginalisation of the poor is accompanied by a blasé indifference on the part of the rich and powerful. (Harvey 1997: 20)

This is not a view held only on the left. American conservative Charles Murray talks of the transition to 'custodial democracy whereby the mainstream subsidises but also walls off the underclass. In effect, custodial democracy takes as its premise that a substantial portion of the population cannot be expected to function as citizens.' (Murray 1999: 5). Though here it is the characteristics of the poor themselves, rather than the dynamics of capital accumulation, that determine their exit from democracy. It is not of course that capital loses altogether its interest in *cities* or in what goes on in society in general. It needs to protect its means of communication, defend the consumption and dormitory areas of the middle class and wealthy, the shopping precincts, leisure facilities and business districts which function as the command and control centres for global operations. However, the disconnection of the rich from the city as collective living space, shared by social classes, is a reflection of the disconnection of capital from the city as the site for the reproduction and socialisation of labour. One of its spatial indications, as Harvey mentions, is the growth of gated communities and fortified urban areas. Such a development is a global phenomenon of which the most spectacular examples are to be found in Third World countries (Caldeira 1996; Martin and Schumann 1997). In the United States something approaching 10 percent of the population live in gated communities (Thurow 1996: 264; Gray 1998: 116; see also Alexander 1997: 223). The ability of the rich to separate themselves *physically* from the poor is, of course, easier in America with a relative abundance of land (Kaplan 1998). Nevertheless the process of institutional separation as part of the collapse of organised modernity and the Keynesian welfare state, is a generalised phenomenon. In Britain the demand by the very rich for luxury-house 'sealed communities for the gated garrisons of the "overclass"' (Thomas 1998) is on the increase in both suburban and outer city dormitory locations as well as in newly renovated – and fortified – inner city areas (Orr 1999).

It would be a mistake to see gated communities as simply the very rich opting out and leaving the rest of urban society unchanged. As the city fragments and the substantive economic and social interdependence between social groups and classes gives way to relations of insecurity and risk, it is not simply the rich of course who inhabit such areas. The gated community or well guarded apartment block is a mirror image of the old criminal rookery or the modern ghetto or 'sink estate' in which outsiders are subject to a high level of threatening surveillance. Indeed, many of the problems of poverty and crime in poor areas are exacerbated by the isolation of large, decaying public housing areas. Meanwhile stable working-class and middle-class communities also attempt to fence themselves off from what they regard as adjacent dangerous areas. It is not simply capital protecting itself against the poor but different strata of the population protecting themselves against each other. Pressure to restrict entry to public spaces such as parks, amusement arcades or shopping precincts is another element of the tendency. The 'moral economy of place and space' as an ordered public terrain, in which multi-class participation in the circulation of commodities took place and through which the social relations of crime control could be generalised, fragments into mass private property (Shearing and Stenning 1987) and a 'piecemeal spatial mosaic of the safe and the unsafe … dominated by security cages and a honeycomb of residential and business fortresses' (Christopherson 1994: 421).

The Debilitated Authoritarian State

These dynamics are reflected at the level of the state and politics, though not in a direct unmediated way, but rather as the outcome of tensions and conflicts. The key tensions are, firstly, as I have noted, the global mobility of capital, and the declining importance of a well-paid, stable, Fordist, labour force leads to a loss of interest by capital in expenditure on socialisation and welfare. However, democratic capitalist states with substantial welfare activities still attempt, under pressure from electorates, to sustain a social policy aimed at social integration and citizenship rights.

Secondly, global mobility enhances the power of capital in relation to the state as evidenced in declining levels of corporate taxation. This is often associated with a thesis of the essential redundancy of the state in a new world order of 'hyperglobalisation'. Critics point out that though the power relation between capital and the state has shifted in favour of the former, a stage has certainly not been reached in which capital can entirely emancipate itself from dependence on state power (see Gray 1998; Held et al. 1999; Lloyd 2000). It is rather what capital demands of the state which is changing. That change can be characterised as one from *social integration* to *security and the management of risk*.

The outcome of these contradictions is that the state moves in the direction of what might be termed 'debilitated authoritarianism'. It becomes weaker in relation to capital, continually less able to pursue policies that significant sections of the electorate demand. This leads to profound changes in the nature of politics in capitalist democracies, changes which have important implications for criminality. At the same time the state moves, under pressure from capital, to fulfil new roles in the control and management of population, in an authoritarian direction exemplified in new forms of governance and sovereignty and new relations between private and public power.

The crisis of politics and social policy

The traditions of social policy and the institutions, discourses, and frameworks of state-led governance, which reached their high point in the Keynesian welfare state, become subject to increasing tensions and pressures as the requirements of capital accumulation and social cohesion move in different directions. The result is mounting social problems which increase the burdens on states still committed to social policy at the same time as their ability to actually solve such problems weakens. Governments are continually pressured to yield to the requirements of capital, to force growing numbers of workers to accept low-wage, insecure employment or none at all, while maintaining a cynical pretence at ameliorative social policy. As taxes on capital are forced lower, welfare expenditure is more directly linked to *personal* taxation. The middle classes, under conditions of growing insecurity, increasingly make their own provisions and object to paying for the very poor. In attempting to reconcile these contradictory pressures, different national traditions are of major importance. The decline of the welfare state and the arrangements of organised modernity have been especially severe in societies where the ascendancy of the neo-liberal 'New Right' was established during the 1980s. The polar case, either celebrated or dreaded, is the United States in which the last residues of the New Deal are being buried and in which the state has virtually abandoned any involvement at all for the governance of large sections of the population (see Hardt and Negri 2000). Britain has tended to follow but from a higher threshold of entrenched welfare rights and public spending.[2] But the same tensions are inevitably present.

Social democrats and liberals continue to make the assumption that support for ameliorative policies can be mobilised by pointing to the consequences of their absence. For example, a major British policy report on poverty and social exclusion published in the mid-1990s argued that

> [r]egardless of any moral arguments or feelings of altruism, *everyone shares* an interest in the cohesiveness of society. As the gaps between rich and poor grow, the problems of the marginalised groups which are being left behind rebound on the more comfortable majority. Just as in the last century it was in the interests of all to introduce public health measures to combat the spread of infectious diseases fostered by poverty, so in this century *it is in the interests of all* to remove the factors which are fostering the social diseases of drugs, crime, political extremism and social unrest. (Barclay 1995: 34, my italics)

The repeated reference is to an assumed consensus, as if a smooth *continuity* with the concerns of the nineteenth-century bourgeois philanthropists still existed. Rather the situation, increasingly in Britain and even more acutely in the United States is one in which:

There is no crusade against poverty.... No leading politician demands full employment for the country's workforce. No prominent public figure insists that the wealth which was taken from the poor and given to the rich during the Conservative years should now be returned. There is only the immense jabber of the powerful who are surrounded by the victims of their affluence and who yet continue to know nothing of the undiscovered country of the poor. (Davies 1997: 305)

Capital is increasingly unwilling to provide resources for such social engineering. The rich will indeed attempt to protect themselves from 'drugs, crime, political extremism and social unrest', but they will decreasingly seek to do so through *welfare* as a public good and increasingly through (physical) *security* as a private good: through moving to secure locations and diverting remaining state spending to repressive policing. They have made great progress in segregating themselves from the poor who increasingly remain 'out of sight, out of mind' (see Murray 1999). Despite the attempt to maintain a public commitment to the solution of social problems and to ameliorate the fracturing of social integration, the state is increasingly subordinated to the logic of the market, the rigours of privatisation and dismemberment of public welfare, and the channels of negotiation and compromise between social classes and groups.

More and more, the main economic functions of the state must ... be geared towards ensuring the institutional and ideological conditions of the internationally-imposed deregulation of economic and labour relations, as well as to contributing to the general acceptance of the alignment of public policies to the norms of international competitiveness.... In this sense, the most pressing ideological task of the state is to convince everyone of the need to de-institutionalise and 'de-substantialise' all previous forms of consensual negotiation i.e. to *dis*-incorporate social classes. (Tsoukalas 1999: 65)

Increases in state expenditure certainly occur but they are channelled towards risk management, law and order, rising prison populations. Meanwhile responsibility for remedying poverty and social exclusion is deflected from public policy and refocused on the individual through a shift in emphasis from strengthening the community towards strengthening the family. The object of policy is thus displaced from the *social* to *individual* responsibility and manifested in family dysfunction, absent fathers, single-parent households, etc. (Wacquant 1999).

The crippling of the ability of the state to engage in social policy underlies a growing crisis of democratic politics. As Susan Strange put it:

Today it seems that the heads of governments may be the last to recognise that they and their ministers have lost the authority over national societies and economies that they used to have. Their command over outcomes is not what it used to be. Politicians everywhere talk as though they have the answers to economic and social problems, as if they are really in charge of their country's destiny. People no longer believe them. (Strange 1996: 3)

There is a progressive 'death of the social' (Rose 1996) as the terrain for solution of collectively recognised *social* problems. Individuals and groups are rather expected to produce their own solutions. Politically this appears as the weakening of the public sphere of democratic discussion and opinion formation (see Habermas 1989).

During the 1970s Habermas (1976; see also Lea 1982) had argued that this growing *rationality crisis* of the state – its inability to manage effectively the economy and social system – would result in a *legitimation crisis*, a growing public disillusionment with conventional politics and state agencies and a growing public demand for the discursive justification of values and policies and a renewal of the public sphere. There is certainly evidence of disillusionment with existing political structures in such phenomena as declining voter turnout at elections and growing distrust in political representatives (Pharr and Putnam 2000; Hertz 2001).[3] But while in most western capitalist democracies public opinion polls suggest a strong continued commitment to welfare services, the mobilisation of this commitment finds a powerful obstacle in the fragmentation tendencies noted above which tend to prioritise issues of public insecurity and dangerousness. Meanwhile governments exhibit a growing uncertainty about public support for various operations they undertake. There are increasing attempts to stifle public debate with a new politics which maximises the distance between policy making and traditional processes of democratic discussion and accountability. The emerging characteristics of this process include: reference to global forces beyond the control of the national state which close off political options and dictate that, 'there is no alternative'; ideological incoherence as in doctrines such as the 'Third Way' in which the demands of capital and the requirements of social integration are reconciled by magic incantations; the relative decline of parliaments and legislatures as sites of effective policy making in favour of focus groups, polls and other mechanisms which substitute political debate with the mere registering of opinions.

State and private bureaucracies alike take refuge in a pseudo-reduction of complexity, which takes place not in the real world of actual solutions to social, economic and environmental problems, but in the largely self-referential world of performance indicators, frequently massaged, and measured outcomes which evaluate simply the capacity of the organisation to produce statistics and devise indicators. The appropriate mind-set for the twenty-first-century bureaucrat has moved from the traditional ethic of public service and commitment to pragmatic social reform to the evasive cynicism of the spin doctor.

In the meantime the debilitation of the state as effective mechanism for steering *or* rowing the economy and social system renders it vulnerable to systems of organised clientelism and corruption. Political parties are able to secure less funding from the public, trades unions, small businesses, etc., finding it increasingly difficult to justify the provision of such funding given its lack of substantive outcome, while the costs of political organisation and mobilisation in media-dominated communications rise continually, so that only the best funded can afford to enter national political contests (Tsoukalas 1999). The result is that traditional forms of state corruption whereby favours were *secretly* purchased from individual politicians and state bureaucrats by businessmen seeking lucrative public contracts for goods or services are joined by an overt public clientalism in which backing for political parties is secured from wealthy individuals and interests with a façade of denials concerning any particular favouritism. This is accompanied by the increasing fusion of public civil service with private commercial interests, celebrated in the name of bringing 'the efficiency of the private sector' into government. The role of the state as an institution whose resources are to be pillaged by powerful interest groups begins to displace the state as the effective agent of social cohesion.

The new governance

The fact of capital's declining interest in sustaining the institutions of organised modernity does not imply that it no longer needs the state. The state is, to be sure, becoming weaker in relation to globalised capital but it remains a crucial institution. It is pushed in the direction of new types of coercive and authoritarian policy arising from a preoccupation with risk and security.

The collapse of organised modernity has seen the partial displacement of the state by capital with increasing forms of direct rule by private property. The privatisation of public utilities and welfare services is complemented and reinforced at the global level by organisations, such as the World Trade Organisation, which are simply forums for direct deliberation by the representatives of private capital and increasingly lay down the law to nation states on issues concerning international trade and the opening up to private capital of lucrative opportunities in newly privatised public utilities and welfare. While globalisation is accompanied by new forms of economic regulation which necessitate the off-loading of welfare functions, the latter are not being taken up by global welfare organisations but are rather being taken off the agenda (see Mishra 1999).

Such institutions and arrangements are, however, guaranteed by nation states which still provide the ultimate back-up in terms of armed force – even if the relevant force is the 'visiting' military of another state – as well as essential supports of legal title to property, deregulation of financial institutions and their protection from 'political interference', licensing private welfare or security companies, guaranteeing rights to defend private space, and so on (see Sassen 1996, 1999). Thus the state moves back towards the 'government at a distance' of the nineteenth century in which it 'steers' rather than 'rows' the economy and social system (Osborne and Gaebler 1992) and concedes much governance to private organisations. However, it would be a mistake to see present developments simply as a return to an earlier stage of capitalism.

In Foucault's conception, discussed briefly in earlier chapters, the form of rule characteristic of modern society involved a governmentalisation of the state: the assimilation of direct coercive domination or sovereignty to wider strategies of governance aimed at shaping the institutions and processes through which social groups regulate their own conduct. This subordination of sovereignty to 'government at a distance' (Rose and Miller 1992) was located within the boundaries and interests of the nation state and national community. It comprised a diversity of institutions and social relations, including those of crime control, and a diversity of modes of operation. Thus the operational principles of the family and the commercial company differed strongly from those of crime control. Nevertheless all these structures formed part of a project of governance within the nation state and concerned with the socialisation of populations, their education and disciplining as required by capital accumulation and its management. The Keynesian welfare state of organised modernity closed the distance between public and private by involving the state more directly in the workings of both the family and the company.

The present shift back towards 'government at a distance' is in some ways a strong reassertion of the semi-autonomy of the company and the family and the forms of governance they entail, in the face of the decaying Keynesian welfare state. But two characteristics distinguish current developments from the strategies of governance characteristic of the nineteenth century. Firstly, government at a distance is no longer necessarily a distance bounded by the nation state. While the family remains largely a private institution within the national terrain – though large-scale labour migration with family members spread out across the globe modifies this – the commercial company increasingly does not. Globalisation brings, as I have noted, a mobility of capital between regions with the establishment of linkages and dynamics that threatens the ability of the state to pursue a coherent economic policy, even one that is 'hands off' (see Castells 1996). Some forms of governance no longer 'governmentalise' the state but ignore it altogether. Linkages forged by capital accumulation, global communications networks, cultural transmissions, cut across and ignore the terrain of the nation state rather than complement it, albeit usually relying upon it for legal title to property or security back-up of last resort. Thus:

> Within nominally sovereign territories today ... new flows of communication and information are decentering once sovereign authorities, multiplying operational spaces, dividing ties of belongingness, and mixing zones of rules. These flows provide new alternative codes of contragovernmental legitimacy,

desire and power over new populations in many places to operate against 'old sovereignties'. (Luke 1996: 23)

Secondly, the concern of private capital is increasingly that of security rather than socialisation. The great engines of discipline embodied in the school, the hospital, the prison, the factory and the family have been displaced by a combination of parasitic short-term profiteering from newly privatised public goods and the replacement of a concern with the reproduction of the working class to one of neutralisation of populations who may constitute any risk to profit-taking. Rather than governance being a modification and widening out of sovereignty as in Foucault's account, a preoccupation with issues of sovereignty brings about substantial modifications in strategies of governance. The new unity of purpose between governance and sovereignty and between state and private governance centres on the management of risk, the latter having become the new, perhaps overused, concept in social theory (Beck 1992). The popularity of the concept of risk to describe relations between social groups reflects the fact that social and political fragmentation is producing a society in which the relations between individuals, social groups and classes are increasingly governed not by structured channels of interaction and trust in which certain actions, decisions and responses can be reasonably expected and comprehended but by the risk that undesired collisions and interruptions will occur.

The elements of discipline and socialisation that remain are, meanwhile, increasingly dedicated to the negative tasks of encouraging young working-class people to revise downwards their employment expectations and accept low-paid insecure work. The residue of the Keynesian welfare state is transformed into the 'workfare state' (Jessop 1994). The destruction of welfare and social engineering appears as its continuation. Political fanfares about education for the masses mean in fact, outside the increasingly privatised provision for the upper middle class and very rich, the displacement of education by varieties of mindless 'skills training'. In a similar way social work as the reclamation and reintegration of clients as citizens is displaced by a managerialist assessment, classification and management of problem individuals in terms of their likely risk to public security (see Froggett 1996). Discipline and socialisation merge into strategies concerned with the management, assessment and classification of populations in terms of their destabilising potential and the taking of appropriate risk-neutralisation measures.

Such measures take on an *actuarial* orientation. That is to say the concern is less with the characteristics of individuals but rather with those of groups and the aim of policy is not to change those characteristics so much as neutralise their disturbance effect on the rest of society. Traditional social policy was governance oriented to socialisation: that is, changing the characteristics of populations, mainly but not exclusively the working class, through various types of discipline and socialisation. By contrast, the aim of risk management is to plot the characteristics of groups, develop predictors of the likelihood of disruptive activity, and to devise strategies for its minimisation. Jonathan Simon (1988) specifies the main difference between disciplinary and actuarial power as follows:

> Disciplinary practices focus on the distribution of a behaviour within a limited population (a factory workforce, prison inmates, school children etc.) ... with the goal of ... narrowing the deviation and moving subjects toward uniformity (workers are to be made more efficient and reliable, prisoners more docile, school children more attentive and respectful). Actuarial practices seek instead to map out the distribution and arrange strategies to maximise the efficiency of the population as it stands. Rather than seek to change people ('normalise' them in Foucault's apt phrase), an actuarial regime seeks to manage them in place.... While the disciplinary regime attempts to alter individual behaviour and motivation, the actuarial regime alters the physical and social structures within which individuals behave. (Simon 1988: 773)

The actuarial management of risky populations embraces a wide spectrum, far beyond traditional ideas of dangerousness. The key move is that 'the notion of risk is made autonomous from that of danger' (Castel 1991: 288). Risk is no longer based on the presence of concrete dangerous individuals or groups but on a combination of abstract factors making more or less probable certain occurrences. 'One does not start from a conflictual situation observable in experience, rather one deduces it from a general definition of the dangers one wishes to prevent' (Castel 1991: 288).

Membership of a group defined as risky leads to many forms of social exclusion. This is reinforced by the network society and information technology whose effects lie not so much in exclusion *from* information sources as exclusion *by* information technology which facilitates the storage and accessing of detailed profiles such as criminal records, employment history, credit ratings, educational credentials, residential area, etc., which enable decisions about *individuals* – such as refusal of credit – to be made on the basis of actuarial statistics about *group* characteristics. Information technology facilitates and exacerbates social exclusion (Perri 6 and Jupp 2001). Actuarialism reconnects in many ways with traditional ideas of sovereignty displaced during the nineteenth century by more sophisticated notions of governance aimed at socialisation. Just as sovereignty is concerned with the conformity of the population to the law and authority of the state, actuarial strategies aim simply to minimise the risk various sections of the population present to property and security. Both strategies have in common that, in contrast to socialisation and discipline, there is no attempt to change the general behavioural characteristics of the poor. Actuarialism is one of the key forms in which governance is re-subordinated to older notions of sovereignty (see Stenson 1999: 64). It is less important that the poor acquire skills and abilities they will never use in the global labour market than that they learn passivity and obedience to the law. Indeed, that is precisely the 'skill' required. Social policy returns to an emphasis on *police*, now taking the form of a combination of border patrol for the secure sites of capitalist production or financial activity, and the pacification of risky populations. As Zygmunt Bauman puts it:

> state governments are allotted the role of little else than oversized police precincts, the quantity and quality of policemen on the beat, sweeping the streets clean of beggars, pesterers and pilferers, and the tightness of the jail walls loom large among the factors of 'investors' confidence', and so among the items calculated when the decisions to invest or de-invest are made. To excel in the job of precinct policeman is the best (perhaps the only) thing state governments may do to cajole nomadic capital into investing in its subjects' welfare; and so the shortest roads to the economic prosperity of the land, and so hopefully to the 'feel good' sentiments of the electors, lead through the public display of the policing skill and prowess of the state. (Bauman 1998: 120)

Thus political concern with 'law and order', the size of prison populations, etc., and public fears about crime, begin to lose their connection with actual crime rates and risks of victimisation – which in most industrial countries have been falling in recent years – and become a vehicle for more general themes of security in the face of social fragmentation. They increasingly merge into fears of unknown populations, and the preoccupation with their management.

The increasingly actuarial nature of policy enables it to be shared between state and private institutions. The privatisation and marketisation of public goods turns the citizen into the customer purchasing personal security in the same way as private health care. The commercial organisation, rather than being a form of private governance linked to the nation state as part of the governmentalisation of the latter, becomes an independent form of governance of growing importance. The privatisation of urban space, the linking of private service provision to global capital movements and profit concerns beyond the remit of the national state, is expanding while, at a local level, the 'social contract' as the basis for citizenship rights is displaced by commercial 'governance contracts' (Shearing 1995) oriented to security as, for example, that entry to gated communities, shopping malls, transport networks, etc., be subject to vetting or electronic monitoring. As long as the state retains a monopoly of the use of legitimate force then only its officials can apply direct coercion. State actuarial policies are able to deploy sovereignty in the form of legal coercion such as mass incarceration, intrusive technological surveillance, and heavy policing of certain zones. But private institutions deploy forms of rule based on civil property rights to increasing effect.

The shift from citizen to customer also displaces the focus of social and political activism. The civic privatism of the old welfare state consensus which sustained the passive expert–client relationship between state and social groups transmutes into newer forms of political apathy based less on the feeling that government expertise has taken care of matters than on a cynicism, manifested in declining voter turnout and the transformation of political communication into media hype, rooted in the perception of the declining role of government in the general determination of life chances. At the same time the decline in the old taken-for-granted securities of welfare state social citizenship brings forth a new activism, particularly on the part of the middle-class communities who realise they have to purchase their security, and even if it is still provided by the state can no longer take for granted the efficiency of service delivery. At a local level communities may both purchase the services of private security companies and enter into an active partnership with local police and business for the defence of property. Such alliances involve an *active community* in a more equal partnership relation with state agencies, themselves acting with increasing degrees of local autonomy (see O'Malley and Palmer 1996).

A final important characteristic of the new governance/sovereignty is its increasingly *episodic, contingent* and *fractured* nature. This is related, firstly, to the privatisation of provision. Universal social rights to citizenship have to be constantly available to all. They presuppose some form of communicative public sphere as the basis of their legitimation. Citizens who lack resources, fall upon hard times, do not forgo these rights, they actualise them through claims on the appropriate authorities. But customers only get what they pay for and if they can't pay then they cease to be customers. Private services, and security, will *only* be provided to those who pay. Behind these developments lies the fact that it is less important to capital that all sections of the working class are properly fed, educated and ready for labour that requires certain minimal skills. A new division of labour develops in which the state provides a minimal safety net, whether of income support or police back-up, but an increasing number of everyday essentials will be privately paid for. If residents or property owners want twenty-four-hour patrol or surveillance then they can hire private security. The police will come if there is a perceived threat of wider disruption. Services can, of course, be more readily provided to active communities with whom various forms of political alliance have been established, while the poor can be left, in all but the most acute emergencies, to fend for themselves. Meanwhile, risky populations can be dealt with as and when trouble breaks out. There is no need for all areas of cities to be effectively policed, indeed no need for continuous domination of urban space. Such developments change the relationship between state action and discourses concerning rights and moral values. Juridical and moral discourses about universal entitlements are displaced by discourses about effectiveness in the containment of risks and problem outbreaks.

This shift in the direction of a plurality and discontinuity of power is repeated on a global scale. Areas inessential to capital accumulation can be left to degenerate into the wild zones of ghettos and inner cities, or even whole countries in some areas of the Third World as 'ungovernable chaotic entities' (de Rivero 1999). There is a *re-mediaevalisation* of space (Kaplan 1998) in which key zones and communications networks are defended, like mediaeval walled towns, against a surrounding 'bandit country'. These areas, uncoordinated by capital and only episodically by the state, are fertile ground for alternative forms of 'governance from below' (Stenson 1998, 1999) in which criminality, terrorism, corruption and violence may proliferate.

Again, the existence of counter-tendencies to a pure and simple politics of risk management needs to be stressed. Even populations redundant to capital accumulation may still have political power and be able to pressure the state, or the international community, to take ameliorative action. Such resistances vary between states and regions. Where redundant populations can be entirely geographically segregated, pressure is minimal. Where the middle classes and the poor intermingle more, as in western European cities, pressure is greater. The salient point is the decreasing ability of either the state or private capital effectively to contain these contradictions in the long run.

Identity and Aggression

The final area in which the destructive self-reproduction of capitalism makes an impact is in laying the ground for the growth of forms of personal identity which legitimise aggressiveness and short-termism. In Chapters 2 and 3 it was argued that a key component of the development of capitalism and emergence of the social relations of crime control was the long-run tendency to restraint and non-violence as general characteristics of inter-personal relations (see Elias 1982, 1994). Violence by capital became institutional, bureaucratised and instrumental – a 'violence without passion' (Collins 1974) exemplified in the clinical violence of the military and state agencies of repression, in the cynicism of multinational corporations pillaging the environment and impoverishing the poor. For the working classes the situation described by Engels (1845/1975) in the earlier nineteenth century was replaced by rising wages, stable communities and habituation to work and passive consumption. Individual violence and aggression became dysfunctional, aberrant and criminalisable.

These tendencies were reinforced and consolidated in the organised modernity of the Keynesian welfare state. Economic and social life were essentially predictable enterprises in which the long-term project made sense. Large companies and governments made massive investments with a view to maturation over long time periods in stable and predictable market conditions (Galbraith 1967). Social and personal life also conformed to a predictable cycle. Choices were made at certain key points in the life cycle such as what to specialise in at college and what job to take. For men the subordination of self to the organisation was an essentially similar process for working- and middle-class man, for 'Fordist man' and 'organisation man', while for women the more restricted world of the family was determined once the choice of spouse had been made. In addition to work, participation in community and public life, the essentially passive process of voting, involvement in trade union and other local activities, the sharing of welfare rights and a relationship to the state as client to expert or as supervisor of negotiated compromise over a fairly restricted agenda of monetised needs, complemented the orientation to consumption and the growing affluence of the post-war boom as a source of the conservatism, uniformity and stability of these identities. Identity formation was a process of linkage to stable communities from which were derived meaning, trust, standards of ethical conduct. It was also a process that linked the individual to the state and civil society.

The debilitation of the structures of organised modernity has created new dynamics of identity formation. The hegemony of 'impatient capital', short-termism, personal insecurity, the co-ordination of economic activity by global networks, the weakening of communities, has created a disjunction between economic co-ordination and the social production of identity. Hegel, among other philosophers, understood that freedom and self-identity were associated with recognition, approval, trust, etc., from others. Individual freedom presupposed a community of others (see Honneth 1992: 169). The problem is that it is difficult to build such structures on the basis of the disjointed logics of the network society of globalised capitalism which have undermined the older linkages of community, society, politics and the nation state. Identity formation today, unlike that of the 'imagined communities' of modern nationalism (Anderson 1983) or traditional class politics, is less based on linkages to civil society and the nation state. The centres of power are not where communities can be formed. As Castells observes,

> the network society is based on the systemic disjunction between the local and the global for most individuals and social groups.... Therefore reflexive life planning becomes impossible, except for the elite inhabiting the timeless space of flows of global networks and their ancillary locales. And the building of intimacy on the basis of trust requires a redefinition of identity fully autonomous *vis à vis* the networking logic of dominant institutions and organisations. (Castells 1997: 11)

The search for stable identity becomes more pressing as a way of dealing with individual uncertainty, insecurity and risk. While global network society does show the possibility for new forms of virtual – internet-based – communities and oppositional political identities, these are only at an embryonic stage. Meanwhile the reconstruction of a sense of community *in the face of* the fragmenting tendencies of capital becomes harder with the 'fundamental irony that the solidity of identity deteriorates in proportion to its very urgency' (Young 1999: 166).

For those with resources, the elite, the plurality of identities, constant choice and the celebration of *difference* fit easily with the notion of post-modern society as mobile, fluid and continually being re-made: a sort of laissez-faire world of infinite possibilities, in which 'the pluralisation of life expands the potentialities and identities available to ordinary people in their everyday working, social, familial and sexual lives' (Hall 1989: 129). But for the poor this fluidity and constant re-making of life involves moving constantly between the legal and illegal economies of short-term employment, wheeling and dealing, coping with short-term threats and instabilities which become the normal everyday character of life.

Identity formation is thus decreasingly linked to restraint and the learning of communal moral standards. The weakening of the social is at the same time a weakening of the moral community which leads to a decline in empathy and the understanding of others' problems as socially produced rather than the result of individual failure. There is 'no shared narrative of difficulty, and so no shared fate' (Sennett 1998: 147). A growing support for punitive as opposed to welfare responses to social problems reflects, in turn, an orientation to the short term, to the shifting contingencies of life rather than sustained commitments to others. Thus,

> it is wise and prudent not to make long term plans or invest in the distant future; not to get tied down too firmly to any particular place, group or cause, even to an image of oneself, because one might find oneself not just un-anchored and drifting but without an anchor altogether.... In other words 'to be provident' means now, more often than not, to avoid *commitment*. To be free to move when opportunity knocks. To be free to leave when it stops knocking. (Bauman 1994: 12)

Or, as Robert de Niro's gangster advises his young accomplice in the film *Heat*, 'Don't get into any relationship you can't walk out of in thirty seconds.' The insecure lifestyle of the gangster migrates from the underworld to the upperworld. In this context older structures of restraint and socialisation, crucial in earlier arrangements of governance for socialisation and integration can now be dispensed with as redundant impediments, or even criticised themselves as forms of violence. Bauman again:

> Marriages, families, parenthood, neighbourhoods, work places have lost much of their role of the frontier outposts of the societally managed factory of order. Coercion applied there daily and matter-of-factly lost its function as the vehicle of 'law and order' and so can be challenged as gratuitous violence and unforgivable cruelty. The once uncontested hierarchies can be challenged anew, habitual patterns of relations renegotiated, old rights to coerce and demand discipline vociferously questioned and violently resisted – so that the overall impression is created that the sum total of violence is on the increase

while the previously complied with or just unnoticed exercise of superior power is being reclassified as illegitimate violence. (Bauman 1995: 156)

The increased struggle to stand out in an uncertain and competitive world when the old certainties and status of career and community have been undermined increases the recourse to aggression as often the only thing that enables the individual to attract attention or to alter situations. Thus 'Descartes' cogito has been rephrased as "I am noticed, therefore I exist" (and for practical purposes unpacked as "I shout, therefore I exist")' (Bauman 1995: 157). The role of 'expressive violence' and an aggressive masculinity, formerly thought of as a subcultural phenomenon associated with the attempts of male youth in poor marginalised communities to express identity and elicit respect (Cloward and Ohlin 1960), is now becoming a more widely generalised form of behaviour; part of a resurgent aggressive individualism. It is less dysfunctional to economic processes than might otherwise be thought. The historical decline of aggressiveness in favour of restraint, deferred gratification and the location of violence either in criminal subcultures or in institutional bureaucracies is being undermined. Governance is less reliant on the long-term integration of individuals into complex organisations and social contracts and more characterised by short-term locations, opportunism, insecurity and competitiveness while the overall co-ordination of the system is increasingly located in markets and communication networks rather than in *social* cohesion.

This attempt at the construction of identity involves drawing on a constantly shifting *bricolage* of elements drawn from global mass media, ethnicity, religion. Some is highly innovative, but much is dominated by superficiality, the loss of historicity in favour of a cannibalisation of the past, the loss of meaning and the dominance of reproductive technologies (Jameson 1984). Such a negative freedom of constant self-recreation is contradictory. It is predicated on the dissolution of the social lifeworld as source of mutual recognition and affirmation of stable individual identity. But unable to achieve any stability it continually collapses into its opposite: a nostalgia for community represented frequently in conservative revivals and attempted reappropriations of the language of earlier stages of modernity. These include forms of authoritarian ethnic and religious reaction and range from the peaceful nostalgia of communitarianism (Etzioni 1993) to the violent nostalgia of the extreme right for a clearly defined visible ethnic community which attempts to secure recognition by the forced exclusion of ambiguity and diversity, rather than finding in them new resources for community and mutual recognition. Such violent authoritarianism responds to the process of social exclusion by trying simply to replace capital as the excluder.

What should be avoided is any notion that the working class or the socially excluded poor are the unique repository of such violent attempts to recreate community and personal identity. True, the image of the violent husband, the 'lawless masculinity' of inner city youth (Campbell 1993) or of the fascist vigilantes, are all working class. But that is largely because the notion of violent identity is operationalised in such terms. As feminists have pointed out, domestic violence is not a unique characteristic of the poor but is to be found in all classes (Mooney 2000). Yet the convention among many social commentators remains that of locating the sources of aggression in those who have somehow deviated from, or become disconnected from, the mainstream. The old tradition of the residual pathology, or culture of poverty, of the poor as a self-generated obstacle to integration into modernity is now reproduced in a new form. For some conservatives the frightening spectre is that the pathologies previously unique to the more or less permanently unemployed 'underclass' now threaten to pollute the normal.

Thus Charles Murray, the American conservative, talks of 'cultural spillover' and asks 'How much has the culture of the underclass already spilled over into the mainstream?' In his opinion:

> most disturbing is the widening expression, often approving, of underclass ethics: Take what you want. Respond violently to anyone who antagonises you. Despise courtesy as weakness. Take pride in cheating (stealing, lying, exploiting) successfully. I do not know how to measure how broadly such principles have spread, but that they are more openly espoused in television, films, and recordings than they used to be is hard to deny. I am suggesting that among the many complicated explanations for this deterioration, cultural spillover from the underclass is implicated. (Murray 1999)

Murray is not unaware of some of the objections to his thesis but nevertheless persists:

> It should also go without saying that vulgarity, violence, and the rest, were part of mainstream America before the underclass came along. But these things always used to be universally condemned in public discourse. Now they are not. It is not just that America has been defining deviancy down, slackening old moral codes. Inner-city street life has provided an alternative code and it is attracting converts. (Murray 1999)

But that is precisely the point. The lack of condemnation of vulgarity and violence could hardly be due to the poor and marginalised groups who have very little influence over the mass media or 'public discourse'. It is rather the fact that such values are generated at the core of an increasingly harsh capitalism. The poor and marginalised reproduce and innovate on the basis of the dominant values and the means of achieving them: they produce another variety of them. The 'lawless masculinity' of rioting youth in Beatrix Campbell's study of deprived housing estates in the north-east of England in the early 1990s (Campbell 1993) is a culture not markedly distinct from that of the financial dealing rooms of the City of London. Indeed, it is in the expanding role of finance capital that we see some of the most blatant examples of the culture of 'lawless masculinity'.

During the 1980s the City of London and other world financial centres witnessed the advance of the new globally mobile speculative finance capital, what I earlier referred to as 'fictitious capital', which brought to prominence a new breed of operatives. Thus '[t]he chief beneficiaries of world trade were not the company men but the dealers ... spending their day yelling and swearing as they moved millions in bonds across the globe' (Sampson 1995: 151). In a polemical view of the new forces at work in the world of finance, Christopher Stanley brilliantly draws out the similarities between the new aggressive culture of the financial class and that of the 'underclass' in a comparison between the financial City and the 'inner city' of East London, where

> [t]he terrain may be different but the tensions and processes of fragmentation consequent upon economic and ideological change are very similar. A previously stable (mythological) subculture generated a series of codes of conduct. The fragmentation of this cultural stability has accentuated the contours between previously generated normative behaviour and new forms of arbitrary violent behaviour. The old forms of customary practice (traditional 'wheeling and dealing, ducking and diving') have been eroded given the invasion of more violent forms of entrepreneurial-criminal behaviour in the form of drug related transactions. The violence in the streets of the East End may be more 'real' in the sense of a growing physical fear but it is only a shadow of the 'symbolic' violence being waged in the dealing rooms of the finance houses of the City. (Stanley 1996: 72)

Meanwhile, the aggressive masculinity of the financial dealing rooms is arguably more serious than that of the socially excluded housing estates. The latter are still recognised at least as a social problem and governments still attempt to find ways of channelling young men into more constructive activities. More important, in the poorest communities such aggressive individualism is at least tempered by elements of collective solidarity and resistance born of the need to survive. The aggression of the rich, characterised by its 'anomie of affluence' (Simon and Gagnon 1976) leads, notwithstanding the occasional punch-up in a City of London wine bar, to less overt physical violence, but is symptomatic of a socio-economic system locked in destructive self-reproduction.

Conclusion

In this chapter I have looked at a number of features of capitalism in its phase of destructive reproduction. Socialisation and homogenisation are replaced by social polarisation and fragmentation. The welfare state and political compromise between social classes as stabilising mechanisms are replaced by the direct power of private property and market mechanisms, turning the citizen into the customer. The state becomes both more authoritarian in its substitution of social policy for security and risk management, and weakened by the global power of private capital and the crippling of the political process. An important consequence of the latter becomes the weakening of the social or the public sphere of politics as a form of negotiation and compromise between social classes and other groups and as the terrain of policy formation and implementation. Public communication becomes increasingly a form of cynicism, obfuscation and contentless babble. It now remains to move on to a consideration of some of the impact of these developments on both criminality and its control.

Notes

1 The shift of funds from productive investment to financial speculation has in recent years been dramatic. In 1979, 30 per cent of global foreign exchange transactions were accounted for by trade in goods and services. By 1995 this was only 1.5 per cent (Khor 1997; see also Kennedy 1998).

2 In Britain, where, as noted previously, the welfare state was open to all social classes rather than being targeted on the poor, large sections of the insecure middle class support the improvements of public services and utilities but are more hesitant about the levels of personal taxation actually required to deliver such improvements.

3 The General Election in the United Kingdom in May 2001 achieved a record low turnout of 58 per cent of the population eligible to vote. The 'landslide' victory for the Blair government was delivered by precisely 25 per cent of the British total population.

6

Varieties of Normalisation

The changing direction of development in modern capitalist societies, discussed in the previous chapter, impacts directly on the social relations of crime control as a system of governance organising the population around the management of certain types of harms and conflicts. The tendencies outlined in the previous chapter – the fragmentation of communities and growing social polarisation, the changing nature of politics and the strength of the state, the legitimisation of aggression – have led to the social and economic relations underpinning crime control beginning to crumble. In many ways modernisation is moving into reverse. The phrase 'back to the future' comes readily to mind as we see some of the characteristics of the *pre-modern* reasserting themselves in new forms as part of the *postmodern*.

It is usual to associate the type of changes discussed in the previous chapter with rising *rates* of crime which, until recently, characterised most countries. This relationship has been ably summarised by the American criminologist, Elliot Currie, for whom 'market society' (that is to say, unrestrained capitalism) is one 'in which the pursuit of private gain increasingly becomes the organising principle in all areas of social life ... [and in which] all other principles of social or institutional organisation become eroded or subordinated to the overarching one of private gain' (Currie 1998: 134). He emphasises the criminogenic character of market society which fosters crime, firstly 'by increasing inequality and concentrated economic deprivation'; secondly by 'eroding the capacity of local communities to provide informal support, mutual provision and effective socialisation and supervision of the young'; thirdly by 'stressing and fragmenting the family'; fourthly by 'withdrawing public provision of basic services from those it has already stripped of livelihoods, economic security and informal communal support'; and finally by 'magnifying a culture of Darwinian competition for status and resources and by urging a level of consumption that it cannot provide for everyone through legitimate channels' (Currie 1998: 135–42).

Rising crime signifies the growing ineffectiveness of the social relations of crime control as a system of governance – the first stage of their decomposition. In the short term there may still be clear, shared conceptions of the boundaries of crime, a willingness by communities to collaborate with a coherently functioning set of criminal justice institutions, even if such an alliance of forces appears to be fighting a losing battle. But even when actual crime rates are falling, as in recent years in most countries, the social relations of crime control themselves begin to decompose and it becomes increasingly difficult to respond to crime in traditional ways because of the *qualitative* changes in the relationship between criminality and social life which eat away at the very notion of crime control as an identifiable process. This is our emphasis here. In this chapter I shall look at the impact of changes in the organisation and socio-economic role of criminality. I shall underline three developments in particular; first, the weakening of the *identity* of the criminal, and the clear definitions of crime and offenders shared by most sections of society as the basis for practical criminalisation; second, the undermining of the *marginality* of crime as exogenous and disruptive of normal social processes; and finally the undermining of the *weakness* of the criminal offender, not in relation to the victim but in terms of the capacity to neutralise the activities of law enforcement agencies and communities.

Blurring Identities: Crime and Risk

The social relations of crime control depend on reasonably clear notions of the identity of criminal offenders and criminal activities shared by the majority of the population and coherent with legal norms as the basis of collaboration between communities and the state. In our brief treatment of historical conditions predating modern crime control we saw how criminal identity emerged gradually as an aspect of modernisation. In doing so it overcame on the one hand forms of popular censure in which criminalisation was limited by locality, kinship or social status and, on the other hand, the indiscriminate application, by the state authorities and the ruling class, of criminalisation to the working class as a whole as the 'dangerous classes'. These dissolved as the modern notion of criminality developed. But now the tendency is in the opposite direction: we are moving back towards a blurring of the identity of criminality. This is an obvious consequence of the factors mentioned in the previous chapter in which social groups increasingly encounter one another as risks. A confusion between actual criminality and a diffuse notion of the need to fortify oneself, one's family and neighbourhood, against risky people, against the new 'dangerous classes', with the latter often taking on ethnic as well as class connotations, is widespread. And as the other side of the coin, those who have money and property, and are members of groups with whom one has no social relations of trust and dependency, increasingly appear as fair game. People who are not known or interacted with become the vehicle for suspicion and fear. This echoes the 'society of others' characteristic of early capitalism captured by Frederick Engels' portrayal of urban life in the English industrial city, characterised by '[t]he brutal indifference, the unfeeling isolation of each in his private interest.... The dissolution of mankind into *monads*, of which each one has a separate principle, the world of atoms, is here carried out to its utmost extreme' (Engels 1845/1975: 329).

The boundaries of practical criminalisation become blurred and applied to wider categories of behaviour and people who are then read as risks, ultimately of some diffuse notion of crime occurring. There are several elements to this. Firstly, as David Garland has remarked,

> [f]or most people, crime is no longer an aberration or an unexpected, abnormal event. Instead, the threat of crime has become a routine part of modern consciousness, an everyday risk to be assessed and managed in much the same way that we deal with road traffic – another modern danger which has been routinized and 'normalized' over time. High rates of crime have gradually become a standard, background feature of our lives – a taken for granted element of late modernity. (Garland 1996: 446)

Secondly, the anticipation or fear of harm becomes disconnected from organised space and person. There is a fracturing of the moral economy of place and space with its clear signals of who should be where and when, doing what, into a chaos of intermingled security and insecurity. You are not only likely to be robbed in the red-light district but also on your own doorstep. This new experience turns generalised middle-class insecurities based on changing labour market conditions towards a new support for both prevention and punitive measures against crime (see Garland 2000). Criminal subcultures lose their distinctiveness; the features of the subculture become the features of normal life. But, thirdly, it is not simply a question of collective fortification against outsiders. Anyone is likely to be aggressive, or to defraud or swindle you. Getting away with it is increasingly normal behaviour, in business and in life, less the exception that proves the rule. The offender is as likely as not to be someone legitimately present at the scene rather than an invader or outsider. What were seen as the special characteristics of business and family crime become generalised to wider spheres of harm and violence. An increasing proportion of rapes, for example, are by men known to their victims (Lees 1996). The visual sign of dangerous individuals or groups fragments into ever wider categories of risk including those with whom one interacts on a daily basis or in whom one places trust. This gives a particular salience to sexual crimes, for which

> the degenerate on the social margins, has been replaced by the anonymous abuser, the pervert all the more dangerous in that he knows how not to cause alarm. The fear long focused on the public enemy has been transferred to the man in the street, the neighbour of whom one must beware ... a culprit with no special features, socially integrated and professionally accepted.' (Vigarello 2001: 235)

The result is that

> the offender is seemingly everywhere in the street and in high office, within the poor parts of town but also in those institutions which were set up to rehabilitate and protect, within the public world of encounters with strangers but within the family itself in relationships between husband and wife and parent and child. We are wary of scoutmasters, policemen, hitchhikers, babysitters, husbands, dates, stepfathers and stepmothers, people who care for the elderly – the 'other' is everywhere and not restricted to criminals and outsiders. (Young 1999: 66)

The fragmentation of the local community of certainty and trust is reproduced in wider networks of interaction. It appears on a global scale in the form of the internet which brings the possibility of completely undisclosed identities. A professional and respectable looking website can be rapidly assembled by unknown fraudsters. The global network society, like the seemingly normal family, obliterates the signs of crime and the identity of the criminal. Violence too becomes delivered in new ways through the networks. The increasing isolation and fragmentation of everyday life contrasts with the anonymity of networks and all forms of electronic communication to produce new fears of aggression. Verbal aggression, magnified by the telephone conversation and the email message becomes a

> true 'phenomenon of the age' … linked to the new coverage of the telephone network and electronic messaging, it becomes violence through the feelings of unease and insecurity it provokes … psychological aggression is taken as the first threshold of violence and counted as such, words are converted into violence, no longer seen as an affront but as brutality. (Vigarello 2001: 219)

It is important to understand the dyadic nature of the weakening identity of criminality. That is to say, it affects not just a widening and diffuse fear of the other, but also weakens restraints, and indeed awareness of entering into criminality. There are at least three aspects of this. Firstly, the weakening of family and community governed norms of predictable behaviour increases the difficulty of reading the signs of dangerousness and risk, and the likelihood of misunderstanding by both parties to the interaction. For example, in the area of sexual assault the rise of 'date rape' is symptomatic of the breakdown both in clearly prescribed standards of behaviour and signs of risk. Secondly, this lack of clear definitions of risk and danger puts resources in the hands of offenders. An example, again from the area of sexual assault, is the recent concern with 'acquaintance rape' which constitutes a growing proportion of rapes but for which conviction rates are low. Conviction by the courts will be less likely if it is known that the victim 'knew' the offender. But what does 'know' mean in the context of weakening norms of behaviour? Serial rapists, as Sue Lees (1996) points out, become skilled at 'getting to know' their victims as a precursor to rape. This is considerably easier where, if a victim has met her attacker for the *first time* on the day of the rape, the relationship will be classified as acquaintance (Lees and Gregory 1999: 101), and where the existence of clearly demarcated rules of social engagement sustained by a community is reduced to zero, to the advantage of offenders who no longer have to violate social restraints.

Finally, just as encounter with criminality is increasingly a normal expectation, it is also becoming something increasingly normal to be entered into. The identity of criminal offenders and activities becomes blurred not only by the lack of clear signs of criminality or criminals but also by the normalisation of activities and motivations hitherto considered criminal. There is a new contingency to criminality as a solution to normal problems or as an aspect of normal everyday activity reminiscent of pre-modern and early industrial society. The precursor is the growth of the ethic of short-term gratification and risk-taking combined with the increasingly fractured nature of governance.

An example of the normalisation of previously distinct subcultural activities can be found in the widespread taking of recreational drugs as part of a process of 'the accommodations of previously "deviant" activities into mainstream cultural arrangements' (Parker et al. 1998: 156; see also Wainwright 1999). In a similar way, large numbers of low-paid workers may move in and out of informal and criminal economies of theft and illegal labour without even realising it, far less feeling the need to rationalise their activities (Ruggiero 1997, 2000).

The normalisation of criminal risk-taking occurs throughout the social structure. Similar dynamics characterise the commercial organisation, in particular the changing world of finance capital. The old culture of the City of London, which had insulated the deviant from criminalisation but which had also acted as a system of informal self-regulation, collapsed in the face of globalisation and became an environment in which '[t]he game became ... how much one could consume, and how many opponents one could annihilate' (Stanley 1996: 88). The result in the dealing rooms was widespread willingness to violate financial regulations, such as those prohibiting money laundering, in an environment in which

> [t]heir risk taking culture ... coupled with the highly competitive environment within which they work ... predisposes them to break the rules more readily than practitioners in other commercial sectors. These are the traders to whom the compliance officer [responsible for ensuring adherence to regulations against money laundering] is generally seen as 'the business prevention officer'. (Bosworth-Davies 1997: 7)

As far as finance capital is concerned, the socialisation of entrepreneurs into an ethic of restraint and deferred gratification, an important aspect of the nineteenth-century development of governance, is moving into reverse. Aggressive individualism and short termism are the key criminogenic orientations. The assimilation of criminality in this context to just another variety of risk-taking activity, rather than any sort of subcultural deviance, is reflected at a theoretical level in the rise of an 'administrative criminology' unconcerned with the motivation (either psychological or subcultural) of criminality but simply with strategies of prevention which seek to discourage crime – or for that matter any other behaviour regarded as risky or dangerous – by raising its costs and reducing its benefits to the perpetrators. The economist Gary Becker, in his classic application of the economic theory of *rational choice* to criminology claimed that 'a useful theory of criminal behaviour can dispense with special theories of anomie ... and simply extend the economist's usual analysis of choice' (Becker 1968: 169). People will commit crime when the benefits outweigh the costs. The aim of administrative criminology is simply to work out how to increase the costs of those activities regarded as crime. However, Becker proceeded to add a 'willingness to commit an illegal act' as a variable in the formula for the calculus of rationality of criminal action. This undermined his whole attempt to dispense with sociological or psychological theories of criminal motivation since it was precisely the willingness to break the law, rather than simply the calculus of costs and benefits, which was the issue in explanations of crime, particularly in the sociological analysis of criminal subcultures. But once that willingness becomes normalised then rational choice theory approaches a step closer to reality.[1] Certain types of criminal offending have been traditionally understood as forms of risk-taking from which perpetrators derive thrill and excitement (Katz 1988). It is also well understood that offenders frequently attempt to normalise or rationalise their behaviour through denial and 'techniques of neutralisation' (Sykes and Matza 1957). But increasingly there is no need to neutralise that which is already normal and expected.

Criminals are no longer innovators in the Mertonian sense, seeking status by deviant means; they are just doing what everyone else is doing. Crime is increasingly 'generated less by a deficit than a hypertrophy of opportunities. It could be seen as the effect of the gigantic and uncontrolled proliferation of ways in which status can be achieved' (Ruggiero 1993: 135). Offenders are hardly aware of crossing the criminal threshold and their activities are normal, to be expected, and merging into wider categories of risky behaviour. The 'community' fragments into a diversity of activities and individuals taking and avoiding risks, victimising and being victimised. Who is a criminal or what is 'crime' begins to lose clarity. Criminalisation is simply a tactic for dealing with groups or individuals who constitute risks or obstructions. Where the poor and the socially excluded, as the new 'dangerous class' are concerned, this means everyone.

Criminality takes its place alongside the proliferations of sexual, ethnic and lifestyle-based identities as part of 'postmodern' diversity. Its normalisation returns us to many of the characteristics of *pre-modern* criminality; back towards the older mass criminality, discontinuous and pragmatic enforcement of law, the predominance of local norms in the practical definition of crime and risk, and away from the marginalised, clearly demarcated, criminality of modernity governed by the social relations of crime control.

Structural Normalisation

I have so far looked at the normalisation of crime from the standpoint of individuals: as problems to be responded to and as actions to be undertaken. This leads on to the further question of the relationship of criminality to the wider dynamics of economic and social life. Behind statistical and cultural normalisation of crime lies the issue of structural normalisation whereby certain types of crime increasingly function as a part of the reproduction of social and economic life rather than its episodic disruption or dysfunctional breakdown, The role of crime both as mode of capital accumulation and as a way of surviving its consequences becomes an increasingly important issue. In this way the criminal offender blurs back into the community not simply as a familiar figure engaged in uncontroversial activities but as a component of the way in which various quite normal communities reproduce themselves.

Social crime revisited

During the eighteenth century, a criminality of resistance to encroaching capitalism appeared as *social crime* (see Chapter 2). While never entirely disappearing in poor communities, it became marginalised with the development of modern institutions of the labour movement and welfare state as collective political solutions to social problems, combined with the generalisation of the wage relationship as the main source of income for the vast majority of the population. However, the decomposition of the welfare state and the return of substantial levels of joblessness or low-wage insecure employment, poverty and widening inequality provides a basis for a return, especially in poor communities, to the search for income sources other than through wages and employment (Vobruba 1998). On the legal side, new subsistence economies of direct exchange of labour and barter are expanding in many urban areas (Bennholdt-Thomsen and Mies 1999; Ruggiero 2001: 69). This has a general legitimising effect on non-market sources of income which, in turn, provide the context for a return to the 'tolerated illegalities' of an earlier period (Lea 1999). Shoplifting, defrauding public utilities such as gas and electricity, social security fraud, tax avoidance by small enterprises, smuggling of alcohol and tobacco to the United Kingdom (where taxation levied on these products is much higher than in nearby

Continental European countries), come readily to mind. Other forms of tolerated criminality which have always been inextricably linked with more destructive varieties are expanding. As Howard Parker and his colleagues noted, local heroin economies may be dependent on the willingness of the local poor to turn stolen goods into cash for the purchase of drugs.

> The presence of the 'straights', the coping poor of a region, particularly in recession and decline, is a prerequisite. The trading system or chain needs customers who will strike a bargain on the doorstep or in the local pub for something they want or need.... For them, taking the opportunity to supplement their often low standard of living seems common sense not crime. (Parker et al. 1988: 179)

In contrast to the social criminality of eighteenth-century England there is no alternative pre-capitalist culture or moral economy to be defended, and hence social crime easily passes, as noted earlier, into forms of petty capitalism and, if the activity is at all profitable, the involvement of professional crime. Elements of social crime, tolerated in poor communities as meeting needs, are likely to be tied up with more organised and harmful activities. The survival strategies of poor communities increase the hegemony of criminal groups as simultaneous sustainers and destroyers of the social fabric. The loanshark and his debt-collecting thugs are not far behind the shoplifter selling cheap stolen goods. But the very poor have little alternative as their social exclusion is reinforced by economic exclusion from access to credit (Leyshon and Thrift 1997). Nevertheless, widespread sanctioned activities which have a low entry cost, such as petty shoplifting or avoiding excise duty at ports, can remain popular pursuits despite the presence of professional organisations. Because the harmful and the beneficial (to the poor) criminal activities are frequently inextricably intertwined, it is necessary to avoid simply conflating them under a more generalised category of 'crime' which presupposes the type of consensus characteristic of functioning social relations of crime control. Like the commercial poachers of the eighteenth century, certain forms of organised criminality may operate against the background of a general toleration of the activity in which they engage. For example, a recent sensitive portrayal of the effects of poverty in a large northern English city reports that:

> The crime still flashed through the estate like flames on oil. One day, it was one of the Hooks using a stolen car as a battering ram to destroy a garage door. The next day, it was a woman who lived with one of the McGibbons, coming round the estate with carrier bags full of shoplifted clothes, selling them on the doorstep and taking orders for her next trip. 'Does your little boy want a tracksuit?' (Davies 1997: 64)

Crime both underlines and accentuates the destruction of community and at the same time provides resources for survival and defence. This reinforces the necessity of exploring the contradictory elements in criminal activities and how they interact. Communities vary as to their ability to withstand the anti-social and sustain the social varieties of criminality. What is undermined, as this type of situation becomes more common as part of the general expansion of the informal economy, is the fixed notions of offender and victim and the loyalties of the community to the latter and to the state which are central to the social relations of crime control. The existence of such economies of social crime has the consequence of weakening the practical criminalisation of forms of activity regarded as harmful. Communities with large economies of social crime may be reluctant to call the police into their areas to deal with anti-social crime for fear that these other illegalities will be discovered.

Forms of criminality differ, of course, in the extent and type of their normalisation. Neither the child abuser nor the rapist make any contribution whatsoever either to the accumulation of capital or to survival by the poor. For these forms of crime, normalisation is essentially a question of increasing frequency and unpredictability of occurrences. The street mugger or petty household burglar may be thought to fall in the same category. But it is here we see the central role played by economic criminality. Petty thieves need to sell their stolen goods for ready cash, frequently to purchase drugs. This links them not only to the locals who buy the stolen goods but to global financial markets, powerful political elites, multinational corporations and institutions not normally considered in any way as criminal.

Eighteenth-century social crime also combined economic with political resistance in conditions in which modern channels of political representation, negotiation and compromise had yet to emerge. The new direction of change outlined in the previous chapter points towards the continued expansion of forms of political and quasi-political protest which blur the boundaries between politics and criminality. Firstly, the growth of marginalised sections of the population, particularly the youth in poor working-class communities, who are effectively outside the channels of political representation, to whom political parties and the dominant political culture make little appeal, and whose experience of the state is most likely to be coercive and law-enforcement agencies,[2] constitute an obvious group to devise forms of rage, riot and episodic quasi-political protest. These necessarily take a theatrical and disruptive form – as in riot – not as a tactic in more organised and bureaucratised politics but as their substitute. They may involve harsh infliction on local communities already fragile through economic and social decay. From the standpoint of modern conceptions of organised political protest they appear unambiguously criminal, the elements of protest being revealed in a closer inspection. Thus the joyriding and racing of stolen cars by sizeable gatherings of unemployed youth in some British cities, mainly in the already deprived poor housing estates, was 'a particularly apt expression of the combination of marginality and relative deprivation, kids who are denied access to the labour market taking the status symbols of the consumer society and testing them to destruction!' (Lea and Young 1993: xxviii). The fusion of social and anti-social is not the collapse of the former without residue into the latter. It is the contradictory nature of such actions that need to be explored rather than dismissing them as forms of one-dimensional violence or a simplistic 'lawless masculinity' (Campbell 1993: 202).

Secondly, there has been a slow but steady growth in recent years of more overtly direct action protest movements, ranging from protests against the criminalisation of certain forms of open-field entertainment to direct action against road construction, blood sports and genetically modified food production. Among those mobilised by these actions involving criminal trespass and violation of property are young people drawn from the ranks of the socially excluded. Added to this, the weakening of the national state in the face of the power of multinational capital, the global interconnections of the latter which transcend national boundaries and forms of political representation, means that such movements can only confront the power nodes of global capital in particularly anarchistic and theatrical forms which usually involve confrontations with police and public order or trespass laws. This has been the case in recent years with forms of 'disorder' at meetings of such institutions as the World Trade Organisation and the European Union. These meetings of the global business and political elites increasingly take place in highly fortified locations secured against the 'political criminality' of the mob outside the barbed wire fences.

Capitalism and organised crime

Capitalism as a system of destructive self-reproduction changes the functionality of crime not only for the socially excluded at the bottom of society but also for capital itself, which is now busily destroying cities and communities, welfare and public goods, laying waste to large areas of the globe, undermining the basis of social cohesion as part of the normal 'legitimate' process of economic development. In such a context the 'innovatory' activities of criminals look increasingly normal from another standpoint: they are not just statistically normalised and familiar, constituting a category of risks to be managed, they are functionally normal, they express the general tendencies of the wider system itself. They are aspects of the form taken by capitalist development rather than its disruption. In the words of Italian criminologist Umberto Santino, we are reaching the stage at which '[e]vents formerly considered as "criminal ways to capitalism", occurring in peripheral zones and in secondary social spheres, have turned into "the criminal ways of capitalism and contemporary society"' (Santino 1988: 232). That is not to argue that crime is becoming less risky or hazardous in its effects, only that such activities are becoming characteristics of capitalism as a whole, something the system depends upon and integrates into its core dynamics, rather than as dysfunctional deviance.

Organised crime today is not only big business, it is part of big business. It has been estimated that by the middle of the 1990s the 'gross criminal product' of organised crime made it the twentieth richest organisation in the world and richer than 150 sovereign states (Castells 1998: 169). If we add such activities as computer fraud, animal smuggling, slavery (Bales 1999) and European Community fraud, the world's gross criminal product has been estimated at 20 percent of world trade (de Brie 2000). The criminal economy is a complex system of trading (in a variety of commodities: drugs, arms, radioactive material, people, body parts, sexual services, rare animals, art treasures) and manufacture, mainly drugs, conducted both at global levels and at micro-levels within inner cities, leisure areas, and in large areas of the legal economy. It is clear that any theory of modernisation predicting the marginalisation and peripheralisation of economic crime in the advanced capitalist societies is seriously mistaken. Such a hypothesis was based, as we have seen, on the assumption that economic expansion and welfare citizenship would undermine the recruitment base for professional or enterprise criminality, while the effective rational administration of the modern Keynesian welfare state would displace archaic patron–client relations characteristic of traditional mafia organisation and eliminate its channels of political influence at national and local levels. A further assumption was that many of the needs catered for by criminal markets would disappear or become legalised in the expanding modern mass consumption society.

The first point that both law enforcement agencies and governments frequently find difficulty in handling is that for those forms of organised criminality which involve clients purchasing services rather than victims being coerced, the demand for the product is a crucial variable. The resistance to starting from consumer demand (particularly in areas such as drugs and pornography) rather than criminal supply is not simply a feeling that this allows criminals to escape blame but also a refusal to engage in a critique of a society which expands and normalises the demand for such commodities. The use of hard drugs, sexual tourism, pornography and trafficking in women for prostitution have all expanded in recent years. All have been aided by the growth of internet communications and the opening up of eastern Europe as well as Africa and Asia (see Hartman 1998; Gery 1999; Hughes 1999). The image of a Fordist mass consumption culture based overwhelmingly on legitimate activities has fallen apart. For the affluent, the 'new times' of diversity of identities, increasing normalisation of drugs, aggression and individualism, meant the end of subcultures and the assimilation of 'perverted' needs to the status of lifestyle choice. Thus as far as organised criminal groups involved in drugs and vice are concerned, '[t]he 1990s is seen as a boom time for them, with the exploitation of a recreational western culture that wants its luxuries and its drugs. The legitimate businesses will run alongside the illegitimate ones.' (Campbell 1990: 8). The same goes for pornography where the illegal sector 'is the trailblazer. Where it goes, legitimate media must follow if they are not to allow the unscrupulous to walk away with the lion's share of the profits, and ultimately the whole business' (Greer 2000). Alongside the lifestyle choices of the rich, growing poverty and inequality have massively expanded the market for drugs and other activities of organised crime in poor communities where the social and physical damage is greatest.

The illegal sector also increasingly acts as an important social cushion against poverty and economic collapse.

> At a time of narrowing economic opportunity across wide areas of the world, participation in the illegal economy furthermore constitutes one of the few realistic options available to many families who simply need to ensure a basic level of subsistence. Illegality makes certain commodities or services unusually profitable. Thus the drug trade has become one of the central economic activities of the late twentieth century, drawing millions of people – from the peasant villages of Third World countries to the inner cities of the industrialized North – into networks of exchange which provide great wealth for some and a tolerable living for many who have limited alternative sources of income. (UNRISD 1994: 3)

Cocaine production acts as a counter to the impoverishment of Latin American peasant farmers, reducing the impact of falling world prices for agricultural products and raw materials in these areas, and so staving off rebellion. Attempts, usually financed by the United States, to eradicate coca production are periodically met with organised resistance (Thorpe 2000), and are in any case more concerned with suppressing political rebellion than drugs production – and may even encourage the latter (McCoy 1991; Scott and Marshall 1991; Monbiot 2001). Illegal imports of hard currency in Latin American drug-producing states, usually in US dollars, may help counteract the effects of export of profits by foreign companies and investors (Keh 1996; Santino 1988). To the extent that a proportion of profits from the drugs trade is reinvested in these countries – particularly in the purchase of newly privatised state assets – the legitimacy of the criminal groups in the eyes of the poor may be consolidated. The laundering of profits from the drugs trade helps sustain the growth of offshore banking facilities whose closure would have a devastating effect on already meagre living standards in the impoverished economies where they are located. In a similar way, drugs profits function, in both producing and consuming countries, as a source of capital and credit for legal enterprise, particularly small business, which also provides conduits for money laundering (Ruggiero 1993; Ruggiero and South 1995). Meanwhile dead-end low-wage jobs in poor communities do not enable escape from poverty into stable legal jobs but rather lead back into the criminal and informal economies. The networks of legal job search are often simultaneously those that yield information about criminal opportunities and the availability of drugs or cheap stolen goods (Smith and Macnicol 1999; Johnston et al. 2000). Organised crime does not simply move into legal business but also into white collar criminality. In the United States and in Italy traditional mafia families, driven out of their older drugs, vice and protection rackets, are moving into sophisticated financial fraud (Weiss 1996; Taylor 1997; Vulliamy 2000).

Drugs syndicates, meanwhile, are not run by philanthropists who invest in poor communities in defiance of the laws of capital accumulation. Workers and producers in the illegal sector are not protected from the rigours of the market and employment insecurity. Drugs are generally carried across international frontiers by unskilled and low-paid couriers, often young women from Third World poor communities who are ruthlessly exploited and end up in prostitution in the country of destination. High levels of burglary to secure money for drug purchases disrupt poor communities. Coca leaf or poppy farmers in Latin America or Asia at one end of the production chain, and street dealers at the other, are paid a pittance compared to the enormous profits made by criminal entrepreneurs, and profits from drug sales are increasingly less likely to be reinvested in local activities, either legal or illegal, than in global financial markets (Hagan 1994: 96). As it expands its scope of activities, organised crime's employment structure assimilates to that of legal employment with unskilled street workers facing scant chance of upward mobility (Ruggiero and South 1995; Bourgois 1996). The role of organised crime as the 'queer ladder of social mobility' is well past.

The fact that crime provides income for its employees and services for its customers does not mean it is not destructive, that it does not ruin lives and destroy already debilitated communities through violence and drug addiction. But legal capitalism does the same things in a less directly violent way and over a longer time span, through global warming, atmospheric pollution and the destruction of urban environments. Economic criminality becomes like legal capitalism because significant parts of the latter are becoming more like crime. Organised crime is increasingly a variant of 'impatient capital' operating under conditions in which violence and coercion in the short term are the viable roots to profits which can then be legalised by money laundering through by no means unreceptive banks and financial markets.

Such a view is anathema to those who insist on identifying a clearly distinct phenomenon associated with a criminal underworld distinct from, and entirely *parasitic* upon, the social and economic system of capitalism, and constituting a *unique threat* to both democracy and the efficiency of legal business (Lee 1999: 6–7). Organised crime is frequently seen as having replaced the old Soviet Union as the 'Evil Empire' (see for example Kerry 1997). For this reason the state chooses to represent organised crime as some alien and illegal financial enterprise, the eventual control of which rests in isolating and removing the key personalities within its organisational structure. In this way the state can rationally remove the focus of its control strategies from the wider reality of universally suspect business practice and bureaucratic compromise.... It can individualise the threat and make personal its motivations. (Findlay 1999: 157)

The more blurred the actual distinction between criminal and legitimate capital accumulation becomes, the higher the moral tone of law enforcement agencies as they desperately seek to retain the old clear distinctions between 'goodies and baddies' (Angell 1996).

The view of organised crime as some sort of exogenous parasite can be reinforced by attributing unequalled powers of corruption and contamination to criminal groups such that, for example, drugs trading is seen as a variety of self-creating pollution of the social body in which drug dealers create their own consumption demand through the diffusion of their highly addictive products (see for example Sterling 1990: 115–16). Even if it is admitted, more realistically, that the demand for drugs results from cultural values and social problems not attributable to organised crime itself, the parasitic view is ideologically sustained: who but criminals would consider responding to such pathological demands, widely agreed to be symptoms of social breakdown, in the first place! Conversely, the argument that organised crime would weaken if hard drugs were legalised and regulated like tobacco or pharmaceutical products sees criminality as the by-product of irrational state prohibition (as with alcohol in the United States during the 1920s). However, in the absence of criminal networks it is clear, as recent alleged bribery and smuggling activities of the tobacco industry might reveal (see Abrams and Rowell 2000), a business dealing in a legal, regulated and taxed drug is perfectly capable of acting like a criminal syndicate if profitability so dictates.

Other forms of organised crime present analogous issues.[3] Recently the smuggling of immigrants has come to be seen as equal to drugs in revenue and disruptive effects. The global mobility of capital and the impoverishment of large areas of Africa, Asia and eastern Europe create pressures for migration. The existence of state borders and immigration controls creates opportunities for criminal groups to turn well established drug-smuggling routes and techniques towards people smuggling. Criminal smugglers notoriously maltreat their human cargoes, many of whom find themselves working in virtual slavery (including forced prostitution) to pay off their debt to the smugglers. Mass-media focus on immigrants suffocating in sealed trucks or drowning at sea in overloaded boats shifts attention away from the fact that ruthless employers in both Europe and North America benefit from the starvation wages that can be paid to clandestine workers in seasonal employment such as fruit and vegetable picking (see for example Garrido and Prats 2000), in a variety of manufacturing sectors such as clothing and food, construction and agriculture, and in 'dirty economies' where semi-legal employment is interspersed with employment in more directly criminal activity (Ruggiero 1997). Again, a key aspect of contemporary capitalism can be presented as a problem of disruptive criminality.

As with the legalisation of hard drugs, the abolition of immigration controls would undercut the smugglers (Hayter 2000: 158). But it would simultaneously drive employers in legal sectors to find new sources of low-wage labour or move to lower-wage areas, where the brutality of criminal entrepreneurs is simply legitimate industrial relations. Indeed the global sphere of operations of multinational corporations enables capital to export its more brutal aspects to convenient locations in the southern hemisphere where 'workers have to contend with thugs hired by the bosses, blackleg trade unions, strike-breakers, private police and death squads' (de Brie 2000: 4). Such brutal labour regimes in Third World countries can then be presented as characteristic of the 'lack of governance' in these societies and nothing to do with the dynamics of global capitalism in general, whereas they are expressions of the fact that 'corporations find it less and less possible to operate without engaging in criminal activity' (Bello 2001: 16; see also Mokhiber and Weissman 1999).

The driving force behind such developments is of course the need to secure the profitability of capital. This leads to intensifying competition and so to the blurring of legal and illegal activity. Capitalism has reached the stage where the incentive to break the very rules it put in place to stabilise the system as a whole is becoming irresistible. But globally there is no 'system as a whole', only the relentless competition between multinational corporations and banks for profits. There is no state apparatus to represent the interests of 'capital in general' (let alone 'society') from which standpoint individual companies or banks must be penalised if they break the rules (see Mészáros 1998). The transition to a globalised capitalism is not, as some writers see it, towards some new stable form of 'empire' (see Hardt and Negri 2000) governed by cordial relations between corporations and banks, articulated through such bodies as the World Trade Organisation with national states in the background as a back-up resource, but a growing anarchy of intense competition in which breaking every rule in the book comes naturally and the power of national states to intervene is debilitated.

It is of course useful if illegal activities by large corporations are farmed out to distinct organised criminal groups who have 'nothing to do' with the legal world and can be kept at a distance, so that it appears that crimes 'that are functional for a particular industry are committed by actors who are not only not of that industry but are of a totally different economic world, the "underworld"' (Szasz 1986: 26). This is only one example of a growing structure of mutual exchanges and a widening spectrum of reciprocal services between the legal and illegal sectors of capital (Ruggiero 1996, 2000). The result is that '[l]egitimate and criminal interests have become so intertwined in some parts of the world that the frontier between the two has become purely theoretical' (Geopolitical Drug Watch 1999: 10).

The legal financial sector meanwhile, with an eye on the growing wealth of organised crime, may go out of its way to attract criminal investments. The closure of the Bank of Credit and Commerce International in 1991 gave a glimpse of the tip of an iceberg whereby legitimate private banks and investment traders openly tout for legal and illegal funds without making a fuss about the distinction between the two (Kochan and Whittington 1991; see also Chossudovsky 1996; de Brie 2000). A further indicator is the fact that legitimate capital is turning to the same tactics as organised crime. The activity of drugs cartels laundering their profits through 'offshore' banking facilities (banks in states which guarantee zero taxation of deposits and absolute secrecy about the identity of investors) 'pales, however, beside the gigantic losses to the public purse that result from the legally organised flight of capital' (Martin and Schumann 1997: 63). Legitimate capital enhances its power over governments to reduce tax burdens not only with the threat to relocate plant but also by adopting the tactics of organised crime. Indeed, criminal capital forces legitimate capital to compete with it to overcome the 'burden' of having to pay at least some minimal tax revenue (Shelley 1998: 608–9).

Finally, the growing interaction between organised crime and legitimate business is reflected at the level of organisation. Rather than modernisation weakening organised crime, much of the latter has modernised in the form of an expansion of an 'entrepreneurial' crime closer to the model of professional crime and characterised by fluid and shifting structures in which [t]here are no key players ... no ring leaders, bosses or godfathers. It is a co-operative, a series of temporary social arrangements that enables a constantly changing group of actors to make money from predominantly criminal opportunities' (Hobbs 1998: 413; see also Carter 1997: 139). The organisational form of entrepreneurial crime, whose aim is simply to accumulate profit, is precisely that of the modern, flexible, postfordist business organised to respond to rapidly changing market conditions as well as to evade the taxation powers of the nation state.

The Resurgence of Criminal Governance

I noted previously Foucault's characterisation of pre-modern society as one in which the emphasis by the ruling class on sovereignty as an 'irregular and discontinuous power ... 'left the subjects free to practise a constant illegality' (Foucault 1977: 88). Growing inequalities of wealth and resources, compounded by the increasingly episodic and fractured exercise of state power, in a growing number of areas from inner cities to chaotic ungovernable regions of the Third World, create spaces in which forms of criminal governance can move from the periphery, to which it was assumed that modernisation would continually relegate them, back to the centre to become increasingly important players in global capitalism.

I have also noted the three strategies whereby criminal organisation can challenge the law enforcement agencies of the modern state to either retain or increase its power and autonomy: by appropriating the functions of law enforcement as a rival system of governance and coercive sovereignty, by neutralising its activities through corruption and intimidation of criminal justice officials or political leaders at a national or local level, and by simply evading the reach of state authority altogether by retreating to areas where it does not reach. Similar processes are at work in the relationship between crime and various types of communities. Let us first deal with the question of evasion.

Sanctuary and disguise

In previous chapters I noted the weakness of the state, its lack of complete dominance over its own national terrain during the early stages of modernisation as an important factor in the power of criminal groups to secure their survival and organisation. Areas of sanctuary, places where criminal fraternities or groups could rest and recoup, relatively secure from the reach of the law enforcement agencies were often areas where criminals had come to some understanding with local communities by, for example, providing some local services, agreeing to keep their criminal activities elsewhere, in return for turning a 'blind eye' and refusal to aid law enforcement. In other cases sanctuaries were also systems of criminal governance either in opposition to the state, as, for example, with coastal smuggling communities in which most local people were involved in economies based on crime, or in various degrees of collusion with the state, as was the case with the traditional Sicilian mafia. I also noted how modernisation involved the national state apparatus consolidating its territorial dominance such that the survival of sanctuaries either at the rural periphery or in urban strongholds was undermined. Old criminal fraternities declined and new forms of professional crime turned increasingly to strategies involving disguise and avoidance of the state while traditional forms of organised crime attempted to confront the state through corruption and intimidation.

A feature of the present period is the re-emergence of some of these older forms of criminal sanctuary. In the context of the modern urban crisis the fragmentation of public space into a mosaic of safe and unsafe, the retreat of citizens behind locked doors and fortified estates leaves the streets, public parks and spaces to the criminal. The modern inner city housing estate and ghetto may become the equivalent of the Victorian rookery. Episodic and fractured governance by law enforcement agencies and private property interests which leave large areas as social and economic rubbish tips create obvious sanctuary to petty and organised crime. Likewise various regions of the globe are in the process of degenerating into 'ungovernable chaotic entities' in which 'huge areas of the world already lie outside the jurisdiction of any state' (George 1999: 13), and provide sanctuaries for powerful criminal organisations alongside terrorists and warlords.

But one of the most important developments of the present period is the reappearance of sanctuary in a completely new guise: that of the network society. As Castells points out:

> The technological and organisational opportunity to set up global networks has transformed, and empowered, organized crime. For a long time, its fundamental strategy was to penetrate national and local state institutions in its home country, in order to protect its activities.... This is still an important element in the operational procedures of organized crime: it can only survive on the basis of corruption and intimidation of state personnel and, sometimes, state institutions. However, in recent times, globalisation has added a decisive twist to the institutional strategy of organised crime... the high mobility and extreme flexibility of the networks makes it possible to evade national regulations and the rigid procedures of international police cooperation. (Castells 1998: 202; see also van Duyne 1997)

The eighteenth-century problem of an ineffective state apparatus, unable to secure the national terrain, now reappears in the form of the absence of a global state. Newer flexible forms of criminal organisation and methods of work, highly adapted to the new fast-moving global networks, find new forms of disguise in sophisticated money laundering techniques and a new virtual sanctuary in the interstices of the global society of nation states and law enforcement agencies. In the use of encrypted electronic mail, anonymous Web sites and the myriad of instantaneous transactions which constitute the Internet in general and financial markets in particular, the legal and the illegal are increasingly indistinguishable and, where distinguished, unpursuable by national law enforcement agencies. Criminality is normalised by the networks: it inhabits a new global 'grey area' where the distinction between legal and illegal evaporates in the absence of the state. The conditions of nineteenth-century Sicily are reproduced in a new form in the global network society (see Cavallaro 2001).

Neutralisation and corruption

But organised crime groups still need to neutralise the state to protect territory and markets, crucial shipments of commodities, or drug-refining laboratories, and corruption by intimidation or bribery is still a vital strategy. There are two aspects to the linkages between the state and criminal enterprise. Firstly, the state is opened up again as a resource for criminal or corporate profit-taking through clientalism and the corruption of state officials. Modernisation theory assumed that the development of capitalism would marginalise clientalism and corruption as impersonal bureaucratic and legal procedures were recognised as the only appropriate framework for the management of a state apparatus which guaranteed the open competition for resources demanded by capital. This thinking also lay behind the assumed decline in the power of traditional organised crime discussed in Chapter 4. The development of even the minimal American version of the Keynesian welfare state was seen as a factor undermining corrupt city politics, while the more elaborate western European welfare systems impeded its emergence. The survival and resurgence of powerful criminal organisations with the capacity to corrupt or intimidate state agencies was widely seen as a symptom of backwardness characteristic of regions as yet unclaimed by modernisation and sustained capitalist development. Italy, where organised crime successfully captured aspects of the modernisation process, such as the allocation of public construction contracts and the development of new mutually beneficial relations with sections of the political elite, or Latin American states with large politically powerful criminal groups sustaining various types of corrupt relations with the state and political parties, could be interpreted as characterised by a 'failure to modernise'.

However, this approach is now superseded by developments in the real world. On a global level, the dynamics of modernisation now accentuate more than ever both global and local inequalities of income and resources, and involve the destruction both of local communities and in some cases of entire territories as functioning socio-economic systems. Backwardness or underdevelopment is thus revealed as an aspect of modernisation itself, including that of the most advanced democratic states. As with organised crime, modernisation, far from eliminating corruption, has simply modernised its forms.

> It appears that corruption has increased – taking on new forms – rather than decreasing or being eradicated, insinuating itself into the increasingly complex relations between state and market, feeding off the changing needs created by new mechanisms of political consensus formation ('politics as spectacle') and the crisis of political activism, and taking advantage of new techniques of mediation and management of the financial resources for corruption. (della Porta and Vannucci 1999: 7)

The weakening of the national state as overall co-ordinator of social and economic policy in the face of globalisation and economic deregulation discussed in the previous chapter and the increased pressure and lobbying by wealthy interest groups able to influence, and on occasion 'buy', ministers and members of parliaments or assemblies, creates an environment conducive to, and partly legitimising of, new forms of clientalism and corruption. This process occurs in all the advanced democracies. The increasingly clientalist structure of the state strengthens organised crime as much as the power of the latter enables it to penetrate otherwise clean government. Alison Jamieson argues that, in the Italian context,

> [t]he growth of the Mafia... is organically linked to a degeneration in the exercise of political power.... The decline of ethics in Italian politics has created a vacuum into which criminality has extended its influence, if not always its presence. More organised crime is the effect, not the cause, of this decline. (Jamieson 1990: 28)

This process takes different forms in different areas. In Italy older traditions of clientalism are continued and modernised and constitute an environment in which traditional forms of organised crime may perpetuate themselves, as with the penetration of organised crime into the allocation of public contracts in Sicily. The same structures also provided an environment for the wholesale bribery of public officials by respectable multinational companies in the 'bribesville' scandals of 1992 in northern Italy. But if the latter was an example of the special pathological backwardness of the Italian political system, then of course ongoing police investigation in Germany of over 2,000 corruption cases a year, many of them linking politicians and industrialists (Griffin 2000), must also be regarded as symptomatic of backwardness. Likewise the revelations of massive fraud in the European Union (Warner 2000). The term becomes entirely vacuous when corruption becomes a general characteristic of the political systems of the most advanced capitalist societies differentiated only by historical and national variations.

Finally, the rolling back of the Keynesian welfare state through increased privatisation of public assets has given massive encouragement to clientalism and corruption at all levels. On a global level recent decades saw the enforcement by the World Bank and International Monetary Fund of the privatisation of state assets as part of structural adjustment programmes enforced upon Third World economies and the former state-managed economies of eastern Europe in return for financial aid. Massive acquisition of privatised state assets by criminal organisations gave an important boost to Russian organised crime (Goldman 1995; Handelman 1995; Williams 1997). At a local level even in the advanced democratic states the subcontracting of services by national or local state agencies gives opportunities to corrupt and criminal business to siphon off resources and engage in fraudulent manipulation of contracts. This in turn fosters the re-emergence of 'machine' politics as politicians become bought by those interests seeking favourable treatment, and those seeking democratic accountability and scrutiny are bribed or intimidated. Democratic scrutiny is undermined by privatisation and subcontracting as local or national political elites can absolve themselves of public responsibility for those activities which have been handed over to private companies. The development of private security also gives new opportunities for organised criminal groups, from providing night club 'bouncers' and private guards. The traditional functions of the mafia of private protection compensating for a weak state now take on new market forms where the state is again privatising and curtailing its protection functions (see Gambetta 1993).

These conditions, combined with the increased income generated by organised crime facilitate the protection of its particular interests through neutralisation and corruption strategies. Again, national peculiarities are important. There is in northern European democracies such as the United Kingdom little evidence of direct relations between organised crime and factions of the political or state elite. Corruption is at a much lower level. But the point is that the tendency, even in this highly 'modernised' democracy, is towards expansion. Low-level police corruption is currently at an all-time high. The UK National Criminal Intelligence Service (NCIS) allegedly recently regarded police corruption as having reached 'third world levels' (Seed and Palmer 1998). In a backhanded acknowledgement of the increasing resources at the disposal of organised crime for corruption purposes the NCIS argued in a recent report that

> [a] development which may affect the liability of police officers to be corrupted has been the restructuring of pay and conditions in recent years. Reductions in pay and allowances for more recent recruits might well result in them being more vulnerable to corruption. (NCIS 2000: 9)

Direct rule and sovereignty

The need to defend terrain, whether for the manufacturing of illegal commodities or protection of market areas, brings us to the question of the revival of criminal rule, of criminal groups substituting for the state and becoming the source of governance and sovereignty in those areas where the state has been kept at bay by various corruption and neutralisation strategies or has simply vacated areas considered no longer crucial to the accumulation of capital. Older systems of criminal governance which formerly accommodated with a weak state may attempt to retain domination of territory in traditional ways. Thus, a recent study of the Sicilian mafia has argued that the organisation has not made a complete transition to a system of entrepreneurial organised crime, but continues to focus on the traditional aims of dominance of territory while 'discarding safer and possibly more profitable investments abroad' in favour of the primary goal of 'the establishment of power over the local community' (Paoli 1998: 279–80; see also Paoli 2000). This strategy has led since the beginning of the 1980s to an increasingly violent confrontation with the state, which of course is strong in peripheral regions, unlike in the earlier epoch of mafia hegemony. Such a conflict is ultimately detrimental to even illegal profit opportunities.

The fact is, however, that increases in global inequality, social fragmentation, and the fracturing of governance both in modern cities and entire regions are now recreating areas in which criminal and other organisation can inaugurate systems of what Kevin Stenson (1998, 1999) has termed 'governance from below', emanating from

> organised crime and other illegal economic networks; gang and subcultural networks of young men on the streets ... paramilitary groups like the IRA and UDA in Ireland, Basque separatists in Spain ... and warlords in ex-Yugoslavia.... In these areas, the authority of the institutions of the nation state have weakened and the dense, relatively autonomous provinces and practices of liberal institutions have yet to develop, or struggle with a variety of authoritarian political movements and social practices. (Stenson 1999: 60)

A weak state apparatus may be simply pillaged and transformed into an instrument of such factions with the result that 'no one can tell any longer which parts of the state apparatus still defend the rule of law, and which have been contracted by one set of criminals to wage war on their rivals' (Martin and Schumann 1997: 210). Such a situation describes the *ungovernable chaotic entities* characterised by

> the state's inability to maintain control of its national territory and population. Whole sectors of the economy, towns, provinces and regions fall under the yoke of new warlords, drug traffickers or Mafia. Respect for law and order and the institutions of civil society evaporate. The people fall prey to armed groups, and then come to rely, not on government or national authorities, but on humanitarian organisations such as the International Red Cross, Médecins sans Frontières and Oxfam, and various branches of the United Nations. (de Rivero 1999)

This weakness is directly related to the dynamics of global capitalism and the policies it forces on Third World countries. In sub-Saharan Africa, for example, the collapse of political rule into forms of criminal activity 'has become the dominant trait of a sub-continent in which the state has literally imploded under the combined effects of economic crisis, neo-liberal programs of structural adjustment and the loss of legitimacy of political institutions' (Bayart et al. 1999: 19).

Forms of counter-governance by 'post-state' organisations (see George 1999: 101) taking the form of organised crime, terrorist or guerrilla groups also enter into conflict situations and the fighting of the 'new wars' which have tended, in the period since the ending of the Cold War, to replace classic conflicts between nation states. New forms of warfare, like organised criminality, exhibit a similar indifference to national state boundaries. Mary Kaldor, observing the wars in former Yugoslavia during the 1990s, describes the ingredients of new military machines as including 'a disparate range of different types of groups such as paramilitary units, local warlords, criminal gangs, police forces, mercenary groups and also regular armies including breakaway units of regular armies' (Kaldor 1999: 8). This blurring of criminality and warfare results in a situation in which

> no one knows who should be considered 'as a criminal', who are 'the police', and who are 'the army'. Criminals become incorporated into formal control agencies and criminal behaviour is not only unpunished – it is even regarded as desirable as a strategy of inter-ethnic war. (Nikolic-Ristanovic 1998: 475)

In short a complete rupture of crime control. Criminality may function as a direct organised component of warfare as in organised rape and mass killings of non-combatant civilians (see Jamieson 1998). Crime is normalised as an essential ingredient of military strategy. Finally, the distinction between economic criminality and political aims such as ethnic emancipation can become intertwined with conflict over access to resources such as oil fields and pipelines (see Luttwak 1998: 171), as well as criminal trading routes for drugs, arms and illegal migration. Guerrilla organisations whose aim is the emancipation of oppressed communities are frequently linked to organised criminal networks who act as their arms suppliers in return for facilitation of drugs production and trafficking routes (Chossudovsky 1999). Such arrangements may constitute a modern variant of the 'social banditry' celebrated by Eric Hobsbawm (Hobsbawm 1969; see Chapter 2 above).

This might seem less a form of governance than chaos. But even in such chaotic zones populations may be managed and co-ordinated by such means, for example, organised into conduits for immigrant or drug smuggling, or into armed groups for the protection of resources vital for multinational capital such as oil pipelines or diamond deposits. Such criminal groups may be regarded by some as forms of 'transitional governance' awaiting the stabilisation of more modern state institutions. Russian organised crime, expanding rapidly after the collapse of the Soviet Union and, as noted already, facilitated by large-scale privatisation of state assets, has been portrayed by some imaginative commentators as a necessary transitional phenomenon between the old Soviet system and a new dynamic capitalism. In this argument organised crime takes the form of an embryonic business class analogous to the nineteenth-century American 'robber barons' who broke every rule in the book but nevertheless developed the capitalist economy. Additionally, the weakness of the Russian state creates a situation, analogous in some ways to nineteenth-century Sicily (Varese 1994), in which the mafia provides the only viable form of governance. From this standpoint

> Russia's criminal world ... has become the only force that can give stability, that is capable of stamping out debts, of guaranteeing the banks repayment of loans

and of considering property disputes efficiently and fairly. The criminal world has essentially taken on the state functions of legislative and judicial authority. (Leitzel 1995: 43; see also Williams 1997: 6–7)

Such a view accommodates easily to a variant of modernisation theory which sees criminality as a feature of rapid *transition* to capitalism rather than illustrative of any general tendencies in mature capitalism. The fact is, however, that at least some of the wealth of American ruthless capitalists such as John D. Rockefeller or Cornelius Vanderbilt (see Abadinsky 1994) was reinvested under conditions favourable to sustained economic development. In Russia the irony of a group of thugs, who have 'contributed nothing, produced nothing, risked nothing … who simply robbed what was there … manipulating the country's currency, destabilising its fragile economy, stripping it of its oil, gold, timber …' (Sterling 1994: 96–7; see also Anderson 1995) being taken seriously as a business class is that they indeed represent something, albeit in an exaggerated form, of the future for capitalism as a whole under conditions of destructive self-reproduction. Capitalism is indeed developing apace in Russia but it is the type of capitalism which portends the future of the system as a whole: increasingly breaking its own rules of legality in order to maintain the short-term rate of profit, the wholesale wrecking of national economies through export of capital, by both legal and illegal means, to areas of higher profitability and the justification of these activities by an aggressive ethic of cynical self-interest. The character of organised crime as fundamentally parasitic, as a variety of 'unfair competition' in which the enforcement of monopolies through bribery and violence increases costs, creates market uncertainties and instabilities, and diverts productive capital to short-term speculative activities aimed at high profits (Drucker 1981; Reuter 1983), is an increasingly important *tendency* of the capitalist system as a whole. If unchecked, the end result will be a new form of barbarism, appropriately termed by Susan George 'gangster capitalism' which

> [i]f it succeeds in supplanting legitimate business, traditional rules of competition would be blasted to bits while corporate terrorism would become the order of the day. Today's relatively predictable business climate would be replaced by durable anarchy and a Hobbesian war of all against all among individuals, firms and nations. (George 1999: 15)

Under such a nightmare scenario law enforcement would be recruited by capital as simply another weapon against competitors. This is at present some way off. But the point is that the tendencies of global development under conditions of destructive reproduction of capital point in its direction: counter-tendencies are much weaker, either in the form of a resurgent organised modernity of strong Keynesian welfare states and economic planning or of new oppositional social movements.

Finally, at a micro and more local level such tendencies are observable in the advanced capitalist countries in the inner cities and ghettos in areas vacated by capital and subject only to episodic incursion by law enforcement and other agencies of legitimate governance. Increasingly secure in these new criminal 'rookeries', linked to public bodies and legal organisation through networks of corruption and clientalism, and dominating communities through fear and intimidation, criminality acts as co-ordinator and regulator. In the United States Tim Luke (1996) describes the extreme variant: a situation in which

> mafia potentates in New York, Asian crime gangs, Jamaican posses, Haitian toughs, Colombian drug lords, and Nigerian syndicates all are exercising extraordinary levels of quasi-legitimate coercive and commercial power in hundreds of housing projects, poor neighborhoods, and city halls all over the United States – those who dissent against them can be tortured, those who oppose them are murdered, those who accept them are exploited, those who openly embrace them can be served. Consequently, everyday politics in many places appears to become what power games always were without a pretext of legitimate governmentalizing authority: the conduct of war, crime, and exploitation by other means.' (Luke 1996; see also Davis 1990, 1998)

This form of surrogate sovereignty is not simply pure force. The control over territory required by a criminality oriented to the manufacture and sale of consumer products such as drugs cannot, on the one hand, simply assume the tactic of disguise and evasion of the state as can the predatory crime of the professional thief. But neither is there any desire for the type of hegemony over *communities* characteristic of the traditional mafia. There is rather a specific need to secure key distribution and sales outlets such as night clubs and other spaces. This can lead to a violent control over territory, pure terror without the functionality – such as mediation of local disputes – which forms of organised crime more closely rooted in communities were, and are, able to perform. It is, nevertheless, even in this negative mode, a form of governance from below, supervising and co-ordinating populations in a spectrum of criminal activities which Manuel Castells has appropriately termed *perverse integration*. In such areas

> [t]he informal economy, and particularly the criminal economy, become prevalent in many poor neighborhoods, which become the shopfloor of these activities, and increasingly influence the habits and culture of segments of their population. The explosion of crack cocaine's traffic and consumption in the black ghettos in the 1980s was a turning point for many communities. Gangs become important forms of youth organisation and patterns of behaviour. Guns are, at the same time, working tools, signs of self esteem, and motives for peers' respect. Widespread presence of guns calls for more guns, as everybody rushes to self defense, after police give up serious law enforcement in a number of poor neighborhoods. Economic transactions in these inner-city areas often become marked by the criminal economy, as a source of work and

income, as demand generating activities, and as the operational unit for protection/taxation in the informal economy. Economic competition is often played out through violence, thus further destroying community life, and increasingly identifying gangs with surviving social networks, with the crucial exception of community-based churches. (Castells 1998: 141–2)

Such phenomena, covering large areas of many American cities stand midway between chaotic ungovernable regions in many parts of the Third World and the smaller, and as yet less organised, criminal ghettos of west European societies.

Conclusion

I have tried to give an illustration of *tendencies at work*, tendencies whose pace of development differs profoundly between countries, communities and types of crime. Nevertheless the tendencies are clear: that the social relations of crime control, rather than being consolidated as in earlier periods of modernisation, are weakening and fragmenting. In this chapter I have focused on changes in the nature of criminal activity and have emphasised three in particular. Firstly, there is the weakening identity of many types of crime and offenders and their blurring into wider categories of risk, such that criminalisation starts to lose its taken-for-granted and accepted sets of definitions about what is crime and who are criminal offenders. As these become more contingent, criminality on the one hand becomes more normal and everyday while, on the other, suitable targets for moral panics can more easily be constructed and public worry about crime can happily co-exist with declining rates of 'real' offending. Crime begins to become a metaphor for general insecurities of life in the fragmenting city.

Secondly, there is the growing reintegration of many forms of crime into the structures of normal social and economic activity. Crime, as social crime, as buying and selling of hard drugs, as money laundering, becomes part of the way the economic system works rather than its breakdown or disruption. As a consequence the sections of the population who have no interest in furnishing an information flow to the authorities about certain types of crime – the poor benefiting from informal economies of stolen or smuggled goods, consumers of hard drugs, employers of low-wage labour, financial dealers turning a blind eye to money laundering, and corrupt officials – tend to expand rather than contract. The working of crime control is weakened.

Thirdly, the power of criminality to establish forms of governance over local communities and to neutralise state law enforcement activities also increases under the impact of the increasing wealth and sophistication of criminal enterprise, the undermining of the competence of national states in a global context, together with the undermining of effective governance in many urban areas and in whole regions. An important effect is to reinforce the decay of politics and the public sphere. Active participation and discourse, the mobilisation of interests in open forums is obstructed by fear, collusion, conspiracy and violence both within the state apparatus itself and in the relationship between the state and communities. The debilitation of the state (see Chapter 5) is further reinforced.

Nevertheless, in democratic states, the state remains the central organisation to which the bulk of the population turn to remedy social problems including crime. This remains the case notwithstanding the changes outlined in this chapter. I therefore turn to the measures which states and communities develop in an attempt to rescue crime control and counteract some of the developments I have briefly outlined in this chapter.

Notes

1 Rational choice theory is still flawed, however, by virtue of its assumption that offenders necessarily calculate the costs and benefits of their actions in a precise way (see Trasler 1986). In failing to behave like accountants they are also, however, acting as entirely normal individuals!

2 See the discussion of socialisation through crime control in the next chapter.

3 Only about 40 percent of the criminal money laundered through international banks is thought to emanate from the drugs trade (Strange 1998: 124).

7

The Decomposition of Crime Control

What are the forces at work governing crime control in the twenty-first century? I have suggested that the social relations of crime control which enable the functioning of criminal law and the state as the regulators of interpersonal conflicts and harms, have moved, during the various stages of modernity from the eighteenth to the twenty-first centuries, from being broadly consolidated to being gradually undermined. The latter process has been reflected, as I argued in the previous chapter, by changes in the nature of criminality itself. These comprised, firstly, the blurring of the boundaries of criminalisation: its increasing normalisation as both experience and motivation, and the loss of clearly marked identities of criminal offenders and the activities they undertake. Secondly, an aspect of this blurring was the increasing integration of criminality into the dynamics of social and economic life. In this process of increasing structural normalisation, criminality becomes, as it was in an earlier period, an increasingly important component of the survival both of poor communities and of powerful business groups. From car-boot sales to corporate tax avoidance, from the aggression on inner city housing estates to the aggression of financial speculation, criminality is part of the way capitalist society works, rather than a departure from the norm. Finally, in such an environment, various types of criminal groups, irrespective of their identities and visibility, were growing more powerful. From local criminals intimidating poor communities to powerful international groups intimidating states or rendering them irrelevant in the global networks, the capacity of organised criminality to secure its environment and protect its activities is increasing. These processes are not taking place evenly or equally either geographically or for all varieties of crime. They impact less on formal legal categories which can remain untouched by the dynamics of actual social relations, but are by contrast crucial for the process of practical criminalisation.

But alongside changes in the nature of crime are the broader social changes, which I argued in Chapter 5 were derived from the dynamics of capitalism in an epoch of 'slow crisis' or destructive self-reproduction. Firstly, there was a decline in socialisation, or the concern of ruling elites with the adaptation and integration of the working class. This is reflected in the decline of welfare citizenship and compromise in favour of a concern for security and the management of risk as the determinant of the relationship between social groups and classes. Under conditions of the 'death of the social', policy becomes increasingly concerned with security, border patrol – keeping risky groups at a distance. The demise of welfare and the weakening of the state has off-loaded many security functions on to private property and individuals, to the detriment of poor communities too fragmented to sustain much notion of collective security. The state, meanwhile, in becoming increasingly concerned with the management of the socially excluded rather than their inclusion, also blurs the boundaries between crime control and the general control of population through various strategies of prevention, which merge the control of criminality with that of a widening spectrum of individuals and activities considered undesirable and risky.

In turning, then, to look in some more detail at changes in the working of the state as regards crime control, we encounter a paradox. Although the shift to risk management has been reflected in various developments which undermine the working of the social relations of crime control, criminalisation as a way of managing an increasing variety of socio-economic problems and behaviours is increasing. The positive aspect of this is a growing concern for social justice while the negative aspect is that criminalisation as a way of achieving *social* justice faces formidable obstacles. In this latter sense the advance of criminalisation is an obvious result of the relative decline of mechanisms of collective negotiation and planning characteristic of the Keynesian welfare state. Social problems are increasingly seen as individual problems of behaviour and responsibility rather than as collective political issues of resource allocation, while the state turns to criminal law rather than to social planning as the preferred form of intervention and regulation of social processes. Thus

> as our social and political institutions resort to criminal enforcement in response to a greater and greater diversity of social problems, so the procedural means of enforcement are developing and diversifying apace. In the face of this diversity it is impossible to identify a unified practice of criminalisation in terms of distinctive procedural approaches. Indeed, it is increasingly difficult to be certain where the boundaries between criminal and non-criminal (administrative, civil, regulatory) enforcement can be said to lie. (Lacey 1995: 21)

Thus in fact increasing criminalisation reflects the same tendencies as resort to risk management and prevention. The former is frequently the legal underpinning of the latter. Social policy as crime control presupposes the translation of social problems into individual actions and responsibilities – and individual private responsibility for taking preventative measures. Social problems appear as crime problems at the same time as crime merges into wider problems of risk and security. The result is the general criminalisation of the socially excluded poor, the new 'dangerous class' (see Gordon 1994).

Dangerous Classes and Powerful Offenders

An important aspect of the increasing authoritarianism of the state involves the devising of new legal and administrative measures to facilitate the working of generalised management of the poor. The dynamic of the social relations of crime control of the criminal as clearly identified and proceeded against by both state and community, never of course completely secured, now collapses into a more contradictory set of relationships which end up leaving the state freer to elaborate its own criminalisation tasks in a more practical, contingent and flexible way. Not all of these are by any means out of tune with popular concerns (but see below), but the autonomy of the authorities, the police in particular, frees them up to respond to the security agenda involving the policing and border patrol of entire communities, a return to the concern with the 'dangerous classes'. The regime in such areas is increasingly *episodic, contingent* and *fractured*. It becomes an erratic oscillation between no policing at all and a punitive sovereignty (Garland 1996; Stenson 2000) of 'military policing' aided by devices such as blanket curfews in poor areas prohibiting young people in general from public places between certain hours, all of which blur the distinction between actual criminal offenders and poor populations in general (Kinsey et al. 1986; Lea and Young 1993). Episodic police forays into poor communities or (largely localised and temporary) regimes of 'zero tolerance' policing in which even minor infringements of criminal law are acted upon, gradually and incrementally replace negotiation, compromise and police–community relations. This continual blurring of criminality and normal life by the law enforcement process, emulating a return to the earliest stages of modernisation, is the driving force of 'actuarial' criminal justice.

> The term 'dangerous classes' was widely used in the late eighteenth and early twentieth centuries to convey that portion of the population that is 'rabble' and inherently dangerous…. Indeed, discussion of crime in late-eighteenth century England may closely parallel recent developments in actuarial justice. (Feeley and Simon 1994: 198)

It is important to avoid a simplistic view of such policing as pure oppression in which criminality plays no part. Poor communities are, as already noted, frequently areas of criminal governance largely left to their own devices by the state. There is a more complex interplay, reminiscent of eighteenth-century social crime (see Chapter 2) in which wholesale criminality – much of it normalised and of a 'social' nature – is the reverse side of episodic general policing. Governance by crime and by the control of crime comes to constitute a self-reinforcing circuit in which poor areas and redundant populations are both left to their own devices and at the same time neutralised as a threat to the zones and activities more productive to capital accumulation.

What is missing from the twenty-first-century version of policing the dangerous zones is therefore the dimension of 'moral improvement by police' articulated by nineteenth-century reformers such as Patrick Colquhoun. It is not that this function has been taken over by social work and the welfare state: these are now in terminal crisis. Policing is the task of minimising the risk constituted by poor populations. Governance as policing no longer counters social exclusion of the poor, but serves to reproduce it. David Garland notes 'the emergence of a more divisive exclusionary project of punishment and police' in which

> [u]nlike the penal-welfare strategy, which was linked into a broader politics of social change and a certain vision of social justice – however flawed in conception and execution – the new penal policies have no broader agenda, no strategy for progressive social change and no concern for the overcoming of social divisions. They are, instead, policies for managing the danger and policing the divisions created by a certain kind of social organisation, and for shifting the burden of social control on to the individuals and organisations that are often poorly equipped to carry out this task. (Garland 1996: 466)

The complaint of residents of poor inner city and other deprived areas is thus as much against under-policing as over-policing (see for example, Campbell 1993; Susser 1995). Policing is of the 'fire brigade' style not because informal crime control can be taken for granted as in the modern middle-class neighbourhood, but because the police in such areas no longer see it as their task to engage in general protection. This is not some special neglect of duty by the police, but rather an echo of the general dynamics of social fragmentation. As with traditional welfare issues such as poverty and social exclusion, the basic question is who has an interest in overall social cohesion as opposed to the containment and border patrol of redundant populations? This is an important political dimension of the 'death of the social': the continual weakening of political concern with overall social cohesion. As far as policing is concerned, even in middle-class areas there is a growing list of 'normalised' crime to which police divert only a purely symbolic attention, shifting the burden on to the community and individual to take preventative measures. Crime control becomes subject to all manner of efficiency audits which legitimise the abandonment of the general right of all citizens to protection. The question of effectiveness is translated, as in other areas of social provision, to one of conformity to internally self-referential performance indicators disconnected from any notion of citizenship rights to protection and safety (see Crawford 1998: 253; Davies 1998; Crowther 2000; Johnston 2000: 57). As with international relations there is no need to intervene against all 'injustices' – only those that constitute clear and present danger.

At the opposite end of the spectrum of criminality similar considerations apply to the policing of certain types of powerful offenders, in particular organised crime. In some cases it is felt that nothing short of militarised warfare will be effective against the organisations of powerful criminal syndicates. On the other hand there is a direct assimilation of policing of organised crime to political relations between states as with the role of United States aid to Colombia for interdiction of the drugs trade (see Chapter 6). In a similar way, military surveillance systems and technology owing their existence to the Cold War period can be turned towards the interception of private and commercial communications and function as a form of state aid in capitalist competition akin to industrial espionage.[1] Finally, the intricate interconnections, already noted, between organised crime and political struggles in various parts of the world together with the activities of legitimate business, further cement the opportunist deployment of interdiction methods by states. Questions of crime control are governed by the requirements of international politics, interdiction measures have to steer a careful course around arrangements central to legitimate business activities (such as some forms of money laundering and offshore banking). The public face of the 'struggle against organised crime' thus tends to focus on those areas, such as drug trafficking, which impinge least on the interests of powerful states or the legitimate business under their protection. These are the areas around which a measure of consensus and global co-operation between criminal justice agencies can be achieved. This episodic and fractured regime is reproduced at local level where the fragmented communities in the grip of criminal governance are also those most socially excluded and most deprived both in economic terms and in relation to capacity to apply political pressure. Policing organised crime is thus an aspect of the episodic forays into poor communities in which police, despite being welcomed by poor communities terrorised by criminal gangs, are scarcely able to rely on public flows of information about organised crime. The public quite rightly conclude that the *continuous* presence of powerful criminals in the area whose willingness to exact revenge is beyond question is hardly offset by *episodic* offers of police support and measures such as witness protection to those willing to provide information, particularly when the police normally ignore the needs of the locality or criminalise its young people *en masse*. The flow of information about crime to the police is further constricted.

Centralisation and Tooling up the State

Thus the generalised policing of the poor and opportunist battles against powerful offenders stretch the social relations of crime control to their limit. In both the policing of the weak and of the powerful there is a growing disconnection between the state and the community – a disconnection which is reinforced by the general social fragmentation discussed in Chapter 5. The reversal of tendencies to social homogenisation and the common social citizenship of the welfare state, the normalisation and reintegration of many forms of crime, all have the effect of weakening a consensual definition of criminality and the taken-for-granted legitimacy of state interdiction. The view that criminal justice policy is backed by the majority of the population 'is regularly repeated and in essence it is barely problematised. The question however is whether this view is morally meaningful in an age of fragmentation' (Boutellier 2000: 40). The state agencies increasingly come to see themselves as the carriers of appropriate norms which justify their actions with minimal necessity to defer to a popular morality. A popular consensus is either assumed or attempts are made at its orchestration through periodic high-profile 'law and order' campaigns and the mobilisation of fear of crime.[2] This then paves the way for assumptions of authoritarian power justified purely by reference to an effectiveness and necessity which tend, unsurprisingly, to veer in the direction of the security agenda of the powerful and less toward the need to integrate and protect the population in general.

One aspect of this is increased centralisation of policing power. This has several dimensions. Firstly, there is a process of continual tooling up against certain 'risky' sectors of the population. Criminal justice legislation moves from an uncontroversial, apolitical and peripheral aspect of the work of parliaments to one of the key areas of legislative output. The content of such legislation is overwhelmingly in the direction of increases in police powers of stop and search, police autonomy to engage in case disposal as with cautioning, revised rules of criminal procedure which generally disadvantage the defendant such as removal of right to silence and reduction in use of jury trial, heavier court sentences combined with automatic incarceration after a certain number of offences.

An adjunct of these developments is a downward pressure on standards of proof in criminal jurisdiction. In Anglo-Saxon jurisdictions this takes the form of expanding use of the civil law criteria of proof on the 'balance of probabilities', displacing the more rigorous criteria of proof in criminal trials of 'beyond reasonable doubt'. This tendency is often accompanied by that of some form of anticipatory criminalisation of those 'at risk' of committing future criminal actions. It is observable both at the level of generalised policing of poor communities and in the more obvious 'warfare' against powerful organised crime. In the context of policing the poor the issue is generally that of likelihood, on the balance of probabilities, of committing a public order offence on the basis of which individuals (mainly young men) may be prevented from travelling to football matches, be constrained to keep away from certain zones, or be subject *en masse* to nighttime curfew. Proof on the balance of probabilities of likelihood of committing a future offence is the appropriate legal accompaniment to the actuarial management of risk groups rather than of offending individuals criminalised on the basis of evidence. Meanwhile, in the 'war against organised crime' the relevant probability is usually that an individual's assets were either derived from or intended for use in further criminal activities. Here the slippage in standards of proof and the burden on the individual, in order to avoid forfeiture, of showing that assets were legally obtained, is intended as a counterbalance to the lack of information flow to the authorities on the activities of organised crime. The actual effectiveness of such methods is of course another question entirely (Naylor 1999).

Similar effects are produced by the blurring of the distinction between individuals and groups as with the Racketeer Influenced and Corrupt Organisation statutes developed in the United States. These, established during the 1970s, enable criminalisation of the *membership* of groups which engage in racketeering (i.e. organised criminal activities) irrespective of individual commission of criminal acts (see Abadinsky 1994). They were allegedly an important device in curbing the power of the traditional Italo-American mafia where membership of a tightly knit group could be shown. Again, their actual effectiveness as a device against more recent 'disorganised' forms of organised crime with shifting groups, lack of permanent membership and global communications networks is open to doubt.

An important aspect of all these shifts in the orientation of criminal law is that even if they derive their initial justification as response to a particular problem such as organised crime, they immediately become generalised resources for the criminal justice system. Thus racketeering can be extended to criminalise membership of street gangs as well as mafia families, criminal asset forfeiture regulations can be directed at small-time criminal entrepreneurs. This is aided by widening definitions of the phenomena concerned. For example a recent report by the UK National Criminal Intelligence Service, using definitions widely accepted in the European Union, defines organised crime as involving at least *three* people whose activity is 'prolonged or indefinite' and motivated by 'profit or power' and involves committing 'serious criminal offences' (NCIS 2000: 4).

The end result is that the careful balance between crime control and due process (Packer 1968) is stretched to breaking point. In the traditional working of the social relations of crime control the two orientations are reconciled. Widespread public consensus as to the parasitic nature of criminality sustains a willingness on the part of the public to provide the authorities with available information about crime. Meanwhile the criminal offender, while capable of intimidating his particular victims, is sufficiently weak to present no threat to the ability of the public to collaborate with the police, or the latter to function free of corruption. Likewise the police can rely on a flow of public information available without intrusive surveillance on their part, and in sufficient quantity and quality to persuade a jury to convict even if offenders exercise their right to remain silent. Not only do the rights of due process and respect for civil liberties not interfere with the effectiveness of crime control but the former are conducive to the latter. Respect for due process and civil liberties secures the public legitimacy of criminal justice agencies and enhances the public willingness to collaborate with them. These two orientations are increasingly difficult to reconcile. Effective crime control requires the dilution of due process.

This can be expected to gradually undermine public respect for police and legal institutions which will in turn undermine the flow of information about crime from communities to the state. This decline is also fuelled by other processes. The complexity and lack of public awareness of many new types of crime, in particular those embedded in global networks such as the internet, the fact that fragmented communities cease to communicate among themselves, the compromise of some communities with criminality both by general participation in social crime and by intimidation by offenders, the effects of the normalisation of crime in creating a divergence of state and popular definitions of criminality, all these undermine the relationship between the state and the community which is key to a functioning of the social relations of crime control.

Police agencies respond to such developments with an attempted self-emancipation from dependence on the flow of information from the public by developing new surveillance resources. One element in this is simply the use of mass media such as television to stage reconstructions of serious crimes as a way of encouraging members of the public to report. Other techniques involve increased use of informers, targeting and continual surveillance of known offenders in anticipation of recidivism, the maintenance of computer databases of personal details such as DNA profiles increasingly held and deployed irrespective of the criminality of the individuals concerned. These enable a flow of information some of which is relevant to crime but which, equally importantly, provides data for actuarial analysis of risk calculation (Ericson 1994; Johnston 2000: 62).

But on an institutional level there is also an attempt to secure through legal compulsion the flow of information from communities to the state that formerly occurred voluntarily. An increasing range of non-state institutions such as banks, firms of accountants, schools, computer networks, become absorbed into a quasi-police apparatus of surveillance. Bank clerks are required to report suspicious financial transactions, Internet service providers to furnish police with encryption keys for email systems. Previously informal structures of community observation become formalised and taken out of the hands of the community itself through such mechanisms as local closed-circuit television systems on housing estates to which police, and private security agencies, have privileged access (see Garland 2000). In a similar way, but without compulsion, the increasing popularity of crime prevention initiatives involving popular participation, such as neighbourhood watch schemes, aim at reconstituting fragmented communities and strengthening informal networks of surveillance and the flow of information to police. Again, as decades of research have confirmed, crime control is a questionable basis for building communities in the face of socio-economic decay (see Crawford 1998).

It is important to emphasise, finally, that these developments do not take place irrespective of the dynamics of criminality itself. It is important to avoid the trap of 'zero-sum' thinking in which authoritarian tendencies in the state can only be demonstrated and condemned as such if it can be shown that they are not responses to a real problem but to some separate, control-oriented, agenda as if to imply that actual increases in crime would somehow legitimise the authoritarian moves (see the critique by Young 1999: 74–6). This is as wrong as its opposite: for example, that rising imprisonment is a simple response to rising crime. The point is that crime is now part of the system: both as a key form of economy, and also a form of resistance. Rising crime, increasing power of criminal offenders, does indeed sustain rising incarceration and authoritarian policing, but this is simply one aspect of a degenerate capitalism reinforcing another. Wider changes, such as the substitution of social integration by criminalisation exemplified in the increasing general policing of the poor as dangerous classes, and the consequent shift of public expenditure from welfare to incarceration, reinforce the tendency. In fact, particularly at the level of ideology, rising crime and a shift to authoritarian control are complementary. The fact that rising crime is a real problem provides the ideological confirmation for the extension of criminalisation as a general form of control.

Tactical sovereignty

The weakening of public participation in the criminalisation process in the form of the social relations of crime control has two important further aspects. Firstly, crime control becomes more autonomous and tactical concerning which demands to meet, which situations to intervene in. It is enabled to become a tactical mobile punitive sovereignty of last resort, able to act with decisive force in situations requiring it, such as communities where public order has temporarily evaporated and which have become ungovernable chaotic entities, or areas plagued by serious criminality in which important property interests are threatened as with shopping and leisure areas. Conversely, poor communities plagued by daily violence and petty theft and drug dealing, and engaging in a good deal of social crime themselves can be disconnected and border patrolled with only the occasional interdiction. In this respect crime control comes to resemble international politics. This is an important aspect because it is widely thought that international politics is becoming less anarchic and more subject to the rule of law and international protection of human rights.

The extension of a practical, rather than simply formal, criminalisation process in the international sphere, particularly in relation to ethnic cleansing and genocide, and whose procedures include the innovatory practice of empowering courts to try non-citizens for crimes committed in third states, does indeed express a growing international communication and a sense of globally shared values and aspirations for 'global justice'. At the time of writing the former president of Yugoslavia is before the International Court in The Hague. What better demonstration could there be of the health and vitality of criminalisation as a way of dealing with harms and wrongs than the fact that it is displacing 'reasons of state' and other forms of turning a blind eye to atrocities in the interests of foreign policy. Such a development seems to complete a final stage in the classic project of modernity. We appear to have nearly moved full circle from Foucault's portrayal of the heinous crime in the Middle Ages as war on the sovereign who takes punitive revenge in defence of his sovereignty (see Chapter 2), to particular types of war as crime: submission of the order of nation states to legally protected human rights and the rule of law.

However, as already noted in Chapter 1, the key question is whether these developments will find expression in a global version of the social relations of crime control as opposed to criminalisation itself becoming a rationalisation for 'reasons of state'. Are international courts and legality powerful enough to progressively link the world population to an embryonic global state and rule of law or will they remain the tools of the most powerful national states and military bureaucracies deploying the language of criminalisation and defence of human rights as a smokescreen for state policies and, not far behind, the interests of significant sections of capital?

Three obstacles facing a new international regime of human rights are clear. Firstly, those organisations, such as the United Nations, which might provide the bureaucratic support for such a regime, are weak and starved of resources. Meanwhile the United States as the de facto global superpower has not only refused to ratify proposals for a world criminal court (unless its troops are excluded from its jurisdiction) but appears intent on expanding those military alliances, such as NATO, over which it exercises decisive influence at the expense of a commitment to the United Nations as the repository of global legitimate force. In such a context the discourse of human rights can function as a cynical cover for the interests of powerful states. The demand that the former president of Yugoslavia be handed over to 'international justice' to be tried for war crimes looks suspicious where none of the other participants in the conflict, in particular the NATO alliance, is offering anyone for similar treatment.

There exist, of course, international institutions which, unlike the United Nations, do exercise significant power. But these institutions, the World Trade Organisation, the World Bank and the International Monetary Fund, embody the direct rule of private capital and are hardly the starting points for international justice. They are now under increasing criticism for their partisan action in attempting to impose, unmediated by any processes of political accountability, the interests of financial and industrial capital on Third World states.

In such a context international human rights enforcement is dragged in the direction of becoming a cover for the ad hoc tactical exercise of punitive sovereignty in which force appears as the servant of law but is in fact its master. As Hardt and Negri put it:

> Armies and police anticipate the courts and preconstitute the rules of justice that the courts must then apply. The intensity of the moral principles to which the construction of the new world order is entrusted cannot change the fact that this is really an inversion of the conventional order of constitutional logic ... we are dealing with a special kind of sovereignty – a discontinuous form of sovereignty that should be considered liminal or marginal in that it acts 'in the final instance' ... to control the marginal event. (Hardt and Negri 2000: 38–9)

Rather than any embryonic structure of social relations of crime control, of citizens and states reporting human rights violations to global authorities who will then act in accordance with the rule of law and attempt to sustain a general regime of legality, police action exhibits a continually negotiated and tactical character: the discontinuous enforcement of law rooted precisely in a sovereignty which, as during the Middle Ages, is only concerned to intervene in those exceptional cases which threaten its ultimate rule rather than sustain a regime of governmentalised sovereignty. Where the smooth automatic rule of capital breaks down, an ad hoc arrangement of instruments will complete a military version of zero-tolerance policing and then move on.

All this might otherwise remain a debate within the study of international politics were it not for the fact that it reflects directly the character of changes within the nation state itself. Rather than the latter sustaining a regime of practical criminalisation and rule of law and presaging a new global state, the tactical and particularistic nature of global law enforcement appears as the future of the nation state. New forms of 'tactical' sovereignty, increasingly deployed by the debilitated authoritarian state, which relate to the final instance and the marginal event, begin to reproduce the character of international relations within national territories. Such developments are understandable in the context of the forms of social polarisation and exclusion in the global network society discussed earlier. The distinction between the national and the international becomes blurred. While the state apparatus remains a vital set of institutions, the terrain it dominates becomes more fragmented and its domination in many areas more episodic. In the international sphere the discourses of criminalisation are subject to the play of powerful state and military machines even though there may exist a *potential* linkage to the global population through, for example, generalised popular rejection of genocide. Likewise within nation states, despite the large area of de facto agreement between the population and the state concerning harmful and criminalisable acts, the community is decreasingly involved in the process of practical criminalisation.

The hysteria of law and order

The second important aspect of the disconnection of crime control from public participation is a new relationship between state and public. The crisis of a form of governance in which the public naturally collaborated with and handed over its problems to the state opens the question of how the state secures legitimacy, to the extent that it does, for its criminalisation processes. Liberal democratic governments make a major attempt to secure public support for state criminalisation and crime control through centralised high-profile politics of 'law and order'. The aim is to mobilise public support for repressive criminal justice in the interests of a consensual 'war on crime' and thus continue, as far as possible, to provide information and engage in the numerous activities of informal control and surveillance without which ultimately crime control cannot function.

The dynamics of mobilisation move in an authoritarian direction by taking on an increasingly distorted form somewhat reminiscent of Habermas' description of what he identified as the doomed attempt by governments at *ideology planning*, which tends to take the form of

> the personalisation of substantive issues, the symbolic use of hearings, expert judgements, juridical incantations and also the advertising techniques ... that at once confirm and exploit existing structures of prejudice and that garnish certain contents positively, others negatively, through appeals to feeling, stimulation of unconscious motives etc. (Habermas 1976: 70)

This involves the repoliticisation of criminal justice through a highly volatile mix of assertions by populist politicians as to the effectiveness of incarceration, further constraints on the rights of offenders, and the necessity and effectiveness of new police powers. These are then given an 'expert' basis in the form of pronouncements by police chiefs as to the seriousness of the situation and consolidated by an appeal both by mass media and – more guardedly – by government to public fears and unconscious prejudices. This *mobilisation* of the public around authoritarian crime control displaces the *subordination* of the public to depoliticised crime control through the informal processes of the social relations of crime control.

The dynamics of such mobilisation are illustrated by recent public reaction to intimate personal crimes involving paedophilia and child murder. The overwhelming emphasis in such cases is on the identification and management of risk which is increasingly seen as requiring a more or less permanent incapacitation of the offender, negating any notion of proportionate guilt and due process. The key is the decay of what Garland (1996, 2000) appropriately terms the 'penal-welfare' strategy which included a strong sense of social citizenship and networks and institutions strong enough to reintegrate the *ex*-offender as a free citizen without future threat to the public. The weakening of the penal welfare strategy is the other side of the coin of the rise of actuarial strategies oriented to the exclusion, management in place, of groups. It also aids a focus on incapacitation as the goal of penal policy and as the aim of sentencing (Vigarello 2001: 237–8).

Finally, it can be seen reflected in postmodern perspectives on criminal justice which see cultural fragmentation as undermining the basis of social integration. Thus 'with the disappearance of ... consensus about crime and punishment, such matters as remorse, forgiveness, and understanding of the perpetrator are left suspended in something of a vacuum' (Boutellier 2000: 67). Hysterical mobilisation, as I have termed it, is an attempt to compensate for this fragmentation. In the absence of the social meaning and solidarity implied in the penal-welfare strategy, it is the dangerousness and the potential recidivism of the offender, to those who feel equally weak and vulnerable, including the insecure middle class, that remains. The state appeals increasingly directly to anger, fear and a nostalgia for social cohesion which expresses itself particularly strongly in those communities marginalised from effective social mechanisms of articulation and representation of interests.

Such mobilisations can lay the basis for further authoritarian shifts by running out of control and turning against the state precisely as a critique of its failure to sustain social integration and defence. Thus Vigarello, commenting on the public outpouring of sympathy for children raped and murdered in Belgium in 1996, notes how the

> sudden emphasis on rape-murder made possible the expression of collective forces that were elsewhere being eroded, gradually fragmented and diluted in a more individualistic society. This explains the obscure revenge of the demonstrators identifying with the victims, massed in a march of 300,000 people on 20 October in Brussels, denouncing a state that was 'powerless to protect its citizens, beginning with the weakest, the children'; rape-murder, once a news item, had become, by its very extremity, the ultimate political path. (Vigarello 2001: 235)

In other situations the public may take matters into its own hands as with outbreaks of vigilante action such as those in which individuals were driven from their homes by mobs following a campaign by a British newspaper to 'name and shame' convicted paedophiles (see McVeigh 2000). The community begins to re-enter as direct participator in the suppression of harms and wrongs, a position from which it was progressively dislodged during the nineteenth century (see Chapter 2). But the re-entry takes a degenerate form, less the enforcement of traditional established norms than a degenerate mobilisation of ignorance and hysteria.

At the same time the transition to authoritarianism is diverted into quite different channels from that of traditional fascist or similar regimes. Firstly the hysteria about the need to incapacitate various types of offenders, even when linked to similar mobilisations against immigrants, asylum-seekers, etc., is not, except on the fringes of the far right, linked to a coherent nationalism. Such ideologies and the groups which carry them are growing in most liberal democracies, but any capturing of political power by such forces will be profoundly affected by the forces of globalisation, privatisation and the weakening of the state discussed earlier. The modern authoritarian state is involved in a tactical deployment of sovereignty rather than an all-embracing penetration and absorption of civil society. It is also a debilitated state. This means that any 'postmodern authoritarianism' will necessarily take very different forms from those statist forms which characterised the dark side of organised modernity, and will articulate itself as much through the direct, decentralised rule of private property as through state power. To find an analogy for the combination of a repressive state which only partially controlled its own population and territory we have to look further back than the Continental European fascisms of the 1930s to the British state in the eighteenth century. The rule of private property is, now as then, every bit a potential basis for authoritarianism as older forms of centralised state power.

Decentralisation: Communities and Victims

Notions of a one-dimensional drift towards an authoritarian criminal justice system are thus one-sided. As argued in Chapter 5, the drift is rather towards the debilitated authoritarian state which combines repressive centralisation with the shedding of functions from the centre. The latter is taking place in two forms. Firstly, a decomposition of the central coherence of criminal justice can be detected, exemplified in the increasing importance of the victim in the criminal justice process. Secondly, there is a shift away from crime control through decentralisation and privatisation and the direct exercise of control by local communities and private property. These tendencies contrast with, but ultimately cohere with, the authoritarian centralising tendencies discussed above in that they both undermine the notion of the social citizenship and governance linking the informal actions of individuals and communities to the state. Authoritarian centralisation absorbs autonomous and informal structures of regulation, discourse, processes of reinforcement and generation of norms into the mechanisms of state surveillance, such that the only discourses left to the masses tend to take a 'hysterical' form. Decentralisation meanwhile undermines social citizenship with the ideology of the responsible individual, the customer and property owner as self-managing their affairs. In terms of crime control the validation of the individual victim, together with ' "the community" as a new territory for the administration of individual and collective existence, a new plane or surface upon which micro-moral relations among persons are conceptualised and administered' (Rose 1996: 331), enables purely local and sectional discourses to define practical criminality and security priorities freed from any wider critique. State authoritarianism is reproduced in the power of private property.

The active victim

Recent years have seen an increased emphasis on the role of the victim in the criminal justice process, both as sufferer of harm and as active participant in the judicial process. There are a number of areas in which this can be observed, such as the growth in importance of services directed to lessen the impact of crime on the victim (see Mawby and Walklate 1993), presentation of victim-impact statements in court prior to sentencing, even consultation with the victim as regards sentence. With the weakening of the social, the state begins to turn to the community and the individual to legitimate its mode of operation. A gradual movement of criminal law towards civil in terms of status of the victim parallels a similar movement, noted already, in terms of standards of proof. The development of victimology has been the theoretical reflection of this (see Walklate 1989; Mawby and Walklate 1993; Boutellier 2000). The result is that the relationship in which the victim remained an essentially passive participant in criminal justice, handing over the problem, and the injury itself, to the state is beginning to be undermined. There is a move, which should not of course be exaggerated, back in the direction of older social relations, predating those of crime control, in which 'crime' was essentially a relationship between victim and perpetrator (see Ness 1990) and in which the notion of the 'social' as a collectivity, both material, with its own dynamics and interests and requiring careful governance, and moral, with the capacity to suffer harm, was much less developed (see Chapter 2).

There are two forces at work in this development. Firstly there is the activity of social movements which consciously portray themselves as victims. This has involved, in particular, feminist campaigns against rape and other forms of male violence, but also includes, in various countries, victims of terrorism (see Pitch 1995) or of ecological disasters. The second factor is the weakening and undermining of the social, under the impact of fragmentation and globalisation, which has been discussed already. I shall deal with the latter first. Pat O'Malley has succinctly described the relationship between a strong notion of social collectivity and the passive role of the victim of crime

> In many important ways, the state represented the social – for it, and only it, could be representative of the collectivity, only the state had the legitimacy and resources to tackle the causes and effects of social problems. The definition of crimes as a social problem thus focused attention not on the individual victim, but on the state–both as the symbolic victim of offences against the collectivity, and as the agent responsible for social rectification…. Relationships of crime were thus almost solely relationships between offender and the state…. The subsequent discrediting of the social … thus made much more visible the relationship between victim and offender – by qualifying the place of the state both as the symbolic victim, and as the agent responsible for all responses to crime. (O'Malley 1996: 6)

Once the problem was handed over to the state the moralisation of the status of victim was a derivative of the injury to the state or the public good. In the absence of this, there are simply two parties to a dispute. The new focus on the victim in crime control is a particular case of a more general re-emphasis on the individual as responsible for their welfare and life chances following the decline of the Keynesian welfare state. Individuals must make provision for ill health and old age just as they must take adequate precautions against becoming a victim of crime. The weakening of the social, the fact that the state is continually less representative of some consensual notion of criminality, leaves the victim as individual aggrieved party suffering *self-defined* harm from another. There has been, in other words, a 'victimalization of morality' defined as a 'shift from moral claims by the community to moral claims by the victim' (Boutellier 2000: 46). This process forces criminal law to move closer to civil law, to appear as a dispute between two parties, no prior judgement of the moral superiority of one party – the victim – being made.

The shift in victim status is also reinforced by the activities of social movements, the most important example of which in recent years has undoubtedly been the campaign by feminists for stronger criminalisation of sexual assault and domestic violence and child abuse. Some sources for this movement were noted in Chapters 4 and 5 – rising divorce rates, growth of female-headed single-parent families, etc., disenchantment with the oppressive aspects of the family institution, in short a crisis in the 'gender order'. In this context the relations between family members are undoubtedly becoming more easy to reconstruct in terms of the criminalising abstraction. Jayne Mooney, in a survey of women's attitudes to domestic violence such as mental cruelty, threats, physical violence and injury in London, finds 'a change in attitude over the years with respect to what constitutes domestic violence and in levels of tolerance over what is "acceptable" behaviour within a relationship [and that] … younger women are more likely to define the behaviours as "violence"' (Mooney 2000: 156).

Violence is becoming more easy to name, family relations and status are continually less of an insulation from practical criminalisation and the involvement of criminal justice agencies.

However, any picture of the social relations of crime control advancing boldly into a new area, demonstrating the vitality of criminalisation in the solution of new areas of social conflict, must be heavily qualified. The extent to which it has actually occurred can be easily exaggerated. The amount of male violence towards women has shown little sign of abatement and is only reinforced by the general legitimation of aggression and short-termism discussed earlier. Criminal justice institutions, police in particular, have, in recent years, come under pressure to maintain legitimacy by taking the criminalisation of domestic violence and sexual assault more seriously. However, what the area of rape and sexual assault illustrates is how the increased role of the victim in the criminal justice process can, paradoxically, be a disadvantage to those who suffer such harm.

The Italian feminist writer Tamar Pitch (1985, 1990, 1995) has noted how the dynamic of feminist campaigns around rape and domestic violence during the 1970s and 1980s involved a shift from the emphasis on oppression to that of victimisation (see also Lasch 1984). Campaigns began to de-emphasise sexual assault and domestic violence as forms of collective structural oppression, implying a political mobilisation to end patriarchal social relations, in favour of an emphasis on the struggle for the recognition of victim status and a demand that the criminal justice system take these forms of harm more seriously. This, in Pitch's opinion, had the effect of demobilising the political struggle by substituting the category of oppression which 'is totalising; it covers all aspects of identity and all spheres of life' (Pitch 1990: 108) with that of victimisation, in which the social movement becomes demobilised and its members 'disappear as collective actors and assume the individualised and passive role of victims' (Pitch 1990: 113).

This tendency, to the substitution of the mobilised social movement with the passive victim characteristic of the social relations of crime control, meets, however, the tendency to increased victim autonomy coming, as it were, in the opposite direction. The active victim, by substituting rather than complementing a strong notion of the public good or public peace represented by the state and the criminal law, ends up being more isolated and alone than the classic passive victim. Notwithstanding the disadvantages of handing over the issue to the state, and the patriarchal prejudices of police and judiciary, the advantages in the form of the state as stronger agency than the offender and regarding itself as affronted by rape or domestic violence are also lost. The traditional view of rape, if not by strangers in violation of the public peace,[3] as a matter of interaction between two parties over the essentially private issue of *consent*, or of domestic violence as simply a private family *dispute*, is thereby reinforced in a new way. Traditional patriarchal exclusion of domestic and sexual matters from legitimate public scrutiny is reinforced by the notion of private dispute. Rape trials, as Sue Lees (1996) has exhaustively documented, are notoriously a battle between victim and defendant in which the tables are often turned, with the victim on trial. The equalisation of the victim paradoxically compounds this disadvantage. The effect is that the undermining of the social and the shift of responsibility on to the potential victim to manage prevention, avoid conflict, not to put themselves in a dangerous situation, acts to generalise the features of essentially *private* governance to social relations as a whole.

The active community

The victim is important in a second context, that of the resurgence of decentralised community and private systems of risk management. The decentralisation to community of responsibility for the security of property and individuals, through various mechanisms of crime prevention is well documented (Crawford 1997, 1998; Hughes 1998). It is part of the wider decentralisation of responsibilities, including various welfare and care functions, which has been a major consequence of the decline of the Keynesian welfare state. The salience of community has increased in inverse proportion to its material decomposition and fragmentation as a local structure of networks and support mechanisms. Much of the assertion of the new viability of community, drawing on a communitarian nostalgia for Victorian ideas of self-help hides a reality of decomposition into, on the one hand, the wasteland areas effectively abandoned to criminal governance and, on the other, largely middle-class and residual Fordist working-class areas held together increasingly by fear of crime rather than by cultural or economic cohesion.

These 'communities of risk', replacing traditional 'communities of sentiment' (see Johnston 2000: 67; Rose 2000: 329), are preoccupied with keeping out risks from their areas. Those risks may be physical such as pollution, obtrusive motorways and architecture, but will crucially focus on groups of people: young people from adjacent poor areas hanging around shopping precincts, bail hostels and halfway houses for mentally disabled or ex-offenders being constructed next to residential property, drug dealers, etc. The crucial characteristic of such communities is their 'active' nature. As people who may have little in common apart from shared notions of risk, they exist by virtue of their mobilisation around fears and issues. Of these, crime and risk are core priorities. Their leading participants may consist of commercial and residential property owners, many living in fortified areas and drawing in local schools, insurance companies, real-estate agencies, and various providers of private security for property protection. These then forge links with agencies of local government and community organisation bringing in wider participation organised around gender, ethnic or other interest groups, but most importantly with local branches of state agencies such as the police who themselves may have increasing autonomy as regards policy implementation on the ground. Such an amalgam may be formalised through various official structures such as consultation committees or partnerships sponsored by local government and police agencies.

The most important characteristic of these 'active communities' (O'Malley and Palmer 1996) and where they differ from the middle-class neighbourhood discussed in Chapter 4, is the abandonment of the old civic privatism which subordinated social groups and areas to the expertise of the planner state of organised modernity. Active communities exhibit, by contrast, a knowledge of local conditions, the ability to articulate interests and engage in local activism, particularly as regards crime. In local partnerships with police 'the community and its leaders are to be involved in determining what are the policing needs of the locale, and what styles of police work are seen to be effective in these terms, and forms of intervention are regarded as desirable or undesirable' (O'Malley and Palmer 1996: 145).

What is replaced is the old 'Keynesian policing' in which the civic privatism of the citizen related to police as client to expert, and in which the social relations of crime control linked citizens and communities to centralised notions of public good and public peace which were to be generally applied to all sections of society. The active community is by contrast the customer, appropriating the mobile resources of state sovereignty, along with those of private security and a plethora of privately provided instruments of crime prevention (see Rose 2000: 329) for its own independent local governance: defending the housing areas and shopping precincts against the disadvantaged mob of the poor areas. In the latter areas, however strong the concern with risk and crime, the market will not deliver private security. Large increases in state investment in environmental improvement and radical reorganisation of the accountability of policing to such communities would be necessary to assimilate these areas to the status of 'active communities' (see Lea and Young 1993).

Not all innovations are of this directly exclusionary nature. For example, locally based forms of restorative justice and conflict resolution through mediation (see Braithwaite 1989; Hahn 1998) aim to use precisely the resources of local communities to disconnect the solution of a wide range of harms and conflicts from the state and the discourses of criminal justice and the criminalising abstraction and to bring perpetrators and victims together as fellow community members. In this sense there appears to be a return to pre-modern systems of community control. But again the problem facing such innovations is that both in communities whose only uniting factor is risk and fear of crime, and in those fragmented out of existence by socio-economic decay and ethnic conflict, the 'weakest point of many of the restorative justice formulations, is thus ... what is the community; what is community interest and how can it be represented?' (Hudson 1998: 251).

In some communities it can, but in a large number of cases it cannot (see also Baskin 1988). Increased sensitivity by police to the priorities of local communities may, for example, create pressures for sidelining of sexual assault or racial violence.

Hence the overall effect of measures based on both community and private property is often to exaggerate rather than ameliorate social fragmentation and division since the aim of active communities and of all entry-control systems involves a heavy emphasis on border patrol and the exclusion of outsiders, most crime prevention initiatives being predicated on the assumption that risk and threat originate outside the defended and fortified area. The 're-mediaevalisation' of terrain is reinforced as active communities 'form a complex and expanding archipelago of private governments that together establish what we might term an emerging "neo-feudalism"' (Shearing 1997: 271).

There is thus a move back from the modern social relations of crime control to the arrangements which preceded them and in which the community defined its own priorities and settled them in its own way. Privatised local governance based on the active participation of local property owners in crime prevention and police priority setting has precisely this effect. The ostensible purpose of such innovations may be to shore up and revitalise criminal justice structures such as local policing. However, rather than the social relations of crime control linking citizens and communities to the general 'public good' from which are derived centralised consensual definitions of crime, the state itself decentralises by paying increasing attention to the particular concerns of powerful communities and groups as de facto customers.

Geographical communities are not the only form of decentralisation. Private or semi-private property such as commercial institutions, banks, and transport systems engage in a growing proliferation of entry-control systems designed as border patrol of risky individuals and activities. Such control systems mobilise normal civil law powers of private property in the establishment of what Clifford Shearing (1995, 1997) calls 'contractual communities' in which entry or participation is predicated upon agreement to be scanned, searched or to obtain valid entry tokens (see also Lianos and Douglas 2000). Questions of crime control, the identification of individuals as offenders, only occur in the marginal instance where someone attempts to directly circumvent such control systems.

Globalisation and regulation

In many ways similar to the active community, the self-regulation of the company is a classic form of 'government at a distance' in which private institutions regulated themselves and thereby weakened criminalisation. The company, like the family, was an alternative system of governance: a frontier and barrier to the social relations of crime control. The developments discussed above – tactical deployment of state power, decentralisation of many aspects of crime control to communities of risk, the disconnection of the community from the state under the slogans of self-reliance and privatised crime prevention – are an extension to the community of the principle of autonomy inherent in the governance of both the company and the family in which such institutions develop their own priorities and emphases and methods of conflict-regulation. The new governance is, in a phrase, the autonomy of the commercial company, of capital, writ large.

However, in a similar way to the progress of human rights enforcement in the international sphere, and the increased focus on sexual violence, there has been in recent years an apparent strengthening of criminalisation in the areas of commercial and business activity. In Britain, for example, the establishment in 1986 of the Serious Fraud Office as a specialised investigatory and prosecution authority, together with the recent (2000) consolidation of the regulation of financial markets under the Financial Services Authority, gives the impression that criminalisation strategy is alive and well in the face of the growing power and criminality of corporate capital.

The pressures behind these developments appear, as with the demand for global justice, to include a growing sense of the global dimensions of capitalism, particularly the consequences of destructive self-reproduction of capital in the worsening environmental crisis. Major multinational companies appear increasingly sensitive to a groundswell of opinion concerning environmental issues. The effect of the privatisation of state utilities, pensions, etc., as part of the dismantling of the Keynesian welfare state, intensified popular concern with financial fraud and with the conflict between safety and profitability in what have become large private monopolies. Such developments may appear to create the basis for an informed community ready to advance the social relations of crime control more strongly into the area of business criminality. Meanwhile, the globalisation of financial markets and the increased international mobility of capital might be expected to have undermined any remaining residues of parochialism and cultural exclusivity of the business elite as a host of new entrepreneurs have joined the financial markets and boardrooms of banks and companies.

But here lies the contradiction. Those same forces of globalisation and mobility undermined the very project of regulation at the outset by weakening the management and coercive capacity of the state. Too much regulation would undermine the working of the market. Capital would simply move elsewhere. The very changes which facilitated external regulation by undermining the cultural exclusivity and cohesion of the financial elite have themselves placed new obstacles in the way of effective regulation by nation states. The result is that the semi-autonomous nature of the company as form of governance has been increased rather than weakened. The global mobility of capital constitutes a constant bulwark against too strong a regulatory environment in exactly the same way as it does against high levels of corporate taxation. It is true there have been attempts to establish forms of global regulation and 'good governance' in such matters as intellectual property rights, Internet domain name registrations, regulation of trade disputes, etc. (see Braithwaite and Drahos 2000). These are secure because they are to the advantage of business and indeed, as with US government support for the resistance of major pharmaceutical companies to permit cheap generic anti-AIDS drugs to be manufactured in Third World countries, can be used against the poor (see Mathiason 2001). In other areas of regulation such as labour conditions (despite the existence of the International Labour Organisation as a recognised international body), welfare rights (see Mishra 1999) are far weaker. In areas of criminality in which business is more heavily involved, such as tax evasion through money laundering, then injunctions to 'good governance' by global corporations tend to remain at the level of paper resolutions.

> Specialist organisations have been set up and international conventions signed and ratified for the prevention of corruption on international markets and for police co-operation and mutual judicial assistance while conferences and studies, commissions of inquiry and reports have multiplied. All this has been accompanied by the most strongly worded declarations and promises from those in authority, but the system of financial crime has not been the least bit shaken. (de Brie 2000)

The fact is that attempts to regulate key financial institutions conflict with the interests of global capital. Any tightening up of regulation of business within nation states has leaned in the direction of self regulation. Criminal justice institutions, such as the Serious Fraud Office in the UK or the US Securities and Exchange Commission, only scratch the surface. Business forms the most important example of an 'active community' in support of which state criminal justice and regulatory agencies intervene only as a last resort – and in the minority of cases which become known to them – while a major effort is directed towards the consolidation of international forms of restorative justice such as private dispute settlement and arbitration schemes between companies, private fraud investigations, etc., which form part of 'a new institutional zone of private agents' (Sassen 1999: 11; see also Strange 1996; Shearing 1997; Braithwaite 2000a). In the face of these decentralised arrangements, as with those in local communities, there is little to ensure that the interests of the poor – in this case workers and consumers – are represented adequately or at all. The deliberate weakening of trade union organisation as a matter of government policy, in particular in the USA and Britain, in the interests of wage reduction and profitability, undermines the single most important countervailing power to business criminality and the main community in a position to provide information and demand investigation. The amount of state regulation of business, in areas such as pollution, health and safety, marketing unsafe products, has shown a tendency to decline in a similar way as has corporate taxation, so as not to reduce the competitive position of business in global markets by imposing high regulation costs. The result according to one commentator is that 'the brand of state regulation known as corporate crime has disappeared' (Snider 2000: 170).

Back to the Future?

The extension of private governance discussed above might seem simply a return to classic liberal government as described by Foucault, but on a larger scale with the social relations of crime control being increasingly displaced by forms of governance modelled more on the autonomous self-regulation characteristic of the company and the family. The nineteenth century saw the emergence of a plurality of forms of governance. The social relations of crime control were portrayed as linking autonomous communities to the state through shared definitions and attitudes to crime, forms of appropriate behaviour, informal social control, etc., enabling the criminal justice agencies to function practically. This contrasted with systems of private governance such as the family and the commercial company, which exhibited greater autonomy from the state and regulated conflicts in ways which were their own though which still cohered with state policies. These systems of private governance are displacing crime control but at the same time weakening their role as forms of 'governmentalisation of the state'.

I have already noted some important distinctions from the forms of liberal government which emerged during the nineteenth century. Firstly, the aims of governance have shifted from social integration of population to the management of social exclusion and risks. Secondly, globalisation has produced 'government at a greater distance' in which many forms of private governance have greater autonomy from the national state or ignore it altogether. Finally, the relations between the state and private governance are changing such that the state, equipped with increasingly authoritarian powers, is increasingly a tactical resource for private governance rather than the latter contributing to the ability of the state to manage its population.

However, the return to liberal governance of the nineteenth century is only one of several possible historical analogies. Many of the developments discussed above evoke an analogy with pre-modern or even earlier historical periods. The actuarial management of the dangerous classes or underclass suggests the image of policing in the eighteenth and early nineteenth centuries. Likewise, increased reliance by police agencies on technological surveillance rather than public communication and support suggests the fragmented and episodic policing based on an army of spies and informers characteristic of eighteenth-century England. The growing attack on civil liberties and the absorption of informal institutions as arms of state surveillance also compounds this trend. The counter-tendency of increasingly autonomous private governance likewise evokes the earlier stages of modernisation in which the propertied classes made their own arrangements for protection while the masses were left to their own devices. Meanwhile for some commentators such developments are to be characterised as 're-mediaevalisation' or 'neo-feudalism', evoking (metaphorically speaking) a return to even earlier historical periods.

The crisis of criminal justice

The reverse side of the development of private governance is the increasing tensions within the state itself. The shift to authoritarianism seeks legitimacy, in the areas of crime control, in terms of effectiveness. The justification for inroads into due process and civil liberties is continually that of the necessity to combat crime. Crime control has entirely displaced due process in that the latter can now, increasingly, be justified only in terms of its contribution to the former. Yet this drive for effectiveness lacks any evidence of success. There is rather the progressive development of a *rationality crisis* (Habermas 1976). It is widely admitted that criminal justice systems are highly inefficient at controlling the level of crime. There is a constant search to discover 'what works', if indeed anything does, and constant fear that 'nothing works' either in policing or penal policy (Cohen 1997). Rising prison populations seem to have little effect on crime rates and recent relatively small reductions in crime in most industrial countries are difficult to attribute to action by police or penal systems (see, for example, Massing 1998; Bowling 1999). Despite increased surveillance and interdiction powers, there is little evidence of the effect of police interdiction in dealing with money laundering and drugs dealing (Rose 2001). But the same is true of the various systems of private governance and self-regulation which seem to have little tangible overall effect on crime rates despite 'successes' for particular projects in particular areas (see Reiner 2000: 86).

But not only do the criminal justice agencies seem to have little effect in regulating crime levels, they begin to have their own criminogenic effects. Thus generalised policing of whole communities as 'dangerous classes' with its blanket strategies of indiscriminate stop and search (stop and frisk) acts to further blur the boundaries between offenders and non-offenders and consolidates community support for offenders (Lea and Young 1993). When large numbers of young men fill up the prisons, these institutions turn into simple devices for managing and warehousing the poor rather than for punishing or rehabilitating offenders. This trend has, unsurprisingly, reached its furthest development in the United States (Feeley and Simon 1992; Parenti 1999; Wacquant 1999; Bauman 2000). When something like 1 in 4 young Afro-American males are incarcerated, the role of the prison becomes what Simon (1997) calls 'governance by crime' in which the prison experience becomes the most important socialising institution–far more important than work–as a basis for establishing networks, learning roles and attitudes, etc. Large-scale incarceration of the poor also helps disrupt family life and fosters criminality (Chambliss 1994). The state ends up complementing organised criminal governance as a key mechanism of perverse integration. The fragmentation and polarisation of society is thus accentuated by both private governance and the state agencies. The state no longer acts in practice as social unifier and guardian of general citizenship rights but as an agency for the reproduction of social fragmentation.

Yet the obvious rationality crisis of criminal justice has yet to lead to a full-blown legitimation crisis in the sense that there is a widespread demand for something else. During the 1980s, in many countries the failure of the criminal justice system as a crime control mechanism was used to reinforce and legitimise the push to the self-responsibilisation of individuals and communities for crime control and the consequent expansion of private governance based around prevention. A full-scale legitimation crisis of the criminal justice system was avoided by first, its retreat to self-referential internal performance indicators, second, the increasingly hysterical mobilising politics of law and order and, third, the emphasis on victim responsibilisation and decentralised prevention schemes disconnecting from the state (see Crawford 1995). Finally, for those who actually suffer violence of theft, despite the widespread cynicism about the effectiveness of the criminal justice system, there is no obvious alternative to calling the police, even if the latter never arrive, or arrive too late to have any effect. The social relations of crime control are in decay but they have yet to be annihilated. We are rather in the throes of a transition in which both the old and new can be seen side by side in new relationships involving 'fragmentations, pluralist systems of control, the historical continuity of old and the emergence of new forms of crime' (South 1997: 117).

Celebrating fragmentation

It is clear that the social relations of crime control as the predominant form of governance of interpersonal harms and conflicts are weakening in the face of profound obstacles. In some areas they are being gradually displaced by other forms of regulation. This, as should be clear from preceding arguments, blurs the notion of crime into more general categories of risk. Crime is in fact being deconstructed into the variety of conflicts and harms that constitute it. This can of course be construed as a purely theoretical process in which concepts are taken apart to reveal the various hidden assumptions behind them. Thus crime can be subject to a theoretical deconstruction in which we abandon the idea of crime as a unified problem which requires a unified solution – at least at the theoretical level' (Smart 1995: 36).

The problem with a purely theoretical deconstruction is that if the only way of dealing with harms and conflicts is by handing them over to the criminal justice agencies, then, having deconstructed crime theoretically, it has to be reassembled as practical criminalisation (Lea 1998). Practical deconstruction occurs when harms and conflicts can no longer practically be dealt with as crime, that is, when the social relations of crime control no longer effectively function.

That is the process I have been describing here. In Chapter 1 I recalled the Russian Marxist legal theorist, Evgeny Pashukanis, who argued that we will be able to dispense with the concept of crime when the social relations which sustain it have been overcome. He saw the social relations of crime control and the state withering away because in a communist society capital and the inequalities and conflicts it generates would have been abolished and power over social processes would have been reappropriated by the people, rendering the state unnecessary. Communism would provide the material conditions for a radical abolitionism in which the substantive equality of individuals would enable them to sort out conflicts and problems without recourse to the state.

However, capitalist society has continued far longer than either Pashukanis or any other classical Marxist ever anticipated and has developed new forms of degeneration and new configurations unanticipated by them. One of these is the way in which the state has indeed partly withered but rather as part of a redistribution of rule in the direction of private property unmediated by politics. Under such circumstances the retreat of the state accentuates inequalities and conflicts by freeing them from any regulation in the interests of general social cohesion. As regards the regulation of interpersonal harms and conflicts, the ascendancy of private governance sustains a 'perverse abolitionism', a crumbling of the social relations of crime control but without new forms of conflict resolution that could effectively replace them, and with a strong tendency to resort to avoidance, segregation and management of risks.

One response to this situation popular at the present time is that of attempting to work in various ways with the new forms of private governance. The starting point is often the assumption that current fragmentation, rather than being a symptom of the degeneration and crisis of capitalism, is rather itself a new, relatively stable, post (or late) modernity in which the over-complexity of organised modernity is being resolved through forms of decentralisation and privatisation (see, for example, Crook et al. 1992). The decentred and fragmented nature of postmodern society is seen as a strength rather than as a symptom of crisis. Such views echo neo-liberal theories which see the market as the only mechanism capable of co-ordinating a complex economy. Postmodern theories apply similar concepts to social systems as a whole with the conclusion that only capital itself, acting through decentralised governance by private property, is capable of co-ordinating society. Centralised political and state institutions, structures of political compromise, in particular those that characterised organised modernity and the interventionist state, are no longer up to the job.

Such thinking has recently been influential among criminologists and others attempting to think through the changes taking place in the areas of crime control and criminal justice. I have noted the view that the state is less important as the repository of 'community' values when increasingly crime is seen as a violation of autonomy of the victim (Boutellier 2000). This is seen not as a crisis or breakdown of social order but rather a shift in its dynamic, a shift that, in principle, facilitates decentralised forms of restorative justice which can concentrate on relations between the parties rather than refer to a centralised criminal justice legitimised by shared public morality.

One response to decentralised private governance is the attempt to democratise it. Paul Hirst, for example, deploys the concept of associative democracy (Hirst 1994, 2000) as a blueprint for the organisation of society into 'self governing communities of choice' which, apart from a 'thin common morality' concerning crimes we all agree about such as 'murder, theft and fraud' (Hirst 2000: 289), can enforce their own local moralities and injunctions agreed through democratic deliberation. It is not necessary to apply the same criminal law between different communities of choice. What has long been the practical wisdom of police officers – do not attempt to enforce the liquor licensing laws in the ethnic ghettos during Mardi Gras – as a practical local compromise designed ultimately to retain community respect for state institutions of criminal justice, now becomes the principle of governance itself, implemented through localised systems of restorative justice and dispute mediation.

These themes are echoed by more mainstream criminologists such as Clifford Shearing who envisages the transition to 'a complex and expanding archipelago of private governments that together establish what we might term an emerging "neo-feudalism"' (Shearing 1997: 270). These involve 'contracts of governance' setting out the duties of membership of these communities which would include agreement to resolve disputes through appropriate procedures of restorative justice. Shearing is clear that such forms of dispute resolution are the extension of principles already at work in the commercial company as a model of private governance of long standing. 'Restorative Justice seeks to extend the logic that has informed mediation beyond the settlement of business disputes to resolution of individual conflicts that have traditionally been addressed within a retributive paradigm' (1997: 275; see also Braithwaite 1989).

These proposals appear practical and workable in the sense that they are essentially extensions and modifications of forms of governance already in existence. But for this reason their weaknesses are also evident. The familiar criticisms that have been levied against existing examples of such arrangements (see, for example, Baskin 1988; Matthews 1988; Hudson 1998) are valid for their extension as a general principle of governance and, in turn, imply a critique of the vision of a stable postmodern society. Basically, such schemes, in order to function as their supporters would wish, presuppose that the fundamental problems of power, social exclusion and fragmentation, social inequality and conflict have been solved. There is remarkably little focus on conflict and exploitation based on class, gender or ethnicity, conflicts which may be heightened rather than ameliorated by the present phase of capitalist development but which are glossed over in much writing on 'late modern' or 'postmodern society'.[4]

An important motive in the formation of 'communities of risk' or 'active communities' is, as noted in the preceding discussion, the management of borders with the poor and keeping them out of middle-class housing and shopping areas (see Hope 2000). The socially excluded populations of inner city areas, or even whole regions, do not feature prominently in the discourse of the extension of private governance. The question therefore is less the portrayal of a possible future of a non-oppressive plurality of decentralised communities than that of overcoming the global forces of impoverishment and social fragmentation which render such a future an impossible utopia. Under present conditions a shift to private governance accentuates inequalities, both between rich and poor communities and within them. Forms of interpersonal violence such as domestic violence and child-abuse could face reduced surveillance in forms of private governance oriented to keeping outside risks at bay. Meanwhile the decentralised and fragmented communities of the poor could merge even more with forms of criminal governance and become, like the smuggling communities of eighteenth-century England, entirely dependent on social crime.

Redistribution of economic and crime control resources to weak communities is minimised without a strong welfare-oriented state. One is reminded that Foucault, focusing more on the stability of classical modernity, saw the issue as the 'governmentalisation *of the state*' rather than the *substitution of the state* by private governance. Arrangements such as those portrayed in Shearing's 'archipelago of private governments' actually require funding from a strong state capable of levying tax revenues, to secure full employment, and to fund state courts that will function effectively in a more rights-respecting way than markets or communities: 'Restorative justice founders when the welfare state is not there to support it' (Braithwaite 2000a: 233). And the fact is that it is not there. Without either a welfare state or a new *substantive equality* between communities, social groups and individuals, an equality requiring major social reorganisation and the checking of the destructive dynamic of capital accumulation, any attempt to devise a form of regulation which might replace the social relations of crime control and the state is undermined. The private governance perspective ignores both the absence of a welfare-oriented state and the presence of a state continually appropriating more repressive powers directed to the management of the poor and the combating of organised criminality. It ignores the question of power.

The Rebirth of the Social

The struggle for the future starts from the necessity to defend aspects of the present, combined with the realisation that this will involve profound social and political change. The need is to defend and consolidate a variant of the social relations of crime control. The respect in which these relations were a gain for humanity rested, it will be recalled, on their underpinning the rule of law. The handing over of conflicts to the state was a form of guaranteeing this. There remains a necessity of a public power to defend the rule of law and to handle relations between communities. Within this – what Hirst (2000) refers to as the 'thin common morality' of basically agreed human rights – local norms can exist. Here the decentralisers and abolitionists are correct. Locally based systems of restorative justice are, in principle, much better than criminal justice agencies at sorting out conflicts. The passivity of the victim in the traditional social relations of crime control is a form of oppression. Communities could take the law into their own hands again. Our conflicts would no longer be their (the state's and the criminal justice agencies') property. There is no problem about constraining those who refuse to confront their accusers. But these systems will function *only* if substantive equality exists between groups and individuals such that disputants have equal power and some willingness to sort out conflicts. This requires fundamental social and political change.

There must be a fundamental redistribution of economic and welfare resources to poor communities, both within advanced capitalist countries and on a global scale. This will enable the disconnection from dependence on criminality, violence and the violation of the rights of others like oneself as a survival necessity. Relations of trust and solidarity will be enabled to replace those of risk and unpredictability. Social inclusion will enable robust communities to sort out a large proportion of their own disputes.

But there will be a need for criminal justice agencies to facilitate dispute resolution by providing legal resources, to track people down and bring disputants together, and to furnish legal frameworks and resources for handling disputes between communities, strangers, countries, etc. This means that people must be brought back into contact with the state. The state must be re-democratised, the corruption and pillaging of the state by powerful interests must be curtailed, politics must be reinvented as a process of democratic involvement, with more decentralisation of control to local communities at the same time as opening up central institutions to popular control and scrutiny. Most important is the development of real international institutions through which disputes can be resolved in a framework of the rule of law. The local and the global must continually be brought into relation with one another with global links between local communities and the local impact of global economic activities being made transparent. The elimination and weakening of the trades union movement as a key community in a position to increase the surveillance and flow of information about criminal activities of corporations must be reversed.

Finally, there must be a remarginalisation of crime. Criminality must be peripheral, not central, to economic, social and political life. The disconnection of criminality from the core processes of global finance and manufacturing, whether as tendencies towards gangster capitalism or as powerful organised crime, must be checked. Reliance on the state armed with increasingly repressive powers, whose only effectiveness will be their inevitable deployment against the poor, must be reversed.

These developments involve tackling the autonomy and destructive power of capital accumulation which has undermined communities, corrupted the state and merged criminality and violence as a normal feature of the social system. The issues of crime control and the resolution of conflicts and harms cannot be separated from the achievement of the conditions necessary for effective dispute resolution. This means, it cannot be said often enough, substantive social equality. Under such conditions, other forms of power and conflict such as gender and ethnic conflict will not simply evaporate but can be more effectively tackled. Furthermore, the element of truth in the project, discussed in Chapter 1, of extending the scope of crime control to include violations of human rights such as imperialism and poverty, can be realised. The violation of social rights can be criminalised if such violation is less the outcome of impersonal market forces than deliberate action traceable to organisations and individuals who have violated democratically sanctioned norms concerning distribution of resources.

All this is simply a restatement of a radical Left Realist agenda for change. Until recently the achievement of such an agenda might have seemed to be some distance away, almost as utopian as the peaceful continuation of the present state of affairs. But during the last few years the beginnings of a reconstruction of the social have been visible on the horizon. The new social movements against global capitalism which have begun to take shape around the world start from the appropriate terrain from which to confront capital: not the increasingly debilitated standpoint of the nation state but from capital which in internationalising and globalising itself inevitably reproduces its own opposition in the form of the global 'multitude'

(Hardt and Negri 2000). These movements, fragmented and episodic as they are at present, make possible a growing challenge to the hegemony of global capital as the *organising force* which in the last instance determines developments. The importance of this movement is the challenge to the tendencies of destructive self-reproduction: global pollution, massive impoverishment and inequality and the contrast between destruction of community and social life in large areas of the planet and the wealth, opulence and arrogance of the ruling elites, the growth of lawlessness and violence.

I do not wish to conclude with a call to arms or a manifesto for the future development of this movement. Whether the successful challenge to the power of capital will most likely involve a global conflagration of class struggles or whether it will involve a variety of social groups, political and voluntary organisations, non-governmental organisations acting as a sort of countervailing power to capital (see Braithwaite 2000b) is a discussion for another place. The important issue is the growth of global resistance movements into a 'global civil society' in which direct power of private capital is effectively countered (Lipschutz 1996). Of one thing we can be certain; as the revolutionary socialist Rosa Luxemburg stated at the turn of the last century, the choice facing humanity is simple: socialism or barbarism.

Notes

1 See, for example, recent discussion of the ECHELON surveillance system (European Parliament 2001).

2 See p. 172 on 'The hysteria of law and order'.

3 See the remarks on stranger rape in Chapter 6.

4 Well known exceptions being the perceptive writings of Zygmunt Bauman (1991, 1995, 1998 in particular) and Frederic Jameson (1984, 1998).

Bibliography

Abadinsky, Howard (1994) *Organized Crime* (4th edn). Chicago: Nelson-Hall.

Abrams, Fran and Rowell, Andy (2000) 'Tobacco firms face quiz in cigarette smuggling inquiry', *Independent on Sunday*, 24 September.

Aglietta, Michel (1979) *A Theory of Capitalist Regulation*. London: New Left Books.

Ahire, P. (1991) *Imperial Policing: the Emergence and Role of the Police in Colonial Nigeria 1860–1960*. Milton Keynes: Open University Press.

Alemika, E. (1993) 'Colonialism, state and policing in Nigeria', *Crime, Law and Social Change*, 20 (3): 187–219.

Alexander, G. (1997) 'Civic Property', *Social and Legal Studies* 6 (2): 217–34.

Almond, Gabriel and Verba, Sydney (1963) *The Civic Culture: Political Attitudes and Democracy in Five Nations*. Princeton, NJ: Princeton University Press.

Anderson, A. (1995) 'The red Mafia: a legacy of communism', in Edward P. Lazear (ed.), *Economic Transition in Eastern Europe and Russia: Realities of Reform*, Stanford, CA: Hoover Institution Press.

Anderson, B. (1983) *Imagined Communities*. London: Verso.

Angell, Ian (1996) 'Economic crime: beyond good and evil', *Journal of Financial Regulation and Compliance*, 4 (1): 2–6.

Archer, J. (1989) 'Poachers abroad', in G.E. Mingay (ed), *The Unquiet Countryside*. London: Routledge.

Archer, J. (1999) 'Poaching gangs and violence: the urban–rural divide in nineteenth-century Lancashire', *British Journal of Criminology*, 39 (1): 25–37.

Arlacchi, P. (1988) *Mafia Business*. Oxford: Oxford University Press.

Aron, Raymond (1967) *The Industrial Society: Three Essays on Ideology and Development*. London: Weidenfeld & Nicolson.

Arrighi, Giovanni (1991) 'World income inequalities and the future of socialism', *New Left Review*, 189 (September/October): 39–65.

Atkins, S. and Hoggett, B. (1984) *Women and the Law*. Oxford: Blackwell.

Baldwin, Rob and Kinsey, Richard (1982) *Police Powers and Politics*. London: Quartet Books.

Bales, Kevin (1999) *Disposable People: New Slavery in the Global Economy*. Berkeley: University of California Press.

Barclay, Peter (ed.) (1995) *The Joseph Rowntree Inquiry into Income and Wealth* (vol. 1). London: Joseph Rowntree Foundation.

Baskin, Dorothy (1988) 'Community mediation and the public/private problem', *Social Justice*, 15 (1): 21–34.

Bauman, Zygmunt (1991) *Postmodernity: Chance or Menace?* Lancaster University Centre for the Study of Cultural Values.

Bauman, Zygmunt (1994) *Alone Again: Ethics after Certainty*. London: DEMOS.

Bauman, Zygmunt (1995) *Life in Fragments: Essays in Postmodern Morality*. Oxford: Blackwell.

Bauman, Zygmunt (1998) *Globalization: the Human Consequences*. Cambridge: Polity Press.

Bauman, Zygmunt (2000) 'Social issues of law and order', *British Journal of Criminology*, 40: 205–21.

Bayart, J., Ellis, S. and Hibour, B. (1999) 'From kleptocracy to the felonius state?' in *The Criminalization of the State in Africa*. Bloomington: Indiana University Press.

Beccaria, Cesare. (1764) 'On crimes and punishments', in John Muncie, E. MacLaughlin and M. Langan (eds) (1996) *Criminological Perspectives: A Reader*. London: Sage.

Beccaria, Cesare (1804) *Elementi di Economia Pubblica*. Milan (quoted in Pasquino, Pasquale 'Theatrum Politicum: the genealogy of capital', in Burchell et al. 1991, pp. 105–18).

Beck, Ulrich (1992) *Risk Society*. London: Sage.

Beck, Ulrich (2000) *The Brave New World of Work*. Oxford: Polity Press.

Becker, Gary (1968) 'Crime and punishment: an economic approach', *Journal of Political Economy*, 76: 169–217.

Behr, Edward (1997) *Prohibition: a Failure to Learn the Lessons of History*. London: BBC.

Bell, Daniel (1961) 'Crime as an American way of life: a queer ladder of social mobility', in *The End of Ideology*, pp. 127–50. New York: Collier.

Bello, Walden (1994) *Dark Victory: the United States, Structural Adjustment and Global Poverty*. London: Pluto Press (with Food First and the Transnational Institute).

Bello, Walden (2001) 'The global conjuncture: characteristics and challenges', *International Socialism*, 91: 11–20.

Bennholdt-Thomsen, Veronika and Mies, Maria (1999) *The Subsistence Perspective: Beyond the Globalised Economy*, London: Zed Books.

Benson, John (1989) *The Working Class in Britain 1850–1939*. London: Longman.

Benton, Ted (1998) 'Rights and justice on a shared planet: more rights or new relations?' *Theoretical Criminology*, 2 (2): 149–75.

Bergreen, Laurence (1994) *Capone: the Man and the Era*. London: Pan Books.

Bittner, E. (1975) *The Functions of the Police in Modern Society*. New York: Jason Aronson.

Bloch, Marc (1961) *Feudal Society*. London: Routledge & Kegan Paul.

Blok, Anton (1974) *The Mafia of a Sicilian Village 1860–1980: a Study of Violent Peasant Entrepreneurs*. Oxford: Oxford University Press.

Bosworth-Davies, Rowan (1997) 'Deviant legitimacy – a theory of financial crime', *Journal of Financial Crime*, 4 (1): 7–16.

Bottoms, Anthony (1983) 'Some neglected features of contemporary penal systems', in D. Garland and P. Young (eds), *The Power to Punish*. London: Heinemann.

Bourgois, Philipe (1996) *In Search of Respect: Selling Crack in El Barrio*. Cambridge Cambridge University Press.

Bourke, Joanna (1994) *Working Class Cultures in Britain: Gender, Class and Ethnicity*. London: Routledge.

Boutellier, Hans (2000) *Crime and Morality: the Significance of Criminal Justice in Post-Modern Culture*. Dordrecht: Kluwer Academic Publishers.

Bowlby, John (1953) *Child Care and the Growth of Love*. Harmondsworth: Penguin.

Bowling, Ben (1999) 'The rise and fall of the New York murder: zero tolerance or crack's decline?' *British Journal of Criminology*, 39 (4): 531–54.

Box, Steven (1983) *Crime, Power and Mystification*. London: Tavistock.

Box, Steven (1987) *Recession, Crime and Punishment*. London: Macmillan.

Braithwaite, John (1989) *Crime, Shame and Reintegration*. Cambridge: Cambridge University Press.

Braithwaite, John (2000a) 'The new regulatory state and the transformation of criminology', *British Journal of Criminology* 40: 222–38.

Braithwaite, John (2000b) 'NGOs and corporate power: is there a win–win solution?' Speech to Global Economy Forum, Australian Council for Overseas Aid. Melbourne: ACFOA.

Braithwaite, John and Drahos, Peter (2000) *Global Business Regulation*. Cambridge: Cambridge University Press.

Brenner, Robert (1998) 'The economics of global turbulence', *New Left Review*, 229 (May/June), pp. 1–265.

Brenner, Robert (2000) 'The boom and the bubble', *New Left Review* (second series) 6 (November/December): 5–43.

Brewer, John (1994) *Black and Blue: Policing in South Africa*. Oxford: Clarendon Press.

Brewer, John and Styles, John (eds) (1980) *An Ungovernable People: the English and their Law in the Seventeenth and Eighteenth Centuries*. London: Hutchinson.

Brodeur, Jean-Paul (1983) 'High policing and low policing: remarks about the policing of political activities', *Social Problems* (30) 5: 507–20.

Brogden, Mike (1982) *The Police: Autonomy and Consent*. London: Academic Press.

Brogden, Mike (1991) *On the Mersey Beat: Policing Liverpool between the Wars*. Oxford: Oxford University Press.

Brogden, Mike and Shearing, Clifford (1993) *Policing for a New South Africa*. London: Routledge.

Brogden, Mike, Jefferson, T. and Walklate, S. (1988) *Introducing Police Work*. London: Unwin Hyman.

Buckley, M. (1985) 'Soviet interpretations of the woman question', in Barbara Holland (ed.), *Soviet Sisterhood*. Bloomington, IN: Indiana University Press.

Burchell, Graham, Gordon, C. and Miller, P. (eds) (1991) *The Foucault Effect: Studies in Governmentality*. Brighton: Harvester Wheatsheaf.

Burman, S. and Scharf, W. (1990) 'Creating people's justice: street committees and people's courts in a South African city', *Law and Society Review*, 24 (3): pp. 263–82.

Caldeira, Teresa (1996) 'Fortified enclaves: the new urban segregation', *Public Culture*, 8 (2): 303–28.

Campbell, Beatrix (1993) *Goliath: Britain's Dangerous Places*. London: Methuen.

Campbell, Duncan (1990) *That was Business, This is Personal: the Changing Face of Professional Crime*. London: Secker & Warburg.

Carson, W. (1970) 'White collar crime and the enforcement of factory legislation', *British Journal of Criminology*, 10: 383–98.

Carson, W. (1982) *The Other Price of Britain's Oil*. London: Martin Robertson.

Carter, David (1997) 'International organized crime: emerging trends in entrepreneurial crime', in P. Ryan and G. Rush (eds), *Understanding Organized Crime in Global Perspective*. Newbury Park, CA: Sage.

Castel, Robert (1991), 'From dangerousness to risk' in G. Burchell et al. (eds), *The Foucault Effect: Studies in Governmentality*, Brighton: Harvester Wheatsheaf.

Castells, Manuel (1996) *The Rise of the Network Society* (vol. 1 of *The Information Age: Economy, Society and Culture*). Oxford: Blackwell.

Castells, Manuel (1997) *The Power of Identity* (vol. 2 of *The Information Age: Economy, Society and Culture*). Oxford: Blackwell.

Castells, Manuel (1998) *End of Millenium* (vol. 3 of *The Information Age: Economy, Society and Culture*). Oxford: Blackwell.

Castles, Stephen and Kosack, Godula (1973) *Immigrant Workers and the Class Structure in Western Europe*. Oxford: Oxford University Press.

Catanzaro, Raimondo (1992) *'Men of Respect': a Social History of the Sicilian Mafia*. New York: Free Press.

Cavallaro, Luigi (2001) 'Il Modello Mafioso Nell 'Economia Globalizzata', *La revista del Manifesto*, 23 (December): 18–21.

Cawthra, Gavin (1993) *Policing South Africa: the SAP and the Transition from Apartheid*. London: Zed Press.

CDP (1977) *Gilding the Ghetto: the State and the Poverty Experiments*. London: Home Office (Urban Deprivation Unit).

Chambliss, William (1994) 'Policing the ghetto underclass: the politics of law and law enforcement', *Social Problems* 41 (2): 177–94.

Chesney, Kellow (1972) *The Victorian Underworld: a Fascinating Recreation*. Harmondsworth: Penguin.

Chossudovsky, Michel (1996) 'The business of crime and the crimes of business: globalization and the criminalization of economic activity', *Covert Action Quarterly*, 58 (Fall): 24–30.

Chossudovsky, Michel (1997) *The Globalization of Poverty: Impacts of IMF and World Bank Reforms*. London: Zed Books.

Chossudovsky, M. (1999) *Kosovo Freedom Fighters Financed By Organized Crime*. Ottawa: University of Ottawa.

Christie, Nils (1977) 'Conflicts as property', *British Journal of Criminology*, 17: 1–15.

Christie, Nils (1986) 'The ideal victim', in E. Fattah (ed.), *From Crime Policy to Victim Policy*. London: Macmillan.

Christopherson, Susan (1994) 'The fortress city: privatized spaces, consumer citizenship', in A. Amin (ed.), *Post-Fordism: A Reader*. Oxford: Blackwell.

Clarke, D. (1978) 'Marxism, justice and the justice model', *Contemporary Crises*, 2: 27–62.

Clarke, John and Jefferson, Tony (1976) 'Working-class youth cultures', in Geoff Pearson and Geoff Mungham (eds), *Working-Class Youth Culture*. London: Routledge.

Clarke, Michael (1986) *Regulating the City: Competition, Scandal and Reform*. Milton Keynes: Open University Press.

Clarke, Michael (1990) *Business Crime: Its Nature and Control*. Cambridge: Polity Press.

Clinard, M. and Abbott, D. (1973) *Crime in Developing Countries*. New York: Wiley.

Cloward, R. and Ohlin, L. (1960) *Delinquency and Opportunity*. New York: Free Press.

Cohen, Albert (1955) *Delinquent Boys*. New York: Free Press.

Cohen, Phil (1972) 'Subcultural conflict and the working-class community', *Working Papers in Cultural Studies No 2*. University of Birmingham: Centre for Contemporary Cultural Studies.

Cohen, Phil (1979) 'Policing the working-class city', in B. Fine et al. (eds), *Capitalism and the Rule of Law*. London: Hutchinson.

Cohen, Stan (1980) *Folk Devils and Moral Panics* (2nd edn). Oxford: Martin Robertson.

Cohen, Stan (1985) *Visions of Social Control*. Cambridge: Polity Press.

Cohen, Stan (1988) 'The object of criminology: reflections on the new criminalization', in Stan Cohen, *Against Criminology*. New Brunswick: Transaction Books.

Cohen, Stan (1997) 'The revenge of the null hypothesis: evaluation crime control hypotheses', *Critical Criminologist* 8: 21–5.

Collins, Randall (1974) 'Three faces of cruelty: towards a comparative sociology of violence', *Theory and Society*, 1 (4): 415–40.

Commission on Social Justice (1994) *Social Justice: Strategies for National Renewal*. London: Vintage.

Connell, R. (1995) *Masculinities*. Cambridge: Polity Press.

Cornia, G. (1999) 'Rising inequality in an era of liberalization and globalization', *Work in Progress: a Review of Research Activities of the United Nations University*, 16 (1): http://www.unu.edu/hg/ginfo/wip/wip-win99.html

Crawford, Andrew (1995) 'Appeals to community and crime prevention', *Crime, Law and Social Change*, 22: 97–126.

Crawford, Andrew (1997) *The Local Governance of Crime*. Oxford: Clarendon Press.

Crawford, Andrew (1998) *Crime Prevention and Community Safety: Politics, Policies and Practices*. London: Longman.

Crook, Stephen, Pakulski, Jan and Waters, Malcolm (1992) *Postmodernization: Change in Advanced Society*. London: Sage.

Crosland, Anthony (1956) *The Future of Socialism*. London: Jonathan Cape.

Crozier, Michel et al. (eds) (1975) *The Crisis of Democracy*. New York University Press.

Crowther, Chris (2000) 'Thinking about the "underclass": towards a political economy of policing, *Theoretical Criminology*, 4 (2) (May): 149–67.

Currie, Elliot (1998) 'Crime and market society: lessons from the United States', in P. Walton and J. Young (eds) *The New Criminology Revisited*. London: Macmillan.

Daunton, M. (1983) 'Public space and private place: the Victorian city and the working-class household', in D. Fraser and A. Sutcliffe (eds), *The Pursuit of Urban History*, pp. 212–33. London: Edward Arnold.

Davidoff, L. and Hall, C. (1987) *Family Fortunes: Men and Women of the English Middle Class, 1750–1850*. London: Hutchinson.

Davies, Nick (1997) *Dark Heart: the Shocking Truth about Hidden Britain*. London: Chatto & Windus.

Davies, Nick (1998) 'Watching the detectives: how the police cheat in fight against crime', *Guardian*, 18 March.

Davis, J. (1989) 'Prosecutions and their context: the use of criminal law in later nineteenth century London', in Douglas Hay and F. Snyder, *Policing and Prosecution in England 1750–1850*. Oxford: Oxford University Press.

Davis, Mike (1990) *City of Quartz: Excavating the Future in Los Angeles.* London: Verso.

Davis, Mike (1992) 'The L.A. inferno', *Socialist Review,* 22 (1): 57–80.

Davis, Mike (1998) 'Beyond Blade Runner', in *Ecology of Fear: Los Angeles and the Imagination of Disaster.* New York: Henry Holt.

Dean, Mitchell (1999) *Governmentality: Power and Rule in Modern Society.* London: Sage.

de Brie, Christian (2000) 'Thick as thieves', *Le Monde Diplomatique* (April) electronic edition: http://www.monde-diplomatique.fr/en/2000/04/05debrie.

de Lint, Willem (1999) 'A post-modern turn in policing: policing as pastiche?' *International Journal of the Sociology of Law,* 27: 127–52.

de Rivero, Oswaldo (1999) 'States in ruin, conflicts without end: the economics of future chaos', *Le Monde Diplomatique* ((June), English electronic edition) http://www.monde-diplomatique.fr/en/1999/06/?c=03rivero.

Deflem, Mathieu (1994) 'Law enforcement in British Colonial Africa: a comparative analysis of imperial policing in Nyasaland, the Gold Coast, and Kenya', *Police Studies,* 17 (1): 45–68.

della Porta, D. and Vannucci, A. (1999) *Corrupt Exchanges: Actors, Resources and Mechanisms of Political Corruption.* New York: Aldine de Gruyter.

Devine, Fiona (1992) *Affluent Workers Revisited: Privatisation and the Working Class.* Edinburgh: Edinburgh University Press.

Downes, David (1966) *The Delinquent Solution: a Study in Subcultural Theory.* London: Routledge & Kegan Paul.

Downes, David and Morgan, Rob (1994) 'Hostages to fortune? The politics of law and order in post-war Britain', in M. Maguire, R. Morgan and R. Reiner (eds), *The Oxford Handbook of Criminology.* Oxford: Oxford University Press.

Drucker, Peter (1981) 'What is business ethics?', *The Public Interest,* 63: 18–36.

Elias, Norbert (1978) 'On transformations of aggressiveness', *Theory and Society,* 5: 227–53.

Elias, Norbert (1982) *State Formation and Civilisation.* Oxford: Blackwell.

Elias, Norbert (1994) *The Civilizing Process.* Oxford: Blackwell.

Elias, R. (1993) *Victims Still: the Political Manipulation of Crime Victims.* London: Sage.

Elton, G. (1977) 'Introduction' in J. Cockburn (ed.), *Crime in England 1550–1800.* London: Methuen.

Emsley, Clive (1987) *Crime and Society in England 1750–1900.* London: Longman.

Emsley, Clive (1996) *Crime and Society in England 1750–1900* (2nd edn). London: Longman.

Engels, Frederick (1845/1975), 'The condition of the working class in England', *in Marx, Engels, Collected Works,* vol. 4. Moscow: Progress Publishers.

Ericson, Richard (1994) 'The division of expert knowledge in policing and security', *British Journal of Sociology,* 45: 149–70.

Etzioni, Amitai (1993) *The Spirit of Community: the Reinvention of American Society.* New York: Simon & Schuster.

European Parliament Temporary Committee on the ECHELON Interception System (2001) *Draft Report on the Existence of a Global System for the Interception of Private and Commercial Communications (ECHELON interception system)* 18 May. Strasbourg: European Parliament.

Evans, Karen, Fraser, Penny and Walklate, Sandra (1996) 'Whom can you trust? The politics of "grassing" on an inner city housing estate', *Sociological Review,* 44 (3): 361–80.

Feeley, Malcolm and Simon, Jonathan (1992) 'The new penology: notes on the emerging strategy of corrections and its implications', *Criminology,* 30 (4): 449–74.

Feeley, Malcolm and Simon, Jonathan (1994) 'Actuarial justice: the emerging new criminal law', in D. Nelken (ed.), *The Futures of Criminology.* London: Sage.

Findlay, Mark (1999) *The Globalisation of Crime: Understanding Transitional Relationships in Context.* Cambridge: Cambridge University Press.

Fine, Bob (1984) *Democracy and the Rule of Law: Liberal Ideals and Marxist Critiques.* London: Pluto Press.

Finkelstein, Norman (1997) 'Daniel Jonah Goldhagen's "crazy" thesis: a critique of Hitler's willing executioners', *New Left Review,* 224: 39–88.

Fitzpatrick, Peter (1988) 'The rise and rise of informalism', in Roger Matthews (ed.), *Informal Justice?* London: Sage.

Foster, Janet (1990) *Villains: Crime and Community in the Inner City.* London: Routledge.

Foucault, Michel (1977) *Discipline and Punish.* London: Allen Lane.

Foucault, Michel (1979) *The History of Sexuality* (vol. 1). Harmondsworth: Penguin.

Foucault, Michel (1991) 'Governmentality', in Graham Burchell, C. Gordon and P. Miller (eds), *The Foucault Effect*, pp. 87–104. Brighton: Harvester Wheatsheaf.

Freeman, Richard (1996) 'Toward an apartheid economy', *Harvard Business Review* (Sept.–Oct.): 114–26.

Freund, William (1986) 'Theft and social protest among the tin miners of northern Nigeria', in Donald Crummey (ed.), *Banditry, Rebellion and Social Protest in Africa*, pp. 49–65. London: James Currey.

Froggett, Lynn (1996) 'Instrumentalism, knowledge and gender in social work', *Journal of Social Work Practice*, 10 (2): 119–27.

Fyvel, T. (1961) *The Insecure Offenders: Rebellious Youth in the Welfare State.* London: Chatto & Windus.

Galbraith, John (1967) *The New Industrial State.* Boston, MA: Houghton Mifflin.

Gambetta, Diego (1993) *The Sicilian Mafia: the Business of Private Protection.* Cambridge, MA: Harvard University Press.

Gamble, Andrew (1994) *Britain in Decline.* London: Macmillan.

Garland, David (1996), 'The limits of the sovereign state: strategies of crime control in contemporary society', *British Journal of Criminology*, 36: 445–71.

Garland, David (2000) 'The culture of high crime societies', *British Journal of Criminology*, 40: 347–75.

Garrido, L. and Prats, J. (2000) 'Las cavernas de los explotados.' *El Pais,* 20 December.

Gatrell, Victor (1980) 'The decline of theft and violence in Victorian and Edwardian England', in Victor Gatrell et al. (eds.), *Crime and the Law*, pp. 238–337. London: Europa Publications.

Gatrell, Victor (1988) 'Crime, authority and the policeman state', in F. Thompson (ed.), *The Cambridge Social History of Britain*, vol. 3. Cambridge: Cambridge University Press.

Gatrell, Victor and Hadden, T. (1972) 'Criminal Statistics and their interpretation', in E. Wrigley (ed.), *Nineteenth-Century Society.* Oxford: Oxford University Press.

Geopolitical Drug Watch (1999) *The World Geopolitics of Drugs 1997/8.* Paris: Observatoire Géopolitique des Drogues.

George, Susan (1999) *The Lugano Report: on Preserving Capitalism in the Twenty-first Century.* London: Pluto Press.

Gery, Yves (1999) 'The dark side of Europe: women for sale', *Le Monde Diplomatique*, February.

Goldhagen, Daniel (1996) *Hitler's Willing Executioners: Ordinary Germans and the Holocaust.* London: Little Brown & Company.

Goldman, M. (1995) 'Is this any way to create a market-economy?', *Current History*, 94 (594): 305–10.

Goldthorpe, John and Lockwood, David (1963) 'Affluence and the British class structure', *Sociological Review*, 11 (2): 112–45.

Goldthorpe, J., Lockwood, D., Bechhofer, F. and Platt, J. (1968) *The Affluent Worker: Industrial Attitudes and Behaviour.* Cambridge: Cambridge University Press.

Gordon, Diana (1994) *The Return of the Dangerous Classes: Drug Prohibition and Policy Politics.* New York: W.W. Norton.

Grant-Stitt, B. (1989) 'Victimless crime: a definitional issue', *Journal of Crime and Justice*, 12 (2): 87–102.

Gray, Anne (1995) 'Flexibilisation of labour and the attack on workers' living standards', *Common Sense*, 18: 10–15.

Gray, John (1998) *False Dawn: The Delusions of Global Capitalism.* London: Granta Books.

Greenberg, David (1965) 'Age, crime and social explanation', *American Journal of Sociology*, 18: 256–91.

Greer, Germaine (2000), 'Gluttons for porn', *Observer,* 24 September.

Greider, William (1997) *One World Ready or Not: the Manic Logic of Global Capitalism.* New York: Simon & Schuster.

Griffin, Rob (2000) 'It's an increasingly dirty business', *Guardian*, 15 September.

Gunder Frank, Andre (1967a) 'Sociology of development and underdevelopment of sociology', *Catalyst*, 3 (Summer): 20–74.

Gunder Frank, Andre (1967b) *Capitalism and Underdevelopment in Latin America*. New York: Monthly Review Press.

Gurr, Ted (1989) 'Historical trends in violent crime: Europe and the United States', in T. Gurr (ed.), *Violence in America*, vol. 1. Thousand Oaks, CA: Sage.

Habermas, Jürgen (1976) *Legitimation Crisis*. London: Heinemann.

Habermas, Jürgen (1987) *The Theory of Communicative Action*, vol. 2. Cambridge: Polity Press.

Habermas, Jürgen (1989) *The Structural Transformation of the Public Sphere*. Cambridge: Polity Press.

Hagan, John (1994), *Crime and Disrepute*. Berkeley, CA: Pineforge Press.

Hahn, Paul (1998) *Emerging Criminal Justice: Three Pillars for a Proactive Justice System*. Thousand Oaks, CA: Sage.

Hall, Peter and Pfeiffer, Ulrich (2000) *Urban Future 21*. London: Spon.

Hall, Stuart (1989) 'The meaning of new times', in S. Hall and M. Jaques (eds), *New Times*. London: Lawrence & Wishart.

Hall, Stuart and Jefferson, Tony (eds) (1976) *Resistance Through Rituals: Youth Cultures in Post-War Britain*. London: Hutchinson.

Hall, Stuart, Critcher, Chas, Jefferson, Tony, Clarke, John and Roberts, Brian (1978) *Policing the Crisis: Mugging, the State, and Law and Order*. London: Macmillan.

Haller, Mark (1989) 'Bootlegging: the business and politics of violence', in T. Gurr (ed.), *Violence in America*, vol. 1. Thousand Oaks, CA: Sage.

Hammerton, A. J. (1992) *Cruelty and Companionship: Conflict in Nineteenth-Century Married Life*. London: Routledge.

Hanawalt, Barbara (1979) *Crime and Conflict in English Communities 1300–1348*. Cambridge, MA: Harvard University Press.

Handelman, Stephen (1995) *Comrade Criminal, Russia's New Mafiya*. New Haven, CT: Yale University Press.

Hardt, Michael and Negri, Antonio (2000) *Empire*. Cambridge MA: Harvard University Press.

Harris, Tim (2000) 'The effect of taxes and benefits upon household income 1998–99', *Economic Trends*, United Kingdom Office of National Statistics (April).

Harrison, Bennett (1994) 'The dark side of flexible production', *Technology Review* 97 (4): 38–45.

Harrison, D. (1988) *The Sociology of Modernization and Development*. London: Routledge.

Hartman, Renate (1998) 'Trafficking in women from Central and Eastern Europe to the Netherlands', *Rights of Women Bulletin* (Summer): 23–6.

Harvey, David (1989) *The Condition of Postmodernity*. Oxford: Blackwell.

Harvey, David (1994) 'Flexible accumulation through urbanization: reflections on "postmodernism" in the American City', in A. Amin (ed.), *Post-Fordism: A Reader*. Oxford: Blackwell.

Harvey, David (1997) 'Contested cities: social processes and spatial form', in Nicholas Jewson and Susanne MacGregor (eds), *Transforming Cities: Contested Governance and New Spatial Divisions*. London: Routledge.

Hay, Douglas (1975) 'Property, authority and the criminal law', in Hay et al., *Albion's Fatal Tree: Crime and Society in Eighteenth Century England*. London: Allen Lane.

Hay, Douglas, Linebaugh, Peter, Rule, John, Thompson, Edward and Winslow, Cal (eds) (1975) *Albion's Fatal Tree: Crime and Society in Eighteenth Century England*. London: Allen Lane.

Hayter, Teresa (2000) *Open Borders: the Case Against Immigration Controls*, London: Pluto Press.

Head, Simon (1996) 'The new, ruthless economy', *New York Review of Books* (29 February).

Hertz, Noreena (2001) *The Silent Takeover: Global Capitalism and the Death of Democracy*. London: Heinemann.

Hegel, Georg W. 1817 [1965] 'Who thinks abstractly?' in W. Kaufmann, *Hegel: Texts and Commentary*. New York: Anchor Books.

Heiland, H. and Shelley, L. (eds) (1992) *Crime and Control in Comparative Perspectives*. New York: Walter de Gruyter.

Held, D., McGrew, A., Goldblatt, D. and Perraton, J. (1999) *Global Transformations*. Cambridge: Polity Press.

Henry, Stuart, and Milovanovic, Dragan (1996) *Constitutive Criminology: Beyond Postmodernism*. London: Sage.

Hess, Henner (1973) *Mafia and Mafiosi: the Structure of Power*. Farnborough: Saxon House/Lexington Books.

Hess, Henner (1998) *Mafia and Mafiosi: Origin, Power and Myth*. London: Hurst & Co.

Hills, J. (1995) *The Joseph Rowntree Inquiry into Income and Wealth*, vol. 2. London: Joseph Rowntree Foundation.

Hirst, Paul (1994) *Associative Democracy: New Forms of Economic and Social Governance*. Cambridge: Polity Press.

Hirst, Paul (2000) 'Statism, pluralism and social control', *British Journal of Criminology*, 40: 279–95.

Hobbs, Dick (1988) *Doing the Business: Entrepreneurship, the Working Class and Detectives in the East End of London*. Oxford: Clarendon Press.

Hobbs, Dick (1995) *Bad Business: Professional Crime in Modern Britain*. Oxford: Oxford University Press.

Hobbs, Dick (1998), 'Going down the glocal: the local context of organised crime', *Howard Journal of Criminal Justice*, 37 (4): 407–22.

Hobsbawm, Eric (1959) *Primitive Rebels: Studies in Archaic Forms of Social Movement during the Nineteenth and Twentieth Centuries*. Manchester: Manchester University Press.

Hobsbawm, Eric (1969) *Bandits*. Harmondsworth: Penguin Books.

Hobsbawm, Eric (1972) 'Social criminality: distinctions between socio-political and other forms of crime', *Society for the Study of Labour History, Bulletin*, 25: 5–6.

Honneth, Axel (1992) 'Pluralization and recognition: on the self-misunderstanding of postmodern social theorists', in P. Beilharz et al. (eds), *Between Totalitarianism and Postmodernity*. Cambridge, MA: MIT Press.

Hood, Roger and Robins, David (1997) *Intergenerational Differences in Experiences of Crime Through Life Histories*. ESRC award L210252016, end of award report.

Hope, Tim (2000) 'Inequality and the clubbing of private security', in T. Hope and R. Sparks (eds), *Crime, Risk and Insecurity*. London: Routledge.

Horwitz, Ralph (1967) *The Political Economy of South Africa*. New York: Praeger.

Hoyle, Carolyn (1998) *Negotiating Domestic Violence: Police, Criminal Justice and Victims* (Clarendon Studies in Criminology). Oxford: Oxford University Press.

Hudson, Barbara (1998) 'Restorative justice: the challenge of sexual and racial violence', *Journal of Law and Society*, 25 (2): 237–56.

Hughes, Donna (1999) 'Men@exploitation.com', *Trouble and Strife*, 38 (Winter 1998/9): 21–3.

Hughes, Gordon (1998) *Understanding Crime Prevention: Social Control, Risk and Late Modernity*. Milton Keynes: Open University Press.

Hulsman, Louk (1986) 'Critical criminology and the concept of crime', in Herman Bianchi and Rene van Swaaningen (eds), *Abolitionism: Towards a Non-repressive Approach to Crime*. Amsterdam: Free University Press.

Humphries, Stephen (1981) *Hooligans or Rebels? An Oral History of Working Class Childhood and Youth 1889–1939*. Oxford: Blackwell.

Hunt, Alan (1992) *Explorations in Law and Society: towards a constitutive theory of law*. London: Routledge.

Huntington, Samuel P. (1968) *Political Order in a Changing Society*, New Haven, CT: Yale University Press.

Ianni, Francis and Ianni, Elizabeth (1972) *Family Business*. New York: Russell Sage.

Jachcel, E. (1983) 'Towards a criminological analysis of the origins of capital', Ph.D. Thesis, University of Sheffield, Centre for Criminological and Socio-Legal Studies.

Jackson, Louise (1999) 'Family, community and the regulation of sexual abuse: London 1870–1914', in A. Fletcher and S. Hussey (eds), *Childhood in Question*. Manchester: Manchester University Press.

Jackson, Louise (2000) *Child Sexual Abuse in Victorian England*. London: Routledge.

Jameson, Frederic (1984) 'Postmodernism or the cultural logic of late capitalism', *New Left Review*, 146: 53–92.

Jameson, Frederic (1998) *The Cultural Turn: Selected Writings on the Postmodern 1983–1998*. London: Verso.

Jamieson, Alison (1990), 'Mafia and political power 1943–1989', *International Relations*, 10 (May): 13–30.

Jamieson, Ruth (1998) 'Towards a criminology of war in Europe', in V. Ruggiero, N. South and I. Taylor (eds), *The New European Criminology: Crime and Social Order in Europe*. London: Routledge.

Jenkins, P. and Potter, G. (1986) 'Organised crime in London: a comparative perspective', *Corruption and Reform* 1 (3): 165–87.

Jessop, Bob (1994) 'The transition to post-Fordism and the Schumpeterian workfare state', in J. Burrows and B. Loader (eds), *Towards a Post-Fordist Welfare State?* London: Routledge.

Johnston, Les (1992) *The Rebirth of Private Policing*. London: Routledge.

Johnston, Les (2000) *Policing Britain: Risk, Security and Governance*. London: Longman.

Johnston, L., MacDonald, R., Mason, P., Ridley, L. and Webster, C. (2000) *Snakes and Ladders: Young People, Transitions, and Social Exclusion*. Bristol: Policy Press.

Jütte, Robert (1994) *Poverty and Deviance in Early Modern Europe*. Cambridge: Cambridge University Press.

Kaldor, Mary (1999) *New and Old Wars: Organized Violence in a Global Era*. Cambridge: Polity Press.

Kaplan, Robert (1998) *An Empire Wilderness: Travels into America's Future*. New York: Random House.

Katz, Jack (1988) *Seductions of Crime: Moral and Sensual Attractions of Doing Evil*. New York: Basic Books.

Keh, Douglas (1996), 'Drug money in a changing world: economic reform and criminal finance', UNIDCP Technical Series No 4. Vienna: United Nations International Drug Control Programme.

Kennedy, P. (1998) 'Coming to terms with contemporary capitalism: beyond the idealism of globalisation and capitalist ascendancy arguments', *Sociological Research Online*, 3, (2) <http://www.socresonline.org.uk/socresonline/3/2/6.html>.

Kerry, John (1997) *The New War*. New York: Simon and Schuster.

Khor, M. (1997) 'SEA currency turmoil renews concern on financial speculation', *Third World Resurgence*, 86: 13–14.

Killingray, D. (1986) 'The maintenance of law and order in British colonial Africa', *African Affairs*, 85 (340): 411–37.

Kinsey, Richard, Lea, John and Young, Jock (1986) *Losing the Fight Against Crime*. Oxford: Blackwell.

Kochan, N. and Whittington, B. (1991) *Bankrupt: the BCCI Fraud*. London: Victor Gollancz.

Koonz, Claudia (1988) *Mothers in the Fatherland: Women, the Family and Nazi Politics*. London: Methuen.

Lacey, Nicola (1995) 'Contingency and criminalisation', in Ian Loveland (ed.), *Frontiers of Criminality*. London: Sweet & Maxwell.

Lasch, Christopher (1984) *The Minimal Self, Psychic Survival in Troubled Times*. New York: Norton.

Lasch, Christopher (1995) *The Revolt of the Elites and the Betrayal of Democracy*. London: Norton.

Lea, John (1979) 'Discipline and capitalist development', in Bob Fine, Richard Kinsey, John Lea, Sol Picciotto and Jock Young (eds), *Capitalism and the Rule of Law*. London: Hutchinson.

Lea, John (1980) 'The contradictions of the sixties race relations legislation', in National Deviancy Conference (eds), *Permissiveness and Control: The Fate of the Sixties Legislation*. London: Macmillan.

Lea, John (1982) 'Legitimation crisis and the welfare state: the relevance of Habermas', Middlesex Polytechnic Occasional Paper No. 9.

Lea, John (1987) 'Left realism: a defence', *Contemporary Crises*, 11: 21–32.

Lea, John (1992) 'The analysis of crime' in Jock Young and R. Matthews (eds), *Rethinking Criminology: the Realist Debate*. London: Sage.

Lea, John (1997) 'Postfordism and criminality', in Nick Jewson and Susanne MacGregor (eds), *Transforming Cities: Contested Governance and New Spatial Divisions*, pp. 42–55. London: Routledge.

Lea, John (1998) 'Criminology and postmodernity', in Paul Walton and Jock Young (eds), *The New Criminology Revisited*. London: Macmillan.

Lea, John (1999) 'Social crime revisited', *Theoretical Criminology*, 3 (3): 307–25.

Lea, John and Young, Jock (1993) *What Is to Be Done About Law and Order* (2nd edn). London: Pluto Press.

Lee, R. (1999) 'Transnational organized crime: an overview', in T. Farer (ed.), *Transnational Crime in the Americas*. New York: Routledge.

Lees, Sue (1996) *Carnal Knowledge: Rape on Trial*. London: Hamish Hamilton.

Lees, Sue and Gregory, Jeanne (1999) *Policing Sexual Assault*. London: Routledge.

Leitzel, Jim (1995) *Russian Economic Reform*. London: Routledge.

Lenman, B. and Parker, G. (1980) 'The state, the community and criminal law in early modern Europe', in Victor Gatrell et al. (eds), *Crime and the Law*. London: Europa Publications.

Leps, M. (1992) *Apprehending the Criminal: the Production of Deviance in Nineteenth Century Discourse*. Durham, NC: Duke University Press.

Levi, Michael (1981) *The Phantom Capitalists: The Organization and Control of Long Firm Fraud*. Aldershot: Gower.

Leyshon, Andrew and Thrift, Nigel (1997) 'Geographies of financial exclusion: financial abandonment in England and the United States', in A. Leyshon and N. Thrift, *Money/Space: Geographies of Monetary Transformation*. London: Routledge.

Lianos, Michalis and Douglas, Mary (2000) 'Dangerization and the end of deviance', *British Journal of Criminology*, 40: 261–78.

Linebaugh, Peter (1991) *The London Hanged*. London: Allen Lane.

Lipschutz, Ronnie (1996) 'Reconstructing world politics: the emergence of global civil society', in J. Larkins and R. Fawn (eds), *International Society after the Cold War*, pp. 101–31. London: Macmillan.

Lloyd, Christopher (2000) 'Globalization: beyond the ultra-modernist narrative to a critical realist perspective on geopolitics in the cyber age', *International Journal of Urban and Regional Research*, 24 (2): 258–73.

Luke, Tim (1996) 'Nationality and sovereignty in the new world order', *AntePodium*, March 1996. *http://www.vuw.ac.nz/atp/*.

Lundberg, Mattias and Squire, Lyn (1999) *The Simultaneous Evolution of Growth and Inequality*. Washington, DC: World Bank.

Luttwak, Edward (1998) *Turbo Capitalism: Winners and Losers in the World Economy*. London: Weidenfeld & Nicolson.

Mack, John (1964) 'Full-time miscreants, delinquent neighbourhoods and criminal networks', *British Journal of Sociology*, 15: 38–53.

Mack, John (1975) *The Crime Industry*. Farnborough: Saxon House.

Maguire, M. and Ponting, J. (eds) (1988) *Victims of Crime: A New Deal?* Milton Keynes: Open University Press.

Mannheim, Herman (1946) *Criminal Justice and Social Reconstruction*. London: Kegan & Paul.

Marenin, Otwin (1982) 'Policing African states: toward a critique', *Comparative Politics*, 14 (4): 379–94.

Marshall, T.H. (1950) *Citizenship and Social Class*. Cambridge: Cambridge University Press.
Martin, H. and Schumann, H. (1997) *The Global Trap: Globalization and the Assault on Democracy and Prosperity*. London: Zed Books.
Marx, Karl (1973) *Grundrisse: Foundations of the Critique of Political Economy*. Harmondsworth: Penguin Books.
Marx, Karl (1976) *Capital* (vol. 1). Harmondsworth: Penguin Books.
Massing, Michael (1998) 'The blue revolution', *New York Review of Books*, 19 November: 32–6.
Mathiason, Nick (2001) 'Bush blocks EU Aids drug relief', *Observer*, 17 June.
Matthews, Roger (ed.) (1988) *Informal Justice*. London: Sage.
Mawby, Ron and Walklate, Sandra (1993) *Critical Victimology: International Responses*. London: Sage.
Mays, John (1954) *Growing up in the City*. Liverpool: Liverpool University Press.
McCall, G. (1995) 'Use of law in a South African township', *International Journal of the Sociology of Law*, 23: 59–78.
McCoy, Alfred (1991) *The Politics of Heroin: CIA Complicity in the Global Drug Trade*, New York: Lawrence Hill Books.
McDowell, Linda (1991) 'Life without father and Ford: the new gender order of post-Fordism', *Transactions, Institute of British Geographers*. NS 16: 400–19.
McIntosh, Mary (1975) *The Organisation of Crime*. London: Macmillan.
McMullan, John (1984) *The Canting Crew: London's Criminal Underworld 1550–1700*. New Brunswick: Rutgers University Press.
McMullan, John (1987) 'Crime, law and order in early modern England', *British Journal of Criminology* 27 (3): 252–74.
McMullan, John (1995) 'The political economy of thief-taking', *Crime, Law and Social Change*, 23: 121–46.
McVeigh, Tracey (2000) 'Namers and shamers face their eviction with pride', *Observer*, 24 September.
McWilliams, Monica and Cullen, Carol (1994) 'Women and policing', in *Policing in a New Society*. Report of a Conference held at Belfast Institute of Further and Higher Education. Belfast: Centre for Research and Documentation and Belfast Community Forum on Policing.
Merton, Robert (1957) *Social Theory and Social Structure*. New York: Free Press.
Mészáros, István (1995) *Beyond Capital*. London: Merlin Press.
Mészáros, István (1998) 'The uncontrollability of globalizing capital', *Monthly Review* (February): 27–37.
Mészáros, István. (2001) *Socialism or Barbarism: from the 'American Century' to the Crossroads*. New York: Monthly Review Press.
Miller, Walter (1958) 'Lower class culture as a generating milieu of gang delinquency', *Journal of Social Issues*, 14 (3): 5–19.
Mishra, Ramesh (1999) *Globalization and the Welfare State*. Cheltenham: Edward Elgar.
Mokhiber, Russell and Weissman, Robert (1999) *Corporate Predators: the Hunt for Mega-profits and the Attack on Democracy*. Monroe, ME: Common Courage Press.
Mooney, Jayne (2000) *Gender, Violence and the Social Order*. London: Macmillan.
Monbiot, George (2001) 'Bush's dirty war: Colombia's peasant farmers are being driven off their land. And we are helping', *Guardian*, 22 May.
Murray, Charles (1999) *The Underclass Revisited*. American Enterprise Institute for Public Policy Research: Papers and Studies. http://www.aei.org/ps/psmurray.htm.
Naylor, R. (1999) *Follow-the-Money Methods in Crime Control Policy: a Study Prepared for the Nathanson Centre for the Study of Organized Crime and Corruption*. Toronto: York University.
NCIS (2000) *Organised Crime: UK Threat Assessment*. London: National Criminal Intelligence Service (UK).
Ness, D. (1990) 'Restorative justice', in B. Galaway and J. Hudson (eds), *Criminal Justice, Restitution and Reconciliation*. New York: Criminal Justice Press.

Nicholson, J. (1967) 'The distribution of personal income', *Lloyds Bank Review* (January).

Nikolic-Ristanovic, Vesna (1998), 'War and crime in the former Yugolslavia', in V. Ruggiero, N. South and I. Taylor, (eds), *The New European Criminology: Crime and Social Order in Europe*, London: Routledge.

O'Connor, James (1973) *The Fiscal Crisis of the State*. New York: Saint Martin's Press.

Offe, Claus (1984) *Contradictions of the Welfare State*. London: Hutchinson.

O'Malley, Pat (1981) 'The class production of crime: banditry and class strategies in England and Australia', in R. Simon and S. Spitzer (eds), *Research in Law and Sociology*. Greenwich, CT: JAI Press.

O'Malley, Pat (1988) 'The purpose of knowlege: pragmatism and the praxis of marxist criminology', *Contemporary Crises*, 12: 65–79.

O'Malley, Pat (1996) 'Criminology and the new liberalism', John Edwards Memorial Lecture, Centre of Criminology, University of Toronto.

O'Malley, Pat and Palmer, Darren (1996) 'Post-Keynesian policing', *Economy and Society*, 25 (2): 137–55.

O'Malley, Pat, Weir, I. and Shearing, C. (1997) 'Governmentality, criticism and politics', *Economy and Society* 26 (4): 501–17.

Orr, Deborah (1999) 'A blueprint for the rich', *Independent*, Tuesday 29 June.

Osborne, D. and Gaebler, T. (1992) *Reinventing Government*. New York: Addison-Wesley.

Overbeek, H. (1990) *Global Capitalism and National Decline: the Thatcher Decade in Perspective*. London: Unwin Hyman.

Packer, H. (1968) *The Limits of the Criminal Sanction*. Stanford, CA: Stanford University Press.

Paoli, Letizia (1998) 'The Pentiti's contribution to the conceptualization of the Mafia phenomenon', in V. Ruggiero, N. South and I. Taylor (eds), *The New European Criminology: Crime and Social Order in Europe*. London: Routledge.

Paoli, Letizia (2000) *Fratelli di Mafia: Cosa Nostra e 'Ndrangheta*. Bologna: il Mulino.

Parenti, Christian (1999) *Lockdown America: Police and Prisons in the Age of Crisis*. New York: Verso.

Parker, H., Bakx, K. and Newcombe, R. (1988) *Living with Heroin: the Impact of a Drugs Epidemic on an English Community*. Milton Keynes: Open University Press.

Parker, H., Aldridge, J. and Measham, F. (1998) *Illegal Leisure: the Normalisation of Adolescent Recreational Drug Use*. London: Routledge.

Pashukanis, Evgeny (1978) *Law and Marxism: a General Theory*. London: Ink Links.

Pavlich, G. (1992) 'People's courts. Postmodern difference and socialist justice in South Africa', *Social Justice*, 19 (3): 29–45.

Pearce, Frank and Tombs, Steven (1993) 'US capital versus the Third World: Union Carbide and Bhopal', in Frank Pearce and Mike Woodiwiss (eds), *Global Crime Connections*. London: Macmillan.

Pearson, Geoffrey (1976) 'Paki-bashing in a North East Lancashire cotton town: a case study and its history', in G. Mungham and G. Pearson (eds), *Working Class Youth Culture*, pp. 48–81. London: Routledge.

Pearson, Geoffrey (1983) *Hooligan: A History of Respectable Fears*. London: Macmillan.

Pepinsky, Howard (1974) 'From white collar crime to exploitation: redefinition of a field', *Journal of Criminal Law and Criminology*, 65: 225–33.

Perri 6 and Jupp, Ben (2001) *Divided by Information? The 'Digital Divide' and the Implications of the New Meritocracy*. London: Demos.

Pezzino, P. (1991) 'La modernisation violente en Italie', *Déviance et Société*, XV (4): 356–72.

Pharr, J. and Putnam, R. (2000) *Disaffected Democracies: What's Troubling the Trilateral Countries?* Princeton, NJ: Princeton University Press.

Philips, David (1977) *Crime and Authority in Victorian England: the Black Country 1836–60*. London: Croom Helm.

Philips, D. (1985) '"A just measure of crime, authority, hunters and blue locusts": the revisionist social history of crime and the law in Britain 1780–1850', in S. Cohen and A. Scull, (eds), *Social Control and the State*. Oxford: Blackwell.

Pitch, Tamar (1985) 'Critical criminology: the construction of social problems and the question of rape' *International Journal of the Sociology of Law* 35: 35–46.

Pitch, Tamar (1990) 'From oppressed to victims: collective actors and the symbolic use of the criminal justice system' *Studies in Law, Politics and Society*, vol 10, pp. 103–17. New York: JAI Press.

Pitch, Tamar (1995) *Limited Responsibilities: Social Movements and Criminal Justice*. London: Routledge.

Pitts, John (1998) 'Young people, crime and citizenship', in Alan Marlow and John Pitts (eds), *Planning for Safer Communities*. Lyme Regis: Russell House Publishing.

Piven, F. and Cloward, R. (1971) *Regulating the Poor: the Functions of Public Welfare*. New York: Academic Press.

Posel, D. (1991) 'Curbing African urbanisation in the 1950s and 1960s', in M. Swilling, R. Humphries and K. Shubane (eds), *Apartheid City in Transition*. Cape Town: Oxford University Press.

Power, Anne (1987) *Property Before People: the Management of Twentieth-Century Council Housing*. London: Allen & Unwin.

Randall, A. and Charlesworth, A. (eds) (1996) *Markets, Market Culture and Popular Protest in Eighteenth-Century Britain and Ireland*. Liverpool: Liverpool University Press.

Ranger, Terence (1986) 'Bandits and guerrillas: the case of Zimbabwe', in Donald Crummey (ed.), *Banditry, Rebellion and Social Protest in Africa*, pp. 373–97. London: James Currey.

Ray, Larry (1993) *Rethinking Critical Theory: Emancipation in the Age of Global Social Movements*. London: Sage.

Reich, Robert (1992) *The Work of Nations*. New York: Doubleday.

Reiner, Robert (1992) *The Politics of the Police* (2nd edn). Toronto: University of Toronto Press.

Reiner, Robert (2000) 'Crime and control in Britain', *Sociology*, 34 (1): 71–94.

Reuter, Peter (1983) *Disorganized Crime: the Economics of the Visible Hand*, Cambridge, MA: MIT Press.

Rex, John and Tomlinson, Sally (1979) *Colonial Immigrants in a British City: a Class Analysis*. London: Routledge & Kegan Paul.

Rhodes, H. (1956) *Alphonse Bertillon, Father of Scientific Detection*. London: Harrap.

Robb, George (1992) *White Collar Crime in Modern England: Financial Fraud and Business Morality 1845–1929*. Cambridge: Cambridge University Press.

Roberts, R. (1973) *The Classic Slum*. Harmondsworth: Penguin.

Robertson, Geoffrey (1999) *Crimes Against Humanity*. London: Allen Lane.

Robson, Garry (1997) 'Class, criminality and embodied consciousness: Charlie Richardson and a South East London HABITUS', *Critical Urban Studies: Occasional Papers*. London: University of London, Goldsmiths College, Centre for Urban and Community Research.

Rock, Paul, (1983) 'Law, order and power in late seventeenth and early eighteenth century England', in S. Cohen and A. Scull (eds), *Social Control and the State*, pp. 191–221. Oxford: Blackwell.

Rose, David (2001) 'Opium of the people', *Observer*, 8 July .

Rose, Nikolas (1996) 'The death of the social? Refiguring the territory of government', *Economy and Society*, 25 (3): 327–56.

Rose, Nikolas (2000) 'Government and control', *British Journal of Criminology*, 40: 321–39.

Rose, Nikolas and Miller, Peter (1992) 'Political power beyond the state: problematics of government', *British Journal of Sociology*, 43 (2): 173–205.

Rostow, Walt (1962) *The Stages of Economic Growth: a Non-Communist Manifesto*. Cambridge: Cambridge University Press.

Ruggiero, Vincenzo (1993) 'Organized crime in Italy: testing alternative definitions', *Social and Legal Studies*, 2 (2): 131–48.

Ruggiero, Vincenzo (1996) *Organized and Corporate Crime in Europe: Offers that Can't be Refused*. Aldershot: Dartmouth.

Ruggiero, Vincenzo (1997) 'Trafficking in human beings: slaves in contemporary Europe', *International Journal of the Sociology of Law*, 25 (3): 231–44.

Ruggiero, Vincenzo (2000) *Crime and Markets*. Oxford: Oxford University Press.

Ruggiero, Vincenzo (2001) *Movements in the City: Conflict in the European Metropolis*. Harlow: Prentice Hall.

Ruggiero, Vincenzo and South, Nigel (1995) *Eurodrugs: Drug Use, Markets and Trafficking in Europe*. London: UCL Press.

Rule, John. (1979) 'Social crime in the rural South in the eighteenth and early nineteenth century', *Southern History* 1: 35–53.

Ryan, William (1976) *Blaming the Victim*. New York: Vintage Books.

Sampson, Anthony (1995) *Company Man: the Rise and Fall of Corporate Life*. London: Harper Collins.

Santino, Umberto (1988) 'The financial mafia: the illegal accumulation of wealth and the financial industrial complex', *Contemporary Crises*, 12: 203–43.

Sassen, Saskia (1991) *The Global City: New York, London, Tokyo*. Princeton, NJ: Princeton University Press.

Sassen, Saskia (1994) *Cities in a World Economy*. Oakland, CA: Pine Forge Press.

Sassen, Sasika (1996) *Losing Control: Sovereignty in an Age of Globlalization*. New York: Colombia University Press.

Sassen, Saskia (1998) *Globalisation and its Discontents*. New York: New Press.

Sassen, Saskia (1999) 'De-nationalized state agendas and privatised norm-making', (unpublished). Inaugural Lecture, Division of Social Sciences, University of Chicago, 28 April.

Savage, Mike and Miles, Andrew (1994) *The Remaking of the British Working Class 1840–1940*. London: Routledge.

Saville, John (1994) *The Consolidation of the Capitalist State*. London: Pluto Press.

Schneider, Eric (1999) *Vampires, Dragons, and Egyptian Kings: Youth Gangs in Postwar New York*. Princeton, NJ: Princeton University Press.

Schwendinger, Julia and Schwendinger, Herman (1975) 'Defenders of order or guardians of human rights' in Ian Taylor, J. Walton and J. Young (eds), *Critical Criminology*. London: Routledge & Kegan Paul.

Scott, Peter and Marshall, Jonathan (1991) *Cocaine Politics: Drugs, Armies and the CIA in Central America*. Berkeley, CA: University of California Press.

Seed, Geoffrey and Palmer, Alasdair (1998) 'Police corruption in UK at Third World levels', *Sunday Telegraph*, 27 September.

Sennett, Richard (1998) *The Corrosion of Character: the Personal Consequences of Work in the New Capitalism*. New York: Norton.

Sharpe, James (1984) *Crime in Early Modern England 1550–1750*. London: Longman.

Sharpe, James (1996) 'Crime, order and historical change' in John Muncie and Eugene McLaughlin, (eds), *The Problem of Crime*, pp. 101–41. London: Sage.

Shearing, Clifford (1995) 'Governing diversity: explorations in policing' (unpublished), *Socio-Legal Studies Association* meeting, University of Leeds, March.

Shearing, Clifford (1997) 'Gewalt und die neue Kunst des Regierens und Herrschens. Privatisierung und ihre Implikationen/Violence and the Changing Face of Governance. Privatisation and its Implications', *Kölner Zeitschrift für Soziologie und Sozialpsychologie*. Sonderheft 37, Jg. 49, S. 263–78.

Shearing, C. and Stenning, P. (1987) *Private Policing*. London: Sage.

Shelley, Louise (1981) *Crime and Modernization: The Impact of Industrialization and Modernization on Crime*. Carbondale: Southern Illinois University Press.

Shelley, Louise (1998), 'Crime and corruption in the digital age', *Journal of International Affairs*, 51 (2): 605–20.

Shiva, Vandana (2000) 'Poverty and globalisation', London: *BBC Reith Lectures*.

Simon, Jonathan (1988) 'The Ideological Effects of Actuarial Practices'. *Law and Society Review* 22: 771–800.

Simon, Jonathan (1997) 'Governing Through Crime', in Lawrence Friedman and George Fischer (eds). *The Crime Conundrum: Essays On Criminal Justice*, Boulder, CO: Westview Press.

Simon, W. and Gagnon, J. (1976) 'The anomie of affluence: a post-Mertonian conception', *American Journal of Sociology* 82: 356–78.

Sklair, Leslie (2001) *The Transnational Capitalist Class*. Oxford: Blackwell.

Smart, Carole (1995) 'Feminist approaches to criminology or postmodern woman meets atavistic man' in C. Smart *Law, Crime and Sexuality, Essays in Feminism*, pp. 32–48. London: Sage.

Smith, David and Macnicol, John (1999) 'Social insecurity and the informal economy: survival strategies on a south London estate' (unpublished). Social Policy Association, Annual Conference.

Snider, L. (2000) 'The sociology of corporate crime: an obituary (or, whose knowledge claims have legs?)', *Theoretical Criminology*, 4 (2): 169–206.

Sombart, Werner (1967) *The Quintessence of Capitalism: A Study of the History and Psychology of the Modern Businessman*. New York: Fertig Howard Inc.

South, Nigel (1997) 'Control, crime and end of century criminology', in P. Francis, P.Davies, and V. Jupp, (eds), *Policing Futures: The Police, Law Enforcement and the Twenty First Century*. London: Macmillan.

Spierenberg, P. (1984) *The Spectacle of Suffering: Executions and the Evolution of Repression: from a Preindustrial Metropolis to the European Experience*. Cambridge: Cambridge University Press.

Stanley, Christopher (1996) *Urban Excess and the Law: Capital, Culture and Desire*. London: Cavendish.

Stenson, Kevin (1998) 'Beyond histories of the present', *Economy and Society* 27 (4): 333–52.

Stenson, Kevin (1999) 'Crime control, governmentality and sovereignty' in Russell Smandych (ed.) *Governable Places: Readings in Governmentality and Crime Control*, pp. 45–73. Aldershot: Dartmouth.

Stenson, Kevin (2000) 'Crime control, social policy and liberalism', in Gail Lewis, Sharon Gewirtz and John Clarke (eds), *Rethinking Social Policy*, pp. 230–44. London: Sage.

Sterling, Clare (1990) *The Mafia: the Long Reach of the International Sicilian Mafia*, London: Hamish Hamilton.

Sterling, Clare (1994) *Crime Without Frontiers: the Worldwide Expansion of Organised Crime and the Pax Mafiosa*. Boston: Little Brown.

Steytler, N. (1993) 'Policing political opponents: death squads in South Africa', in M. Findlay and U. Zvekic (eds) *Alternative Policing Styles: Cross-cultural Perspectives* (United Nations Interregional Crime and Justice Research Institute). Deventer: Kluwer.

Storch, R. (1976) 'The policeman as domestic missionary: urban discipline and popular culture in northern England 1850-1880', *Journal of Social History*, 9 (4): 481–509.

Strange, Susan (1996) *The Retreat of the State: the Diffusion of Power in the World Economy*. Cambridge: Cambridge University Press.

Strange, Susan (1998) *Mad Money*. Manchester: Manchester University Press.

Street, Paul (2000) 'Reflections on globalization', *Z Magazine* (February): 56–72.

Sumner, Colin (1976) 'Marxism and deviancy', in Paul Wiles (ed.), *The Sociology of Crime and Delinquency in Britain*, vol. II. London: Martin Robertson.

Sumner, Colin (1982) 'Crime, justice and underdevelopment: beyond modernization theory', in C. Sumner (ed.), *Crime, Justice and Underdevelopment*. London: Heinemann.

Sumner, Colin. (1990a) 'Rethinking deviance: towards a sociology of censure', in Colin Sumner (ed.), *Censure, Politics and Criminal Justice*. Milton Keynes: Open University Press.

Sumner, Colin (1990b) 'Reflections on a sociological theory of criminal justice systems', in Colin Sumner (ed.), *Censure, Politics and Criminal Justice*. Milton Keynes: Open University Press.

Susser, Ida (1995) 'Fear and violence in dislocated communities', unpublished paper to 94th annual meeting of the American Anthropological Association, Washington, DC.

Swyngedouw, E. (1992) 'The mammon quest, 'glocalization', interspatial competition and the monetary order: the construction of new spatial scales', in M. Dunsford, and G. Kafkalas, (eds), *Cities and Regions in the New Europe: the Global–Local Interplay and Spatial Development*, pp. 39–67. London: Belhaven.

Sykes, Gresham and Matza, David (1957) 'Techniques of neutralization: a theory of delinquency', *American Sociological Review*, 22: 664–70.

Szasz, Andrew (1986), 'Corporations, organized crime and the disposal of hazardous waste', *Criminology*, 24 (1): 1–27.

Taylor, Ian (1982) *Law and Order: Arguments for Socialism*. London: Macmillan.

Taylor, Ian (1999) *Crime in Context: a Critical Criminology of Market Societies*. Cambridge: Polity Press.

Taylor, Ian, Walton, P. and Young, J. (1973) *The New Criminology*. London: Routledge & Kegan Paul.

Taylor, Jessica (1997) 'Mafia migrates north to a rich new playground', *Sunday Telegraph* 20 February.

Theweleit, Klaus (1987) *Male Fantasies*. Cambridge: Polity Press.

Thomas, Richard (1998) 'Rich and excluded', *Observer*, 20 September.

Thompson, Edward (1967) 'The moral economy of the English crowd in the eighteenth century', *Past and Present*, 50: 76–136.

Thompson, Edward (1968) *The Making of the English Working Class*. Harmondsworth: Penguin.

Thompson, Edward (1977) *Whigs and Hunters: the Origins of the Black Act*. Harmondsworth: Penguin.

Thorpe, Nick (2000) 'Leaves on the line', *Guardian*, 25 August.

Thurow, Lester (1996) *The Future of Capitalism*. London: Nicholas Brealey.

Titmuss, Richard (1962) *Income Distribution and Social Change*. London: Allen & Unwin.

Titmuss, Richard (1964) 'Introduction' to R.H. Tawney, *Equality*. London: Allen & Unwin.

Tomes, Nancy (1978) 'A torrent of abuse: crimes of violence between working class men and women in London 1840–1875', *Journal of Social History*, 11: 328–45.

Trasler, G. (1986) *Situational Crime Control and Rational Choice: a Critique*, in K. Heal and G. Laycock (eds), *Situational Crime Prevention*. London: HMSO.

Tsoukalas, C. (1999) 'Globalisation and the executive committee: the contemporary capitalist state', in Leo Panitch and Colin Leys (eds), *The Socialist Register 1999*, pp. 56–75. London: Merlin Press.

United Nations Research Institute for Social Development (UNRISD) (1994) *Social Integration: Approaches and Issues*. World Summit for Social Development Briefing Paper 1. Geneva: UNRISD.

US Census Bureau (2000) *The Changing Shape of the Nation's Income Distribution, 1947–1998*. http://www.census.gov/prod/2000pubs/p60–204.pdf.

van Duyne, Petrus (1997) 'Organized crime, corruption and power', *Crime, Law and Social Change*, 26: 201–38.

Varese, Frederico, (1994) 'Is Sicily the future of Russia? Private protection and the rise of the Russian Mafia, *European Journal of Sociology*, 35 (2): pp 224–58.

Vigarello, Georges (2001) *A History of Rape: Sexual Violence in France from the 16th to the 20th Century*. Cambridge: Polity Press.

Vobruba, Georg (1998) 'Income mixes: work and income beyond full employment', *Crime, Law and Social Change*, 29: 67–78.

Vulliamy, E. (2000) 'Kingpins of US crime clean up with Mafia.com', *Observer*, 18 June.

Wacquant, L. (1999) 'US exports zero tolerance: penal 'common sense' comes to Europe', *Le Monde Diplomatique* (April).

Wagner, Peter (1994) *A Sociology of Modernity: Liberty and Discipline*. London: Routledge.

Wainwright, Martin (1999) 'Blighted children who find hope in heroin' *The Guardian*, 26 May.

Walklate, Sandra (1989) *Victimology: the victim and the criminal justice process*. London: Unwin Hyman.

Walklate, Sandra (1998) 'Crime and community: fear or trust?' *British Journal of Sociology*, 49 (4): 550–64.

Walkowitz, Judith (1992) *City of Dreadful Delight: Narratives of Sexual Danger in Late Victorian London*. London: Virago.

Warner, Carolyn (2000) 'Corruption at the expense, or the behest, of the state? Corruption and fraud in the European Union,' Unpublished Paper, Department of Political Science, Arizona State University.

Watkins, K. (1995) *The Oxfam Poverty Report*. London: Oxfam.

Weiss, Gary (1996) 'The mob on Wall Street', *Business Week*, 16 December.

Wettman-Jungblutt, P. (1997) 'Penal law and criminality in Southwestern Germany: forms, patterns and developments 1200–1800' in Xavier Rousseaux and Rene Levy (eds), *Le Penal dans tous ses Etats: Justice, Etats et Sociétés en Europe*, pp. 25–46. Bruxelles: Publications des Facultés universitaires Saint-Louis No. 74.

White, J. (1986) *The Worst Street in North London: Campbell Bank, Islington, between the Wars*. London: Routledge & Kegan Paul.

Whyte, William (1956) *The Organization Man*. New York: Doubleday Anchor.

Wiener, Martin (1990) *Reconstructing the Criminal: Culture, Law and Policy in England 1830–1914*. Cambridge: Cambridge University Press.

Williams, Phil (ed.) (1997), *Russian Organized Crime: The New Threat*, Liverpool: Frank Cass.

Willis, Paul (1977) *Learning to Labour: How Working Class Kids Get Working Class Jobs*. Farnborough: Saxon House.

Willmott, Peter and Young, Michael (1973) *The Symmetrical Family: a Study of Work and Leisure in the London Region*. London: Routledge & Kegan Paul.

Wilson, William Julius (1987) *The Truly Disadvantaged: the Inner City, the Underclass and Public Policy*. Chicago: University of Chicago Press.

Wilson, William Julius (ed.) (1993) *The Ghetto Underclass: Social Science Perspectives* (2nd edn). Berkeley: Sage Publications/Annals of the American Academy of Political and Social Science.

Wood, Ellen Meiksins (1991) *The Pristine Culture of Capitalism: a Historical Essay on Old Regimes and Modern States*. London: Verso.

Woodiwiss, Mike (1988) *Crime, Crusades and Corruption: Prohibitions in the United States 1900–1987*, London: Pinter.

Wootton, Barbara (1959) *Social Science and Social Pathology*. London: Allen & Unwin.

Young, Jock (1987) 'The tasks facing a realist criminology', *Contemporary Crises*, 11: 337–56.

Young, Jock (1992) 'Ten points of realism', in Jock Young and R. Matthews (eds) *Rethinking Criminology: the Realist Debate*. London: Sage.

Young, Jock (1994) 'Incessant chatter: recent paradigms in criminology', in M. Maguire, R. Morgan and R. Reiner (eds), *The Oxford Handbook of Criminology*, pp. 69–124. Oxford: Oxford University Press.

Young, Jock (1999) *The Exclusive Society: Social Exclusion, Crime and Difference in Late Modernity*. London: Sage.

Young, Michael and Willmott, Peter (1957) *Family and Kinship in East London*. London: Routledge & Kegan Paul.

Young, Michael and Willmott, Peter (1960) *Family and Class in a London Suburb*. London: Routledge & Kegan Paul.

Zaretsky, Eli (1976) *Capitalism, the Family, and Personal Life*. London: Pluto Press.

Zedner, Lucia (1995) 'Criminalising sexual offences within the Home', in Ian Loveland (ed.), *Frontiers of Criminality*. London: Sweet & Maxwell.

Zweig, F. (1961) *The Worker in an Affluent Society*. London: Heinemann.

Index